SCIENTIFIC ASPECTS OF MORMONISM

OR

RELIGION IN TERMS OF LIFE

BY

NELS L. NELSON

Professor of English in the Brigham Young University, Provo, Utah
Author of " Preaching and Public Speaking "

COPYRIGHT, 1904
BY
N. L. NELSON

Published, July, 1904

PREFACE

THIS book is offered to the consideration of sane people,—people not willing to hold convictions the premises of which lie in other men's brains; especially when such convictions affect their attitude toward a considerable portion of their fellow-citizens. Needless to say, this is a new kind of "Mormonism Exposed,"—written from the point of view that Mormonism is good, and true, and beautiful; and that, consequently, its detractors should improve their judgment, or mend their manners.

Mormonism claims to be, not a sect, but a religion,—the religion of Jesus Christ. The distinction between a sect and a religion lies in the fact that the sect has no philosophy, no way of looking at the cosmos differently from that of the family of beliefs to which it belongs. Christians generally insist that Mormonism is not to be classed among the sects—or, to use the softer expression, the churches,—of Christianity. In this judgment Mormons willingly concur. Neither in the background of philosophy, nor in the foreground of its doctrine and ritual, does it more than distantly resemble modern Christian churches.

But that it is therefore not the religion of Christ; that it is therefore not built upon the revelations of the Bible, as well as the teachings of modern science, Mormons by no means concede.

The Church of Jesus Christ of Latter-day Saints may be studied from two aspects: from the external aspect, by which are meant its organization as a church and its rites, doctrines, ceremonies, and practices as a social body; or from the internal aspect, by which is meant its philosophy or fundamental principles,—the principles that must be, in order that its forms as a religion may exist.

To enter upon the first aspect would, in this day, be a thankless task. The age of religious polemics is gone. Time was when to prove a doctrine scriptural was to prove it true; now it is merely to prove it scriptural. People are weary of wrangles concerning interpretation. Suppose you show that the Bible is on your side. What then? You have merely shown that the Bible is on your side. The vital question is not, Does this doctrine square with Scripture? but, Does it square with life as interpreted in that newer revelation of God, the book of nature?

I shall therefore discuss the subject from its second or philosophic aspect, and attempt to show what answer Mormonism gives to the questions, "Whence came man?", "Why is he here?", "Whither does he tend?"; at the same time

Preface

making comparisons step by step with what modern scientific thought teaches along the same lines.

N. L. N.

Provo, Utah,
May 2, 1904.

CONTENTS

	PAGE
PREFACE	iii
PROEM: THE EVOLUTION OF TRUTH	xi

CHAPTER I
THE OCCASION FOR WRITING THIS BOOK . . . 1

CHAPTER II
MORMONISM A SCIENTIFIC RELIGION . . . 9

CHAPTER III
THE MORMON CONCEPTION OF GOD . . . 14

CHAPTER IV
THE QUESTION OF GOD'S PERSONALITY ARGUED . 24

CHAPTER V
ARGUMENT FOR THE PERSONALITY OF GOD (*continued*) 34

CHAPTER VI
COMMON GROUND BETWEEN THE TWO CONCEPTIONS 45

Contents

CHAPTER VII
THE PLACE OF RELIGION IN THE ECONOMY OF LIFE 51

CHAPTER VIII
MORMONISM A TRANSCENDENT SYSTEM OF EVOLUTION 61

CHAPTER IX
THE DUAL EVOLUTION OF THE NATURAL WORLD   69

CHAPTER X
MAN'S SPIRITUAL LIFE A PROCESS OF EVOLUTION 78

CHAPTER XI
HOW GOD IS SHAPING THE DESTINY OF MANKIND 89

CHAPTER XII
HOW GOD RULES AMONG THE NATIONS . . 105

CHAPTER XIII
HOW GOD SHAPES THE DESTINY OF THE INDIVIDUAL 117

CHAPTER XIV
THE SCIENTIFIC ASPECT OF FAITH IN GOD . 129

CHAPTER XV
TRUE EDUCATION AND TRUE REPENTANCE IDENTICAL OPERATIONS OF THE MIND . . 147

Contents

CHAPTER XVI
THE LOGICAL NECESSITY OF REPENTANCE AND FORGIVENESS 160

CHAPTER XVII
THE LOGICAL NECESSITY OF BAPTISM . . 173

CHAPTER XVIII
THE NATURE OF SPIRITUAL EVOLUTION . . 185

CHAPTER XIX
SPIRITUAL FORCES ONLY HIGHER POWERS OF FORCES KNOWN TO PHYSICS . . . 198

CHAPTER XX
WHAT INTELLIGENT BEINGS WILL DO IN THE HEREAFTER 216

CHAPTER XXI
PHILOSOPHICAL DIFFICULTIES TO THE CONCEPT OF A PERSONAL GOD 232

CHAPTER XXII
GODHOOD AS INCARNATED 245

CHAPTER XXIII
THE REAL MEANING OF GODHOOD . . . 251

CHAPTER XXIV
GODHOOD INOPERATIVE UNLESS INCARNATED . 258

Contents

CHAPTER XXV
Jehovah, God of Abraham, Isaac, and Jacob . . . 267

CHAPTER XXVI
How Our Father Became God 275

CHAPTER XXVII
The Fullness of Priesthood is Godhood . 284

CHAPTER XXVIII
If not Mormonism—What? 295

CHAPTER XXIX
What Sectarianism Has to Offer . . 303

CHAPTER XXX
Conclusion: Mormonism Destined to Have the Last Word 311

Advertisement: "Social Aspects of Mormonism" 321

APPENDIX A
Spiritual Proofs of Pre-Existence . . 323

APPENDIX B
Contradictions Resulting from the Attempt to Christianize the God of Buddha 330

Index 339

"The time is wracked with birthpangs; every hour
Brings forth some gasping truth, and truth new-born
Looks a misshapen and untimely growth,
The terror of the household and its shame,
A monster coiling in its Nurse's lap,
That some would strangle, some would only starve;
But still it breathes, and passed from hand to hand,
And suckled at a hundred half-clad breasts,
Comes slowly to its stature and its form,
Calms the rough ridges of its dragon-scales,
Changes to shining locks its snaky hair,
And moves transfigured into angel-guise,
Welcomed by all that cursed its hour of birth,
And folded in the same encircling arms
That cast it like a serpent from their hold."

OLIVER WENDELL HOLMES—*Truths*.

SCIENTIFIC ASPECTS OF MORMONISM

CHAPTER I

THE OCCASION FOR WRITING THIS BOOK

"It [the Mormon Church] is not to be educated, not to be civilized, not to be reformed—it must be crushed. No other organization is so perfect as the Mormon Church, except the German army."—A prominent Christian clergyman before the general assembly of his church.[1]

DURING the last three quarters of a century, remarks like the above quotation have formed the staple commentary on Mormonism; and the animus so expressed, bolstered, indeed, by whatever facts could be impressed into such service, has found its way into dictionary, cyclopedia, and general history. It need not be pointed out here that these harsh judgments have almost invariably originated with those guardians of our moral and spiritual civilization, the ministers of the

[1] The author has considered it desirable to avoid for the most part specific mention of living people.

Gospel; nor need it be wondered at therefore that the Mormons credit the unbalanced zeal of the preaching fraternity with being a prime cause of all the mobbings and drivings which have marked them out as the persecuted religion of the nineteenth century.

To the extent that we Mormons are Latter-day Saints, we smile at such ministerial zeal and forget; for our religion teaches us to "do good to them that hate and revile us, and to pray for them that despitefully use us, and speak all manner of evil against us."

But to the extent that we are merely Mormons, that is to say, human beings trammelled by church forms, we keep tab on such utterances—and the deeds which often follow them; whence it happens that by every human law of offense and reprisal, the sins of the clerical profession against the Mormons should have accumulated by now past all hope of their ever establishing among us those bonds of fraternal sympathy which are indispensable to proselyting work among any people.

As mere human beings, we cannot forget that it is their prejudiced views and mistaken zeal that have propagated the hundreds of lurid "Mormonisms Exposed," which have come to be as necessary as narcotics to many good people. Naturally enough, too, we resent the air of superior sanctity, with which these same men condemn our religion unheard. And if our confidence in them is shattered, by the way in which they misrepresent us,—from mere fragmentary and often misquoted passages; and if our respect follows our confidence, when we see the obvious connection between our periodical besmirchment by them, through the eastern press and pulpit, and their ardent need of funds for the "Mormon Crusade," is it not precisely what would happen with any other people under like provocation?

Now if this animus of meddling clergymen stopped with the godly men themselves, one might regard it as a necessary evil,—a sort of escape-valve for the lingering spirit of Adam in them; but it spreads,—much faster than righteousness could,—as any message winged by hate always will; so that more than once in the history of Mormonism a whole continent has been inflamed against an unoffending people behind the Rocky Mountains.

One can readily imagine the mental process by which the opinions of the pastor become the convictions of the congregation. Accustomed—not without good reasons—to consider his judgment as the standard of righteousness, the flock can only reason that what excites godly anger in the shepherd must be bad indeed; and on no other form of sin does the good man usually wax so righteously eloquent as on what he is pleased to call the delusions of Mormonism.

And yet, on the other hand, one cannot help wondering that, in an age of psychic analysis, several palpable phases of this wholesale denunciation are overlooked by the laity in coming to a conclusion. First, the spectacle of a reverend gentleman turning red in the face and breaking out into anathemas against other interpreters of the religion of Jesus Christ, ought in itself to excite a cautious wonder; secondly, the fact that hatred (of Mormons) can temporarily unite sects which love (of Christ) has never hitherto brought together, ought at least to raise a small doubt as to the real source of the inspiration; thirdly, the fact that Mormonism thrives in spite of this combined assault of the other religions, ought to suggest that righteousness may possibly form a considerable part in the system which this ministerial anger denounces; since, by the growing wisdom of the age, sin is coming to be regarded as weak, transitory, wholly incapable of cohesion,—righteousness alone being vigorous enough to form and perpetuate an organic system.

All this negative agitation by ministers of the Gospel could be overlooked, however, as what we ourselves might do under similar circumstances; but it will not down even with the best of us, the fact that in all the drivings, mobbings, and sanguinary tragedies, which have accompanied the ostracism of this people, the sanctified figure in black has invariably turned up as the immediate plotter and arch-villain.

If, on the whole, therefore, Mormons do not rush to fill the sectarian churches established in our midst; if the advances of sectarian ministers are received with an undercurrent of distrust and suspicion; if they fail to interest, let alone convert us,—the evident reason lies, in part at least, in their general attitude of contempt for us; and especially in the history of their dealings with us as a people.

But this, after all, is only the minor, the superficial reason for our mutual antagonism. For we are not morbidly sensitive, nor do we hold a grudge. Were we a secluded or insular people, sect-narrowness might perpetuate the memory of wrongs and stimulate the desire for revenge, as it no doubt did in the older days; but what with two thousand Elders constantly on missions, and returning every two or three years laden with ideas and observations from every quarter of the globe, we are fast becoming the most cosmopolitan people under the sun; and a cosmopolitan people are not likely to cherish sect-resentment.

Besides, we are too often buffeted and bruised to harbor our injuries long. Let any minister meet us fairly and squarely on the plane of equality, and there is no house of worship throughout Mormondom that would be closed against him, as many notable incidents of this kind already attest.

The real reason why the ministers and the Mormons are as oil and water, lies deeper. What the reverend gentleman says, contains a substantial truth. If being "educated, reformed, civilized," means being converted to his way of looking at things, then, indeed, the solution that he suggests is the only one that will be effective; and if it will ease the gentleman's conscience in advocating it, I may add, that Mormons would prefer it as decidedly the lesser of two evils.

The reverend preacher of Christian love and charity must not think, however, that his reasons for crushing us are either new or novel; for such a justification has invariably been the working basis of every religious crusade that has darkened the history of the world; save, perhaps, that where the bigots of former times proceeded in the name of God, this later Dominie invokes the name of civilization.

It is by no means impossible that we are on the eve of a new crusade; especially in view of the painful memories of Mormons still living. Do you think the thorns and thistles of the Middle Ages forgot to cast their seed? Neither did the Inquisitors and witch-burners. The present universal prate about liberty of conscience signifies nothing. No persecutors ever proceeded as conscious persecutors; nor did contemporary popular sentiment recognize them for what they were.

Religious bigotry is discernible, save by a few, only in perspective. It is ever a past, never a present vice of any people. Couched in the cant phrases of the prevailing popular movement, it seems the very incarnation of purity and progress. The one persistent element in it, if, indeed, we may not call it the motive power, is hate —an element which should make even enthusiasm pause; but then this very quality itself masquerades as the supreme religious virtue,—a righteous valor against iniquity.

Now as the crushing process has more than once been tried against the Latter-day Saints, why should it not be tried again? And as the "reform" demanded of us in the past, has merely meant "conform," and consequently has failed,—I am grateful for the opportunity of pointing out in this book why any new attempt to crush ought not to be made, and if made, why it ought to fail, as it surely will.

In other words, I am grateful for this opportunity of putting the Church of Jesus Christ of Latter-day Saints into sharp contrast with the *isms* whose efforts thus far, instead of having added to the extremely small sum of Christian patience and long suffering in their promoters, have so far as I have been able to learn ended only in balked and vindictive rage.[1]

Mr. Elbert Hubbard (*Cosmopolitan*, October, 1902), in reviewing with Philistine pen the factors that would make for the Millennium, places this condition first: "Men will decline to join any social club that calls itself a 'Church'."

---

[1] Let me disclaim any intention of arraigning ministers of the Gospel in general, save as they resemble those in Utah. These latter have declared war on us, and are therefore legitimate targets for counter attack. Unable to agree among themselves on tenet and doctrine, they have yet found, deep in their spiritual bosoms, a common bond of union—hatred of the Mormons.

I do not take it that Mr. Hubbard condemns churches *in toto*—only those which have degenerated into fashionable clubs, and so are hindering social progress. Let us, then, take this admirable criterion of the fitness of any Church to survive: viz., its social effectiveness or inherent power to help usher in the Millennium; not on some world-to-be, but here on the third planet of the solar system. And by the result of such a comparison, let it be judged whether Mormonism ought to be crushed or cultivated.

CHAPTER II

MORMONISM A SCIENTIFIC RELIGION

SCIENCE and religion have so long been thought of in contrast, that is, as systems of thought more or less irreconcilable, that I shall perhaps provoke a smile from the critical reader when I unite the two concepts as I have done in the title of this introductory chapter. I shall even commit myself further, however, by taking the ground that a religion which is not scientific is scarcely worthy the credence of our enlightened age.

To demonstrate that Mormonism is such a religion is perhaps too large a task for the limit which I have allowed myself in this volume. The utmost I can hope to do, is to show that its basic data are not out of keeping with those general laws of nature on which all the conclusions of scientists rest.

To begin with, the fundamental conception of Reality is alike in science and Mormonism. Joseph Smith defined truth as an account of "things *as they are, as they have been, and as they will be.*" In other words, truth is not a mystical something behind and below phenomena; truth is nothing else than the impression made on the mind of man by phenomena.

But phenomena are merely appearances, not realities. Theosophy and Christian Science—in fact all idealistic schools of philosophy—will demonstrate this fact, that phenomena are illusory—not things, but the shadow of things. Well, in spite of such demonstration, science proceeds to build up these illusions,—these shadows,—into a great many correlated classifications, known as astronomy, geology, biology, chemistry, and so on, through the long list of human investigations. All things seen, heard, smelled, tasted, and felt may, in fact, be illusions,—"wrought of such stuff as dreams are"; but while human nature is organized as it is, they are extremely satisfactory illusions, worthy of all study, and capable, when properly manipulated, of bringing out other and still more satisfactory illusions, which we sum up in the name of enlightened civilization.

Besides, if science were to give up dealing with phenomena, it would have to go out of business for want of raw material. These unrealities—if such they are—constitute the only reality in the universe that man, as man, is fitted to apprehend. Scientists might follow the example of Buddha, or Mary Baker Glover Eddy, and weave a marvellous system out of the entrails of that mystical thing called mind. But the product would not be science; it would be,—well, a web woven from the entrails of that mystical thing called mind.

"Things as they are, as they have been, and as they will be"—let them be shadows, illusions, or what not—will therefore continue to be the warp and woof of science. It cannot afford to give up hungry facts for hectic fancies, no matter what dire predictions hinge on the consequences.

And no more can Mormonism. It finds mankind located in a most beautiful world, albeit a world of phenomena, or illusions,—if you will. It finds those phenomena wonderfully and progressively related. It finds, moreover, that they are always consistent with themselves, and may be absolutely relied upon. If they vary, it is only during vast cycles,—cycles quite beyond the range of any one generation; so that the farmer plants beans absolutely without any lurking fear that the crop may turn out squash.

It finds on the other hand that man is primarily and most emphatically fitted to apprehend these phenomena, and but dimly fitted—perhaps not at all—with powers for apprehending the occult; and to the extent that he forms harmonious correspondences with these same illusions, it finds that he grows in wisdom, power, and happiness. And so it reasons that the objects of sense proclaim their own mission—the development of man; and consequently that the experiences of this world constitute a fabric entirely worthy of religion,—especially as there is no other, save the gauze material of metaphysical dreams.

Thus it will be seen that science and Mormonism

see things in this world primarily in the same way, and also reason as to the purpose of things in the same way; the one naming its product civilization, the other religion; both coinciding in the final generalization, viz: The uplifting of the human race.

But Mormonism does not forget that "things as they are, as they have been, and as they will be" result, when interpreted by man, only in relative truth—truth subject to constant modification. Absolute truth it defines to be "things as they are, as they have been, and as they will be," when interpreted by God. And right here rises the problem of religion—the only reason, in fact, for its existence. Can man come into possession of absolute truth? In other words, can he come to look at things from God's point of view? For, if he cannot, then science is the very best religion he can have.

Here the two systems of thought divide: Science is sceptical, Mormonism confident. Briefly generalized, the teachings of Mormonism on this point are: (1) that apprehension of truth is the means whereby man is perfected (is made like unto God); (2) that God makes use of relative as well as of absolute truth to this end; (3) that while God's point of view might guide men in all their investigations (should God so will), the unity of His purpose respecting the race would preclude such divine guidance, save only as man directs his attention to what God would have him learn next;

(4) that relative truth, resulting from man's point of view, and absolute truth, resulting from God's point of view, are both concerned with the much contemned phenomena, or so-called illusions of our senses—such phenomena having in fact been created for no other purpose.

With this brief general statement by way of justifying the title for this book, I am ready to pass on to more specific matters in the domain alike of science and religion. While this single fundamental instance of agreement could not have convinced the reader respecting the thesis of this chapter, I hope it may have served to arouse interest in other notable instances which are to follow.

CHAPTER III

THE MORMON CONCEPTION OF GOD

Thou shalt have no other God before me.—*Jehovah*.
Let God be true, even though it make every man a liar.—*Paul*.

THE virility of religion, as an ethical modifier of the human family, lies, at the last analysis, in its conception of God. Faith dynamic enough to make for the betterment of the race, must be centred in a Being that can be both loved and feared. The first requisite, therefore, is that He be a Reality, not a metaphysical abstraction; and the second, that He be a sympathetic Reality. In the words of Paul, we must first believe that He *is*, and next that He is a *rewarder* of them that diligently seek Him.

In that word "rewarder" lie summed up the foremost qualities which a live faith requires in its Divine Source. There must be felt, first of all, a relationship equivalent to that of parent and child, with all the best qualities which our own lives have taught us to associate with father and mother; mercy, forgiveness, daily guidance, anxiety, protection, a haven of refuge on earth, and ultimately an eternal home. And we must, moreover, feel that we can safely multiply these parent-qualities as many times in effectiveness, as we conceive God to be greater than man.

On the other hand, as a salutary restrainer of evil tendencies, we must feel God to be the omnipotent creator and preserver of all things; whose omniscient eye beholds even our secret thoughts, and whose omnipresent power and spirit pervade to shape towards righteousness—or else to nullify—all the aspirations and deeds of men.

Along with this conception of God, the man whose faith is to help remove mountains (of sin) must have a conception of mankind equally definite and clear. He must feel himself categorically a child of God; differing, indeed, in degree but not in kind from his Father in heaven; potentially free, as a moral agent, and actually free, to the extent that he has emancipated himself from sin; capable of "becoming perfect as God is perfect" (Matthew v.: 48).

Such faith, and faith in such objects, is enjoined on almost every page of Holy Writ; and as long as mankind worshipped the God in whose image (physical as well as otherwise) man was created; who walked as a man walks, in the Garden of Eden; who conversed with Noah as one man converses with another; whose glorified person Moses beheld on Mt. Sinai; whose voice said in articulate words: "This is my beloved Son"; whom Stephen, the first martyr, looking into heaven, saw side by side with the risen Redeemer; whom John the Revelator saw, seated on a great white throne,—as long, I repeat, as mankind believed actively in the Christ-type of God, their faith was a living, virile force, which shaped their daily lives in directions known peculiarly to themselves and the eye of their Maker.

Then came the expansion of Man's idea of the physical universe, and with it the mistaken demands of reason for a conception of God commensurate with the new ideas of infinitude. Greek philosophy offered such a conception. St. John's remark, that "God is a spirit,"[1] was accordingly made the scriptural point of departure from the "God of Abraham, Isaac, and Jacob," to the God of Buddha.

Into Buddha's cold abstraction, theologians have since been trying to inject the warm qualities of Jehovah,—with what success, from an academic point of view, let the contradictions of metaphysics bear witness; with what failure in the ethical betterment of the race, let the apathy and artificiality of the so-called liberal or intellectualized churches of to-day declare!

[1] This passage, the only one that could be swerved into a support of the Indo-Græchic conception of Deity, ought, in all conscience to be understood in consonance with the rest of the Bible. "God is a spirit." Well, is not Christ also—are we not all spirits? The spirit is the man—the body is merely a house. If this interpretation does not satisfy, there is still another which would leave our Father in heaven a personal being. That is to consider the passage as referring to God, the Holy Ghost.

Mormon Conception of God 17

These latter are, indeed, fine places to be "respectable" in; for which reason they are no longer social or racial workshops. It is not here that movements affecting the destiny of the race originate, but in clubs, guilds, unions, and other secular organizations. True, they still stand on the topmost branch of the social tree, by virtue of past growth; but the vitality of the roots is running into lower branches.[1]

The trouble is, that philosophic theories have supplanted the living faith. That there is left any warmth or virility of faith whatever in such creeds, is evidently owing to the fact that the God of the Bible still lingers, though in a most contradictory fashion, in the person of Jesus the Redeemer. But how long—with the Buddhist conception for a Father—will it be before Christ, too, shall be spiritualized to an essence, boundless as the universe?

[1] It does not follow, however, that because a man's religion becomes perfunctory he ceases to be a factor in social evolution. Rockefeller remained an irreproachable church member, so Miss Tarbell assures us, even during the dark days when the Standard Oil Trust was incubating. In view of the part trusts are to play in future civilization, who will say now that in part, at least, the motive dominating this far-seeing man, was not the ultimate good of mankind? Be this as it may, my point is, his church was evidently not his social laboratory, nor did its atmosphere pervade his business life. It was rather a high, clean, sun-bathed mountain, to which he could retire, at intervals, from the smoke-begrimed sin-bespattered, warring life in the social valley. So far from taking religion with them down into the plains of social and economic strife, men like him would perhaps be the first to say, "Let the Church keep her place!"

Looked at superficially, the question whether God is to be regarded as a boundless spiritualized essence, or as the personal Prototype of man, would seem to be immaterial. As a matter of fact, no question could be more vital to the unity of man's conceptions. It enters into and conditions for him the whole aspect of the universe, from large to small. Let us therefore examine the question more narrowly.

The only conception that any people can possibly have of Deity, is one which comes within their mental horizon—the horizon bounded by their experience. Into His personality they will think their highest and noblest ideals. What they love most, fear most, admire most, will somehow be found among his attributes. To the extent, and in the direction, that they are civilized and enlightened, to that extent and in that direction will He be idealized.

It was therefore a profound remark of our Saviour, that to know God is to have eternal life. No one can know Him save as he becomes like Him. To know Him absolutely, is therefore to be perfect as He is perfect, which of course could be nothing else than eternal life.

By the same reasoning, to know Him in part is to be like Him in part, and therefore to be saved in part; or, to generalize, we are saved (*i. e.*, we have eternal life assured unto us) no faster than we learn to know God; in other words, no faster than we become like Him.

But becoming like Him implies a progressive means of getting ideas about Him. Let us take time to see how this thought works out in practice.

To know God is to have adequate notions of His personality in, say, five different aspects: physically, intellectually, socially, morally, and spiritually. Manifestly these notions can come to man only as God reveals them. The germ ideas respecting His personality are to be found in Scripture; but these are meaningless, save as man thinks into them the content of his experience. The real revelation of God to man is, therefore, to be found in that which gives man experience: in life—nature—law.

If a man would have the noblest ideal of God's physical personality let him master all that is known of physiology and hygiene—and conform his own life thereto; if he would realize His intellectual personality let him become familiar with the elements of intellect in man, then calculate what must be the Intellect that could create and control a solar system, with all the myriad forms of life and being therein manifested; if he would know God's social personality, let him study sociology, determine what qualities in man lead to love and harmony: in the home, in the state, in the nation, in the world,—and then consider that God has so mastered these laws that heaven (ideal social harmony) is His eternal habitat; and so of God's moral and spiritual personalities: to the extent that man discovers and lives moral and spiritual law,—to that extent he will know God.

It follows therefore from the very nature of things, that the honest man's conception of God is a progressively growing ideal. As, day by day, he discovers law (truth), and especially as he conforms his life to law (obeys truth), so must his ideal of the Ordainer of law change; and let no council of ecclesiastics presume to lay an embargo on his soul, by pronouncing once for all what God is or is not.

But this latter was precisely what St. Augustine and his brother monks tried to do for mankind. Consider for a moment with what possible hope of success. How much did these men know of that greater revelation of God, the book of nature, which flooded the last century with light? Interpreting Deity, as perforce they must, by the content of their experience, think what a narrow emanation of the life of the Dark Ages their conception had to be!

What of His physical personality, considered from the standpoint of ascetics,—men who despised the human body as something viler than the rags of a beggar?

What of His intellectual personality, interpreted by an age dogmatic and unscientific to the last degree?

What of His social and moral personality, mirrored in the imaginations of men, whose highest social ideal was to shirk all contact with, and responsibility for the world, by living in caves, convents, and monasteries?

What of His spiritual personality, judged of by beings who wore stones away with their knees, believing that mere adoration was pleasing to Him?

Is it any wonder, then, that when men began to study science; when they went direct to nature for their ideals; when they read God's purpose concerning man by studying man himself, especially in his relation to social evolution,—is it any wonder that they turned away from the artificial conception promulgated by theologians?

For was not this idea of God, after all, only an intensified conception of the mediæval monarch; whose approbation was to be gained, and whose anger appeased, through the mediation of court favorites (saints, angels, the Virgin Mary, the Son of God), who might be bribed or cajoled into pleading the sinner's cause?

Such a conception could not co-exist with ideals attained through the larger generalizations of life. To find pleasure in the servile prostration of multitudes, is not now conceived a noble trait even in kings; less, therefore, in the King of kings.

To make life and death dependent on the mere caprice of human will, we have now come to believe unjust and dangerous, and accordingly have substituted the reign of human law; in the same way, eternal life has come to be conceived as dependent, not upon the favor or anger of Deity (in the mediæval sense), but upon divine law (*i. e.*, the laws of the universe).

But in this shifting of the ultimate Source of volition and responsibility, a great mistake was made. Instead of stripping from the Christ or Bible type of Deity all the vagaries and artificialities in which he had been clothed during the Dark Ages, and then reclothing Him according to the ideals of modern life, scientists overthrew the type itself; and after awhile theologians caught up by substituting a vague generalization,—first fathered by Buddha and afterwards developed by Plato,—under the mistaken notion that such a concession was necessary in order to patch up the breach between science and religion. I repeat that a great mistake was made; for, after all, what type of creative intelligence, other than the man-type, can the race possibly come in contact with? Why, then, throw away the teachings of experience, from some fancy that it may be inadequate, and build upon non-experience, which we know is inadequate?

The point of the foregoing discussion, so far as the present volume is concerned, is this: Mormonism, though starting as it did, in the blaze of a scientific age, yet took for its object of worship the Bible-type of God; but it did not load itself down with the incubus of mediæval interpretation.

Like Christ, God is conceived as the perfected man; but as to the meaning of "perfected," no theologian of the past, however wise in the estimation of Christendom, can have a voice: each man knows God to the extent that he has grown like Him; and he has grown like Him to the extent that he has discovered and obeyed law.

Mormonism thus finds in life, not in metaphysical speculation, its commentary upon Scripture. Accordingly, let the reader come to this book, not with the pre-judgment that he is to witness the setting up again of a conception which has fallen a hundred times in previous polemical battles; but rather with the idea that Mormonism may have something new and entirely worthy of modern thought. For however true of the Augustinian conception, Carlyle's jibe of "an absentee God, sitting idle ever since the first Sabbath on the outside of His universe, and seeing it go"—has no meaning whatever in the conception believed in by Latter day Saints.

CHAPTER IV

THE QUESTION OF GOD'S PERSONALITY ARGUED

IN the preceding chapter I have assumed, partly on the authority of Scripture, partly from the necessity involved in a living, virile faith, that the personal or Christ-type of God is true, and the Buddhistic or universal-spirit type is false.

The proposition is, however, of such vital importance—reaching as it does into every thought and act of our lives—that it should not rest upon these good foundations, if better can be established. Accordingly, I shall, in the two chapters which follow, attempt a series of parallels between the two conceptions in their relation to life itself.

One preliminary, however, needs to be taken into account on the start. Science insists that truth can be known to man only by experience; and that, consequently, the basis for the credibility of any reasoning, speculative or otherwise, must be that its premises are realities. In this discussion I shall insist strongly upon the law of experience being kept in view. A little reflection must show how valueless is any system, however logical, that is not formed on this law.

Buddha, for instance, retires into the darkness of a cave to escape the "tyranny of his senses"; in other words, to escape the truths of experience. There, untrammelled by the necessity of conforming to objective law, his mind weaves a beautiful and most perfect system of soul-evolution; which, because of its unexampled logical unity, he soon comes to believe is real, and in due time, that it is the only reality.

All this is marvellous enough; but what shall we say to the greater marvel of millions of people, in every age since then, disavowing all experience as mere shadows and accepting this dream as the criterion of life! Suppose the first timepiece had been evolved in the same way; should we have apotheosized the watchmaker, and thereafter treated the movements of sun, moon, and stars as base illusions!

To make a beginning then, at the beginning,— let us contemplate the largest truth of which the human mind is capable; a truth, moreover, concerning which all minds must agree, viz., the formlessness, the reality, the unity, the homogeneity, the integrity, the harmony, the infinitude both in time and space, and, withal, the mystery,—of the uncreated universe. We need not reason, indeed we cannot reason, to these aspects of the All-in-All. We have only to open our souls and they pour in to the extent of our capacity. Nor can we reason these intuitions out of ourselves: insanity might temporarily obscure them, but soul-atrophy alone could deprive us of them.[1]

Other aspects, though dependent upon perception and inference, are almost as self-evident. One of these is the fact that the universe is not empty, but full. Full of what? Ah, there we come face to face with the Mystery. We call it ether—quite as if that signified something. Let us rather say, full of power, static, quiescent,—a dark, silent ocean of energy out of which forces rise, and into which they sink, after they have played their transitory parts before the mimic stage of our senses; say rather that the universe is full of the mother-essence of creation, out of which Invention has formed worlds without number, and the resources of which Invention shall never exhaust.

It is precisely at this point—the point at which the uncreated becomes the created—that the problem of religion begins. How and by what agency the "formed" and "limited" comes out of the womb of the "formless" and "limitless"—this is a question that immediately begins to divide mankind. And to this question, therefore, let us first address our attention.

In Salt Lake City is a beautiful temple of gray

---

[1] Let me ask the reader to realize as far as possible the thought involved in this paragraph, by re-reading it and testing each word by introspection; that is, by referring it to his own native intuitions, thereby forming some judgment of its truth.

God's Personality

granite, and in one of the canyons to the east is the quarry whence its massive walls were drawn. Consider then, these two objects: the gray granite mountain in the clouds, the gray granite temple in the valley. What is the relationship between them? Did the mountain brood and bring into being the temple? If not, was there an "All-soul" deep in the bosom of the ancient Wasatch range that conceived this magnificent piece of architecture, then shaped the rugged cliffs into geometrical blocks, and laid them one upon another? Or, if not the soul of the mountain or the soul of the range, perhaps it was the soul of the earth; or of the solar system; or did the universe itself bring about this substantial piece of creation?

If these questions seem palpably absurd, the reader is kindly requested to exercise patience till the analogy is completed.

Science practically agrees with Scripture that there was a time when the space now occupied by the solar system—a very lonely part of the universe, so astronomers tell us—was "without form and void"; that is to say, it exhibited all the formlessness, quiescence, and homogeneity of the rest of the uncreated universe.

Why did it not continue so forever? Who or what caused the change? What is the relationship between that first state and the present? Did the "All-soul" residing within this sphere of pregnant space,—the sphere bounded by Neptune—

conceive the sun and his satellites, then bring them blazing forth in the dark abyss? Or was the moving cause of this transcendent marvel the "All-soul" of the million-fold greater sphere, whose radius sweeps the nearest fixed star? Or did the creative act spring out of the universe itself?

The solar system could not have come about without a cause. To call that cause God, brings us not a single step nearer the solution of the problem; save perhaps that it narrows the question to, What is God?

Of all the conceptions that have at various ages held the attention of mankind, only two survive the enlightenment of the present century, the Buddhistic conception and the Biblical. According to the first, God, if not the universe, is at least co-extensive with the universe; an essence permeating every infinitesimal portion of boundless space; a spirit, dormant or quiescent in the uncreated universe, but active and dynamic—the animating principle—in the created universe; the noumenon, or only Reality; out of which phenomena—that is to say, illusions—arise, and back into which they must inevitably melt or sink; the boundless and eternal uncaused cause of all things.

In so far as a rational conception of God can be gathered from the very irrational definitions given in numerous confessions of faith, this is also practically the conception of modern Christianity;[1] save that its advocates, while they derive all created things—phenomena—from the uncreated universe (or God), have nevertheless not the courage of the Buddhists to carry their premises to their inexorable conclusion, viz., that these phenomena, these semi-illusions exhibited to our senses by form and limitation, must inevitably go back,—melt, sink again,—into the uncreated universe; in other words, that creation must be followed by Nirvana.

Various and fantastic have been the attempts at conveying an idea of the modern Christian God. The Church of England is, perhaps, clearest in its announcement of the immateriality of Deity; declaring Him to be "without body, parts, or passions, and of infinite power and wisdom"; then, very illogically, announcing that in the "unity of

---

[1] Here is the conception set forth in the Athanasian creed, a conception followed, with modifications, by most sects of Christendom: "We worship one God in trinity, and trinity in unity; neither confounding the persons, nor dividing the substance. For there is one person of the Father, another of the Son, and another of the Holy Ghost. But the Godhead of the Father, Son, and Holy Ghost, is all one; the glory equal, the majesty co-eternal. Such as the Father is, such is the Son, and such is the Holy Ghost. *The Father uncreate, the Son uncreate, and the Holy Ghost uncreate.* The Father incomprehensible, the Son incomprehensible, and the Holy Ghost incomprehensible."—To which we may fairly add: this definition is incomprehensible. For how can God be "formed" and "limited" (*i. e.*, as three separate persons), and at the same time be "formless" and "limitless"(*i. e.*, uncreate)? It is stultification of this kind that has brought religion into contempt with thinking minds.

this Godhead there be three persons!"—quite ignoring the distinction between the limited and the limitless.

From current religious discussions may be gathered the notion that He is a being whose circumference is everywhere and whose centre is nowhere; who sits on the top of a topless throne beyond the bounds of time and space. But as there is neither centre nor circumference to that which is boundless, nor top to that which is topless, and no beyond to time and space, such explanations are beneath the dignity of ministers of the Gospel.

Although this conception of God as an immaterial, omnipresent Spirit, is prevalent among modern Christian churches, it is by no means traceable to the teachings of Christ. On the contrary, it represents two distinct compromises of the religion of Christ with secular cosmogonies. The first was with the philosophy of Greece as represented by Athanasius and the school of Greek dialecticians who joined the church during the third and fourth centuries. By the Athanasian Creed (quoted in a footnote) God is called a person, which of course represents the Bible side of the controversy. But in the next breath He is pronounced uncreate, which makes Him without form; the definition thereby violating the second law of thought, viz., a thing cannot be, and not be at the same time. True, by the powerful writings of St. Augustine, the personal aspect was kept in the ascendency down until the eighteenth century. Unfortunately, Augustine associated with the Bible conception such human limitations of Deity,—including also the doctrine of the total depravity of man,—that his ideas became untenable before the onslaught of evolutionary philosophy; and when they fell the idea of a personal God fell with them.

The second compromise—which was all but a complete surrender—was to modern science; for to the extent that science is not agnostic,—that is to say, in so far as science applies the name God to any of its concepts,—it, too, accepts as most rational the Buddhistic idea, that of the immanent God, the indwelling Spirit of life. For does not this idea admirably explain the vivifying principle in nature,—the source and meaning—to borrow Spencer's phrase—of that "infinite and eternal energy whence all things proceed?" Does it not also explain the unity and harmony so manifest in the universe?

Another rapidly growing cult—which might be roughly classed as transcendental, keeping in mind both the good and bad sense of the word; a cult in whose front ranks stand such rational thinkers as Emerson and Carlyle, but whose wings and vanguards are marshalled into line by such dreamers as Madame Blavatsky and Mrs. Mary Baker Glover Eddy—also accept as the basis of their various philosophies this same background of things knowable, the Buddhistic conception of

Deity. So that this doctrine of Pantheism—for such it is, more or less modified,—holds all but universal sway among civilized peoples at the present time.

In view of this fact it would seem to argue unusual temerity for a handful of people like the Mormons to hold up and proclaim the old-fashioned conception of God as a glorified, perfected, personal Being, the Father of the human race and its prototype in every sense; physically, intellectually, socially, morally, and spiritually. To be sure, such is the revelation of Him in the Bible. As before pointed out, from the first page in Genesis, where man is represented as being made in His image, to the last page of Revelations, where He is represented as seated on the great white throne,—in almost every chapter of holy writ we get the conception of a personal God.

Nor do Mormons alone get this idea from Scripture: all men do, who have no esoteric meanings to read into the sacred text. But not all men can withstand the bombardment of speculative philosophy. Let a college professor explain, with his fine air of superiority, that only in a crude age of the world's history did mankind hold so narrow and degraded a conception of Deity, and these honest but entirely exoteric readers of Scripture blush for their ignorance and straightway go over to the popular side.

Only the sturdy convictions of a Mormon can withstand the contempt hurled in the word "anthropomorphism" and similar philosophic brickbats. "Fancy God using His legs!" exclaimed an elegant preacher of righteousness. Well, my fine bird, fancy the Redeemer of mankind not doing so! And yet Jesus is pronounced by Paul to be the "brightness of his Father's glory, the express image of His person." It is not least of the evils of this Buddhistic philosophy that the mental palate becomes so finical as to reject merely natural phenomena as coarse and contemptible.

CHAPTER V

ARGUMENT FOR THE PERSONALITY OF GOD—
(*Continued*)

IT is not my purpose to contend that the Mormon conception of God is that of the revelations of Scripture. This will probably be conceded. The vital question here is, How does this conception work out in the revelations of nature?

In passing, I may merely mention the old philosophic difficulties connected with the non-Mormon or pantheistic conception, viz., that if God is immanent, that is to say, the animating principle in all things, He must be the author both of good and evil; conversely, if man has no psychic existence separate from God, he is not free, and, therefore, not responsible,—either of which destroys a vital principle in the religion of Jesus Christ. These difficulties have never been squared, and it is safe to say never will be, with Christianity's present notion of Deity.

But it would, perhaps, be unprofitable to pursue this dilemma; let us rather take the two conceptions and set before each the problem of creation; and in order to simplify matters, let the problem involve only a single series, such as the creation of our own cosmos, the sun and his retinue of worlds, down to the last ripple of created movement, say of the animalcule swimming, with ocean-like freedom, in a drop of water.

First, then, did the "All-soul," the reservoir of quiescent force, the spirit or essence filling the uncreated universe, brood and bring forth the solar system?

Such a thought is absolutely fantastical. Where in the experience of all mankind, did a block or cube of pure space ever do anything resembling the invention and execution involved in an act of creation? I challenge any philosopher to produce from experience,—and experience, remember, is the criterion of science,—even the remotest analogy for such a thing. It is the absurdity of the mountain creating the temple.

We might indeed imagine intelligent beings walking about this earth, but so hooded as to see results—cities springing up on the plain, locomotives dashing across the continent, steamers plowing the ocean—without perceiving the agents. These might be pardoned for theorizing that somehow an "All-soul" residing in the materials or forces making up a created thing, is the efficient cause of the creation; but how men observing daily the agency involved in ten thousand acts of creation, could come to so crass a conclusion, is explicable only by remembering Buddha and his dream.

Again, by this conception things created take form and outline by virtue of God's being the animating principle. He is conceived as the all-pervading spirit of nature—the noumenon behind all phenomena. The human soul is figured as a breath of Deity breathed into the clay of our mortal habitation, or as a spark struck from the soul of God himself.

Now, what purpose, what possible motive, could a spiritual essence co-extensive with the universe have in creating, say, our solar system or any other system for that matter? It could not have been for His better security, since, by our very conception, He is the All-in-All; and if not for His security, then I can see only two other motives—His improvement or His diversion. The first we may dismiss at once, for how can that which is infinitely perfect have need of improvement by finite entanglements?

There remains then the last consideration. We are to contemplate the probability that the "All-soul" of the universe has involved that infinitesimal portion of Himself which is bounded by the orbit of Neptune, into a blazing sun, a congeries of glowing, dead, and dying worlds, shooting stars and wandering comets, ice-capped poles and belching volcanoes, strutting bipeds and buzzing insects,—all for the purpose of relieving the ennui, the monotony, of eternal bliss!

Is it thinkable? I shall no doubt be charged with blasphemy for daring to ask the meaning of creation. "It is not for the finite to question the Infinite. We do not know—cannot know—what God's motives are." Which objection is precisely the conclusion I have aimed to reach, viz., creation, with the Buddhistic conception of God as Creator, is motiveless, purposeless, from man's point of view.

And if this be so, what assurance, from the standpoint of reason, has man that things formed and limited will endure, *i. e.*, that there is eternal existence for worlds, eternal life for man?

Buddhism answers by flatly denying the possibility; asserting, moreover, that there is eternal life (and bliss) for man only in Nirvana, the uncreated, or, as applied from our present point of view, the decreated state; in other words, that state in which the God-essence forming man's soul is completely disentangled from matter and reabsorbed in God.

This is undoubtedly the legitimate and logical outcome of such a conception of Deity. And yet to the Christian, Nirvana, involving as it does the complete loss of self-consciousness or sense of individual identity, is the worst state imaginable: it is worse than the second death—it is annihilation.

Accordingly, he refuses to follow out the inexorable logic of his Oriental premises, but stops half-way to build him a heaven in which shall reside a risen Redeemer—limited, remember, as to form—with multitudes of other individualized beings, including himself; together with thrones, mansions, cities with pearly gates, and streets paved with gold,—for all which he claims eternal duration; whereby, though he has repudiated the only premises (*i. e.*, the personal God of the Bible) which make possible either the organization or the eternal perpetuity of such a Heaven, he yet very illogically holds fast to the conclusion from the premises set aside.

His clinging to the scriptural Heaven makes him, in fact, twice illogical; first, in repudiating the conclusion of premises he accepts (*i. e.*, Nirvana); and second, in accepting the conclusion of premises he repudiates (*i. e.*, Heaven). But bless him for his inconsistency. It shows that the vagaries of philosophy affect only his head; his heart, which is the altar of the Holy Spirit, still beats loyal to the true God.

Need I point out that from the Mormon conception, creation becomes immediately intelligible? The solar system was constructed in obedience to a necessity similar to that which impels mortals to build colleges and universities; the changes going on in the cosmos, which scientists have collectively named evolution, take place from the necessity of adapting environment to the growing and varying intelligence of God's children; to the end that they may evolve in the direction which He has planned.

We Mormons trust the stability of creation, from the feeling that all this cosmical panorama is but the unfinished work of our Father's hands; for, knowing with what loving tenacity we earth-spirits hold to the working out of our feeble inventions and idealizations, we feel instinctively how dear to God must be the fruition of His perfect plans.

And as to the reality of Heaven, as localized in the revelations of Scripture, if it were not essential to the existence of God himself (as would certainly seem to be the case with the other conception of God), then we might, indeed, fear for its eternal perpetuity; but being in fact that state which is progressively the outcome of evolution, or, as Mormons put it, eternal progress; that state which is the sum-total at any moment of what God has achieved,—it is a necessary part of himself, the very quintessence of His work as Creator, and without which He himself, as well as we, would be homeless; and consequently it is easier to have faith that Heaven will endure than not to have such faith.

By way of bringing out another important relation between Creator and created, consider this illustration: John Jones has lost his way in a blizzard. Feeling a sense of drowsiness stealing over him, and realizing its terrible meaning, he kneels down and prays. Will his life, in consequence, be spared from the fury of the storm?

Before answering, take careful account of all the conditions. First, the storm is only doing the duty God appointed it to do; that is to say, it is the legitimate outcome of law. Law, on the other hand, provides that everything in the blizzard's path that is fitted to survive, shall survive—all the rest shall perish.

But John Jones asks in effect that these laws be set aside for his benefit, *i. e.*, either that the storm be so mitigated that his natural strength may save him, or that he be miraculously raised into the rank of things fitted to survive. Suppose, in addition to praying for himself, he entreats mercy and protection for his horse, for the cattle he is seeking, for the buds in his orchard, will the indwelling soul of the universe stop to consider and act upon his petition?

The example fairly sets forth the inner meaning of prayer and also its conditions. If the Christianized god of Buddha can (and will) act the rôle of Providence, that is, intervene and set aside the operation of his own laws at the request of man, then it is logical to pray—otherwise not.

Is it rational to believe that an infinitely diffused spirit or essence could or would so intervene? Buddhism says emphatically, no. God never acts as Providence, but ever as karma, the establisher of law and dispenser of absolute justice in accordance therewith; and consistently with this view, theosophists, the modern disciples of Buddha, teach that prayer is enervating; that a man can have his way against the universe only to the extent that he himself can influence his environments; to which end let him pray to nothing external,—let him rather assume, not the supplicative, but the compelling mental attitude: so shall the incarnation of Deity within him,—the only God with whom his psychic life can come into contact,—perhaps secure for him his desire.

It is difficult, on *a priori* grounds, to come to any other conclusion. First, there is the bigness of God and the littleness of Jones. Compared with Infinitude the solar system itself is relatively smaller than the smallest microscopic speck discernible to mankind. Where then does the man Jones come in? Secondly, for purposes of answering prayer (as well for all purposes), this Infinitude must be considered Unity, not Plurality; since otherwise ten thousand antagonistic prayers might be granted at once, to the undoing of the cosmos.

But answering a petition involves hearing it, considering it, granting it, and setting in motion the forces necessary to give it effect—in other words, it involves time. Now, Jones' petition is urgent: five minutes' delay may mean death to him. Will the "All-soul" of the universe suspend attention from a million other petitions—to say nothing of temporarily dropping out of mind such trifles as a million solar systems just shaping out of chaos—to listen to a man whose cupidity, perhaps, made him tempt the blizzard?

But even though Infinitude could do such a thing, why should it do so? By the very conception of advanced Christianity, whatever of life is manifested in Jones, his horse, his cattle, and his orchard, is merely the fleeting incarnation of the indwelling Life of the universe. What bond of love or solicitude can be imagined between such a Creator and his creatures—merely limitations of himself—that He, the Infinite, should bend down and heed the selfish cry of the finite? Why should it seem better to Him for them to remain limited and finite than to be changed back to the unlimited and infinite?

But belief in an overruling Providence does not, as it may here be pointed out, result from *a priori* but from *a posteriori* reasoning—that is to say, from experience. "Ask and ye shall receive," said the Saviour, and made the promise seem reasonable by this appeal to common sense: "If ye, then, being evil, know how to give good gifts to them that ask ye, how much more shall your Father which is in heaven give good things to them that ask Him!"

And millions, testing the promise, have found it true. Here, then, we have again the blessed inconsistency of men holding to conclusions derived from premises repudiated and in spite of premises accepted. Another triumph for the human heart!

How much better it would be, however, if man's faith in Providence—that is to say, in the effectiveness of prayer,—were re-enforced by the head as well as by the heart. Observe that the

God to whom the Saviour pointed in the words just quoted was no spiritual abstraction, but a Father whom he compares with our earthly parents.

But, it may be objected, while God's love, out of which grow acts of intervention in behalf of his children, is satisfactorily accounted for by conceiving Him as the personal Father of our spirits; while we may readily believe that the Being who created the solar system for man, would also, were it in accordance with His wisdom, modify or set aside the general application of His will in the interest of individual cases, how is such a thing possible? Millions of petitions go to the Father at the same time, each requiring more or less specific attention.

The objection would hold were God alone engaged in listening to prayer and devising special providences. Let us, however, take a common-sense view of the situation. The President of the United States, for instance, comes, either in person or by agent, into executive touch with every one of our eighty millions of people. Is it possible to conceive God as less resourceful?

I do not pretend to know how God answers all the prayers that should be answered; nor has Mormonism spoken definitely on this point. But the following conclusion may safely be inferred from well-established premises in our religion: Ninety-nine per cent. of our prayers are probably passed upon by our guardian angels; the rest by councils of greater wisdom,—by Jesus Christ, or God himself, if need be.[1]

Nor would providences thus secured be any other than God's providences; for whoever, under God's appointment, does any of the works of God, is to that extent acting by divine authority, which is the very essence of Deity and Godhood.

At any rate, with such a rational view of the *modus operandi* of Providence, one can draw near to God with full confidence that if his petition involves that which will be for his own eternal good, it will be granted. The thought, however, opens up a marvellous new world, a world of beings behind the veil, and their relationship to us, which will be discussed in a later chapter.

[1] "The explanation of how God can hear prayers from millions of worshippers," writes a friend to whom the MS. of this work was submitted for criticism, "has often come to my mind, but I have not dared to put it forth so boldly. I have explained that He has means whereby He can hear us, and read our inmost thoughts; but that those means are in the nature of angels appointed to deal with the prayers or petitions of men, I have not felt at liberty to express. That this is so, is probable; but will it be wise to make the assertion as strong as you have made it? May it not seem a shock to many good people's faith in prayer?"—To which I can only say, that the explanation is put forth, not dogmatically, but only as a suggestion. It is a thought that has helped to make my own prayers more real and vital, and therefore it is hoped that it may also help other doubting Thomases.

CHAPTER VI

COMMON GROUND BETWEEN THE TWO CONCEPTIONS

IT is time now to see what Mormon philosophy and modern Christian philosophy have in common, albeit under different names.

Perhaps Mr. Fiske, in his *Idea of God*, states most clearly a certain Christian hypothesis when he says:

> The world of phenomena is intelligible only when regarded as the multiform manifestation of an Omnipresent Energy that is in some way—albeit in a way quite above our finite comprehension—anthropomorphic or quasi-personal. There is a true objective reasonableness in the universe; its events have an orderly progression, and so far as those events are brought sufficiently within our ken for us to generalize them exhaustively, their progression is toward a goal recognizable by human intelligence. . . . Such a theory of things is Theism. It recognizes an Omnipresent Energy, which is none other than the living God.

With all of which Mormonism is in perfect accord, save the last clause. Instead of being itself the living God, this omnipresent energy is regarded as merely a palpable evidence of the living God.

Suppose no mortal being had ever seen the sun, nor any other heavenly body to give him the suggestion of its existence,—yet its effects on the earth remained precisely as they are, excepting perhaps the phenomena of shadow. Under such circumstances, could the scientist be persuaded that the phenomena of light, heat, actinism, magnetism, and electricity were not immediate expressions of an omnipresent energy, but were in fact effects of a cause localized in space? If he could, it ought not to be difficult to conceive of God, not indeed as that omnipresent energy, nor as the creator of that energy, but as the efficient Cause of its differentiation into the forces known to man.

To quote Mr. Fiske again:

The fathomless abysses of space can no longer be talked of as empty; they are filled with a wonderful substance, unlike any of the forms of matter which we can weigh and measure. A cosmic jelly almost infinitely hard and elastic, it offers at the same time no appreciable resistance to the movements of the heavenly bodies. It is so sensitive that a shock in any part of it causes a tremor which is felt on the surface of countless worlds. Radiating in every direction, from millions of centric points, run shivers of undulation manifested in endless metamorphoses as heat, or light, or actinism, as magnetism or electricity. Crossing one another in every imaginable way, as if all space were crowded with a mesh-work of nerve threads, these motions go on forever in a harmony that nothing disturbs. . . .

It means that the universe as a whole is thrilling with Life—not, indeed, life in the usual restricted sense, but life in a general sense. The distinction, once deemed absolute, between the living and the not-living, is converted into a relative distinction; and Life as manifested in the organism is seen to be only a specialized form of the Universal Life.

All this Mormonism believes implicitly, and goes one better. As early as 1832, five years before Mohr announced the law of the conservation and correlation of energy, Joseph Smith identified all the cosmic forces with which man is familiar as differentiations of one Supreme Force; declaring, moreover,—and this is where Mormonism is still in advance of the age—that man's ability to perceive truth, the power variously known as inspiration, genius, intellectual penetration—is only a higher power of this same "infinite and eternal Energy"; that is to say, just as a certain rate of vibration of the eternal medium gives the sensation of heat, and another rate the sensation of light, so still other rates, progressively varied, account for all the psychic states which result from our perceptions, respectively, of the many-angled aspects of the one universal harmony of Truth.

But this power is not God: it is merely the medium through which He works, plus His will impressed upon the medium. Without the medium God would be helpless to execute, while still retaining all his power to invent. Without God, the medium would remain changeless, inert, throughout all eternity, having no power of initiation within itself.

This medium, which is co-extensive with the universe, would, if unimpressed by God, perhaps present no attrition (*i. e.*, no phenomena) to the present state of our intelligence. The fact, therefore, that this medium does present varied forms of attrition to the human mind is evidence that God by virtue of His will is in all things, through all things, above all things, below all things—the animating principle of the created universe.

To put the distinction in scriptural terms, what Christians recognize as God the Father, Latter-day Saints perceive to be the Holy Ghost (*i. e.*, the universal medium colored by the will of God). Christ himself draws this distinction. "Howbeit when he the Spirit of Truth is come, he will guide you into all truth: for *he shall not speak of himself, but whatsoever he shall hear, that shall he speak.*" Showing that the power of initiation does not lie with the Holy Ghost, but with God.

The failure to keep this distinction in mind is explicable perhaps on the ground that only through this universal medium can God's will be made to bear upon man—just as it is only through the medium of the ether that the sun can influence the earth; nevertheless such failure to perceive the distinction between God and His medium, does not differ in kind from that which should fail to see the architect and builder behind the gray granite temple in Salt Lake City—or the sun itself as the source of sunlight. It is, in fact, a blindness of the same kind that would postulate an "All-soul" residing in the materials used, as the adequate cause of the phenomena presented by such materials.

And yet preposterous as seems this last supposition, let us see how nearly true it is, in fact. The gray granite quarry,—to use my former illustration,—exists only by virtue of the "infinite and eternal energy," which Christians identify with God, but which Latter-day Saints identify with the basic fact of the Holy Ghost; so do all other materials used, and so also do the architect and builders themselves; indeed, the very intelligence necessary to plan the temple, and all the mechanical powers used in its construction, are transmutations, more or less remote, of this same universal spirit.

What remains then for its finite creators? The initiative, and, in a relative sense, the mastery of the materials and forces involved in its construction.

Here we come face to face with the essential characteristic of God: the power of initiative and the mastery of materials and forces. Not, indeed, mastery and control in the clumsy, mechanical fashion in which man seeks to imitate creative intelligence; but in the absolute triumph of mind over not-mind. In these two facts, then, the capacity of mind to invent and the power of will to execute, lies the supremacy of God over the universe, even though He Himself be limited in form to the Christ-type of being.

In no other way are creation and control intelligible to man; for to place initiative and the mastery of materials and forces in the materials and forces themselves, is unthinkable. It is a postulate that never has appealed, and never can appeal, to the *experience* of man, and is therefore no more worthy of credence than are the vagaries of Buddha's dream; among which, indeed, it stands foremost.

For the present, this must end my discussion of God as the source of all light and life, and consequently the source of religion. I am fully aware that there are philosophic questions that I have not touched as yet. These I do not ignore; I only postpone them, while we consider the nature of religion itself as related to man's temporal and eternal welfare.

CHAPTER VII

THE PLACE OF RELIGION IN THE ECONOMY OF LIFE

"RELIGION," says a recent writer, "religion—the childish mistaking of pictures for facts,—the crass materialization of allegory,—the infinite talent of man for humbugging himself,—and underneath it all the shadowy outline of Truth."

It is something to be an iconoclast—there is work for him among the tottering, ivy-grown institutions that are outliving the ages when they really served mankind; it is more to be a builder. The philistine whom I have just quoted assumes to be the arbiter of religion, as well as the oracle of truth. Verily, we have progressed since Pilate's day. Here is a man who not only knows what Truth is, but is able to recognize her outline even when shadowy. Or is he, after all, only a phrase-maker?

It seems to me the utterest folly to attempt a generalization of religion in a single stroke. He who can do it knows too much for this world, and should promptly take his seat among the angels; or else he knows too little, and should have the fostering care of a mental hospital.

Nevertheless, some broad lines of differentiation need to be drawn in religion between what tends to serve and what tends to hinder the evolution of the human race. With this reservation, then, that our findings are to be regarded only as a groping after the truth, let us face the question: What should be the place of religion in the economy of life?

In a previous chapter I took the ground that a religion to be virile enough to make for the betterment of the race, must be founded on a living faith—faith in a Being who can be both loved and feared; also that the first requisite of such a faith is that the Object of it be a Reality, not a Metaphysical Abstraction, and the second requisite that He be a Sympathetic Reality.

But if religion is to be regarded as a gilded something superimposed upon life, a society for the culture, and especially for the display, of a religiously veneered estheticism, then there is little need of real faith—the less indeed the better. Its immaculate pastors can, with a long pair of scriptural tongs dip for themes into the turbid stream of life, and so escape soiling their white hands by contact with men and women still of the earth earthy.

Its votaries, placidly conscious that they are already saved, can sit back in cushioned pews, while sin is idealized, salvation dramatized, and a sense of their own righteousness is distilled upon them like dew.

The Place of Religion

The Church will thus remain eminently holy and respectable, and will draw to its fold all the I-am-holier-than-thou worshippers who can afford the luxury.

True, along with this heaven-tending selective culture, there are likely to grow a few incidental evils; such as artificial righteousness, spiritual snobbery, religious shams and make-believes, a snivelling, psalm-singing cant, and hypocrisy unadulterated; but then who expects in this vale of tears to find any garden of holiness without a few weeds here and there?

It is this conception of religion, so widely prevalent among Christian sects of to-day,—the fashionable church, retaining, to use the language of Scripture, "the form of Godliness, but lacking the power thereof"—that the school of iconoclasts are inveighing against. Lay on, ye philistines; a ranker sham, a more bedizened artificiality does not cumber the field of social progress to-day.

Religion may next be conceived as a divine something which is to be integrated or interwoven with life; a daily and hourly burnisher of the conscience; an unostentatious something that goes with a man to the field, the workshop, or the office, and guides through love or restrains through fear all the thoughts and acts, great and small, which make up the warp and woof of his complex life.

This conception involves on the one side a fervid, perhaps unreasoning, faith in the ever-present love of God, or at least of the Saviour; and on the other, the total depravity or essential vileness of human life, in and of itself.

Man is conceived as belonging to an order of being somewhat above the ants, and somewhat below the angels; with power to rise, through the medium of religion, into the heavenly spheres, but doomed without its power, to sink to the depths of hell.

This conception really represents a stage rather than a kind of religion. It represents the dogmatic, just as the first conception represents the philosophic, stage of almost every sect in Christendom. It is, however, distinctly a factor in the social betterment of the race; as witness the present efforts of the Salvation Army.

The difference between these two conceptions lies in the fact that the first is not only in itself a holy sham, but a breeder of correlative social shams—a religion which at best "but skims and films the ulcerous places" in society; while the second is an earnest, whole-souled effort to probe, cleanse, and fill with health the putrescent moral nature of man. The defect of both alike lies in the fact that they are mere specialized functions of life; seeking to do for the soul by spiritual unction, what the physician tries to do for the body with drop and pill.

There is still a third conception of the right place of religion; not as something superimposed upon life, nor as something integrated with life,

The Place of Religion

but as life itself—life from God's point of view, which is the only real, true, eternal life.

This is the conception of Mormonism. God is conceived as the Father—in a very literal sense—of the spirits of all men. He must therefore be, like Christ, a glorified, perfected man. These spirits, again like Christ their elder brother, lived a spiritually organized premortal life, perhaps for thousands, perhaps for millions of years; and the ego, the I AM, or principle of self-consciousness, never had a beginning.

This earth, by the Mormon conception, is not a pestilent island in the ocean of eternity, where souls are quarantined for sin, as the dismalists among Christians would have us believe; on the contrary, it is a world prepared by our Father in heaven for the transplanting of His children; a glorious university—the only real university—for the development of His sons and daughters.

These sons and daughters do not belong to an order of beings lower than that of God Himself, and are therefore not "totally depraved"; their so-called deformities of sin are, for the most part, merely the deformities incident to growth and development; the deformities of the scaffolding as compared with the perfected house.

Sin itself as ordinarily understood is little else than relative righteousness; that is to say, what would be sin for a higher order of intelligence is often virtue for a lower. This is not denying, however, that there is real sin, recognizable alike in all grades of being; nor that there is a real Devil, capable of tempting men to evil.

From the conception that earth-life is a definitely-planned, and very necessary part in the eternal education of man, it follows that heaven is not some impossible region, remote in time and space, to which the soul flies at death; heaven is the Here and Now, and a million years hence in the life of the soul, will still be the here and now.

That is to say, heaven is always a present, not a future, state of the soul; and if any being would know the extent,—the height, depth, and breadth,—of bliss which the universe has in store for him at any time, let him take stock of how much heavenly beauty he sees, and feels, and Lives, in the creations immediately around him.

His future Here and Now will no doubt be ineffably enhanced in glory; but only on the condition that the beauties and glories between the present and the future state shall have been progressively seen, and felt, and lived; only on the condition that he progressively accumulate in himself, what Dr. Jordan calls the higher heredity.

Let him not foolishly imagine that he can fly from the one state into the other; for the farther he would go, either backward or forward from the here and now of any stage in his progress, the more deeply he would sink into hell.[1]

---

[1] It is not to be inferred, because heaven and hell are here emphasized as states of the soul, that therefore they do not exist as localities. Indeed, a little reflection must show that

For what is the essential fact of hell if not a state of discord with one's surroundings? Just as heaven represents the upward, forward, positive point of view—the life that seeks law to the end that it may come more and more into harmony with God, so hell is the negative, reactionary rebellious point of view—the life which, opposing itself to the harmony of the universe, is in process of being undone. It was with profound insight that Goethe made Mephistopheles declare: "I am the spirit that denies."

It follows from such a conception that there are as many varying degrees of hell as there are of heaven. Our present state, in fact, may be either heaven or hell according to the direction in which the soul's aspirations are pointed. He who says, "Father, thy will be done," is in heaven,—as exquisite a heaven as his soul is capable of,—with angels and all the positive forces of the universe surrounding him. He who has not yet learned to take this mental attitude, is groping in neutral shades; he who denies it, is in hell; for he opposes himself to law, and makes all things eternal his enemies. And as by obedience to law he built up all the power of his psychic life; so now his

---

the states heaven and hell and the places heaven and hell, are irrevocably related to each other as causes and effects. Even in this life we see the tendency of heaven or hell ideals to segregate the men and women holding them into corresponding localities. In the hereafter, that is to say, in any future Here and Now, this tendency will no doubt be much accelerated, for reasons fully set forth in Chapter XX., which see.

opposition to law, must result in stripping him of that power. This latter state is what is meant by being damned,—a state in which the soul has lost the power to repent and come into harmony with God.[1]

The tortures of hell can only be approximately imagined from the relatively short psychic basis of our natural life. Nevertheless, to feel a growing sense of confusion and discord about one; to realize the insidious approach of impotence as revealed periodically in actions which more and more tend to terminate in empty, useless rage; to feel one's power slipping away, and realize that the time will inevitably come when coupled with an awareness that shall know all heights and depths, there will be an absolute helplessness to react upon the universe; in short, to become a keenly self-conscious piece of drift-wood on the waves of eternity—this it is which probably constitutes the supreme agony of the damned.

---

[1] Christ speaks of a sin that is unpardonable—the sin against the Holy Ghost. Paul, in speaking of those who "were once enlightened and tasted of the heavenly gift and were made partakers of the Holy Ghost, and tasted the good word of God and the powers of the world to come, and then fell away, it is impossible to renew them again into repentance." Here then is the unpardonable sin; for manifestly if a man cannot repent he cannot be forgiven. Men in respect of obedience to God are like beacon-fires: as long as a spark of the divine life remains, it can be kindled unto repentance; but suppose it goes out—can you rekindle ashes? The sons of perdition are merely the ash-heaps of divine fires that have gone out.

But in a relative sense, the pains of hell evidently result from being out of joint with one's environment. Such a state would, as before suggested, result from arbitrarily moving either forward or backward from any given point of soul-development. If, for instance, some devout Christian, with mechanical ideas of salvation, should have his prayer granted and suddenly be transported into the presence of God and angels,—supposing that his earthly dross could actually withstand a glory intenser than the atmosphere of the sun,— what would he find in this advanced psychic universe with which to form soul-correspondences? What should he find as food for interest, delight, or comprehension in an environment exquisitely poised to beings psychically millions of ages perhaps ahead of him. Practically he would be in hell—the hell of utter barrenness and monotony.

So, on the other hand, were he suddenly put back into environments whose elementary crudeness once formed delightful soul-attrition, but whose power to shape and modify, and therefore to interest him, he has long outgrown,—what would be the state of his feelings? Fancy a Mozart or Wagner condemned to linger in a plane where *Yankee Doodle* and the *Arkansaw Traveller* were among the highest types of musical concord! Again he would be in hell—this time in the hell of psychic nausea and boredom; than which let no man this side of the gulf of the damned fear a worse fate.

Mormonism, it will thus be seen, has nothing in it to encourage the delusion of those Christians who believe themselves already saved, and who, in consequence, dally with the present life in listless fashion while waiting for the advent of their paradise; Mormonism is pre-eminently the religion of present endeavor.

> Trust no future, howe'er pleasant,
> Let the dead past bury its dead;
> Act—act in the living present,
> Heart within and God o'erhead.

He obeys God best who learns most of the present world, but in such order and relation that the link between him and his Maker becomes daily brighter and stronger. He is in the highest heaven who sees most beauty, feels most harmony, in the creations immediately around him.

Compare, then, with a religion so outlined, a religion vitally interrelated with all real things; indeed, an interpreter of all things in their relation to the soul,—compare with this conception of religion the definition with which this chapter opened: "Religion—the childish mistaking of pictures for facts,—the crass materialization of allegory,—the infinite talent of man for humbugging himself,—and underneath it all, the shadowy outline of Truth."

CHAPTER VIII

MORMONISM A TRANSCENDENT SYSTEM OF EVOLUTION

IT must by this time have dawned upon the reader that Mormonism is a transcendent system of evolution—a system so vast and far-reaching, that by comparison the researches of Darwin and his collaborators, important though they have been, are but as links in an endless chain.

And yet evolution is hardly the word to express our idea of the unfolding of the cosmos. From its derivation (*ex*, out of, and *volvere*, to roll), the word gives no hint of final causes. Its chief aim is to trace modifications and record results; accordingly, as a term in science, evolution stands merely for an unrolling, a coming out, a developing from some centre, of the world and all its forms of life.

This non-committal attitude is certainly a becoming one to the cautious historian of nature; but the mind is hardly satisfied with an account of how things have unfolded: it instinctively seeks for a cause of the unfolding. As a consequence we have, more or less intermingled with the record of evolutionary science, an evolutionary philosophy, which proceeds by speculative theories.

Mormonism accepts all the facts of evolution, but has its own way of accounting for those facts. It cannot agree, for instance, that things happen fortuitously; nor are the present theories of evolution adequate, in its estimation, to account for the status and trend of the universe. Mormonism believes, not only that the cosmos was set going by God, through the agency of intelligent beings, but also that every modification traceable to it since, is likewise the result of intelligent supervision. If, therefore, to the idea of evolution there be added the idea of constant oversight,—that things happen not by drifting, but by direction,—then we have fairly the Mormon idea of evolution; which, however, we are accustomed to speak of under another name—eternal progress. This idea I shall now proceed briefly to outline.

The theme naturally divides itself into two aspects: the evolution of the world as a habitat for man, or as a new set of environments designed for his development; and the evolution of man himself in his relation to this habitat or new sphere of life.

Conceive, then, our Father in heaven, the perfected Man,—not, as Carlyle says, "an absentee God idle on the outside of the universe, seeing it go," but vitally related as Creator and Controller to all His creations: the very Source of all light and

A System of Evolution

life; not isolated in His aspect of perfected Man, but surrounded by millions of just men made perfect,—supreme and alone only in the sense of Godhood, or the power that makes Him God: in the same sense that presidency makes the President of the United States supreme and alone. Conceive also as many million ages of progressive development between Him now and the state when, like Christ, He was man, as are necessary to account for His intelligence and omnipotence as God.

Next conceive as vacant the space now occupied by the solar system: a condition of things which might be represented by matter in its atomic state, or sleeping, as it were, in the bosom of spirit;[1] both matter and spirit quiescent, inert, and literally "without form and void,"—that is to say, presenting no phenomena to beings organized as we are now: a state which science itself postulates previous to the creation of our immediate cosmos.

I choose this small fraction of the universe, not only because it presents a fair sample of creation, but also because it furnishes water deep enough for any sane mortal to swim his ideas in; to say nothing of the further supreme fact that it concerns me immediately, and the Pleiades do not. If I can connect myself and my habitat, the earth, with their adequate Cause, my philosophy is satisfied; I care not a rap how this Cause is in

[1] If, indeed, matter and spirit shall not turn out to be ultimately the same entity. Who shall tell?

turn related to a remoter; I am content to rest in the conviction that the continued existence of our smaller cosmos, is evidence that its connection with the universe is real and vital.

Conceive next, as a motive for creation, millions upon millions of nascent intelligences, the spiritual offspring of perfected beings,—human souls, if you please, in their first or pre-existent estate; needing just such an environment as ours —"a second estate," in the language of Scripture —to further their development in the powers and attributes of Deity.

If this is not the explanation of psychic life, the adequate motive of the creation, will some one rise up and give us a more rational, a nobler, a more exalted conception?

To proceed then. What would be the first step in creation? Manifestly the setting into operation here of a law in force elsewhere in the universe—wherever, in fact, created forms of matter existed—the law of gravitation. For though Newton called this law universal, it is to be thought so only in the fact that it is a condition prerequisite to the existence of any world; but as to whether the law shall operate within any given area (*i. e.*, whether a system of worlds shall come into being), or cease to operate in any given area (*i. e.*, whether a system of worlds shall pass out of being), depends upon the will of God.

Science has traced better than theology can, the history of creation since the beginning of the

A System of Evolution 65

operation of this law; and with the facts of science Mormonism has no controversy. Ask me how God created the world, and I shall answer: In the way it could be created and not in the way it could n't.[1] Ask me how long it took Him, and I shall say: As long as it needed to take. That is the only commentary of Mormonism on the first chapter of Genesis.

We have still thousands among us who cling to the seven-days' notion; thousands of others who are willing to make a day with the Lord a thousand years (which latter concession seems, to the more intelligent among us, as if after discovering that you cannot dam the Mississippi with a spoon, you conclude to use a shovel); but these narrow notions represent, not the ideals of Mormonism, but the remnants of the mechanical theology of sectarianism still clinging to its converts.

Latter-day Saints recognize a great symbolic

[1] On the face of things, this does not seem to say much; but as a matter of fact, it recognizes that there is a "could n't" even for Omnipotence: that things in themselves contradictory are not possible even to the Creator; e. g., the mediæval notion, still held by some Christian sects, that God made the world out of nothing. It also hints that such a passage as that "God is able out of these stones to raise up children unto Abraham," is to be taken as an hyperbole; or if taken literally, that the miracle would imply the reducing of the stones to the atomic state, and then their incorporation first into the plant-world as food for man, and next into the living human tissue,—quite according to natural law. God can, indeed, do all things not contradictory in themselves; but he must do them in the way they can be done, and not in the way they can't.

truth in the Biblical story of creation, but are not dogmatic either as to the way in which God worked or as to the time consumed. Moreover, to the extent that science has read, or shall read, definite concepts into this wonderful chapter, it may rely upon the reverent, grateful attention of Mormonism.

So also of other controverted teachings respecting the order and time of creation. For instance, thousands of books have been written by Christians combatting the notion that species are derived from one another by a process of gradual adaptation. But why should this idea be so strenuously opposed? Because it involves a few million years, instead of seven days, could not God still be Creator? Surely it is a sensible, an economical, a beautiful way, of introducing variety in the flora and fauna of the earth; and if it is God's way—and it surely is, if it is the way at all—let us accept it as a truth with all reverence and humility.

It would be interesting to follow this theme further, but the scope of this work compels me to narrow my discussion to what immediately concerns man. Elsewhere I have maintained that the solar system, and especially this world, was created in obedience to a necessity similar to that which impels us mortals to build colleges and universities; whence the inference is self-evident that the earth and all it contains was created as a means of educating mankind. This was substan-

A System of Evolution

tially one of the doctrines that fell when physical science overthrew the Augustinian theology. It should not have fallen, however; for it is the only concept that gives definite meaning—that is to say, unity and perspective from man's point of view to the work of creation.

But physical science, intoxicated with its success in the rôle of iconoclast, did not stop to balance conclusions with other departments of truth. It rushed headlong to the opposite extreme, declaring that man is a mere incident in the scheme of things; that his pre-eminence over other animals was primarily accidental—due to a lucky differentiation, whereby evolution in him took the form of brain-modification; that the same accident might have happened to the lion, the eagle, or even the star-fish.[1]

There are, of course, many general aspects of nature which lend themselves to this view of creation. It is difficult, for instance, to see what the thousand-fold variety of the butterfly, or the myriad-form aspect of other insects, has to do with man's evolution; other, perhaps, than to furnish him problems for the development of his

---

[1] In accordance with which latter idea, Mr. H. G. Wells has, in his romance entitled *The War of the Worlds*, pictured the inhabitants of Mars as immense, spider-like creatures, with tub-shaped bodies, from which radiate in a dozen directions, scaly tentacles capable of surprising manipulation. Brain-evolution happened to go in that direction on the red planet; producing rational beings of the octopus order, but vastly superior to human beings, nevertheless.

mental life. But, after all, is not this development the very *summum bonum* of existence—that highest good for which all utilitarian goods exist merely as stepping-stones? And toward this *summum bonum*, which of the so-called negative tendencies in life,—weeds and tares in the field of existence—does not contribute its quota of strength and character, if properly met and overcome by man? But if not overcome? Well, it is necessary to eternal progress that offenses come, but woe unto him who does not rise above them.

It is only because man takes a narrow view of life, that created things have no sense of unity to him. If he can understand that the profusion and variety of natural beings are necessary to call out his highest, deepest, psychic powers, this fact alone should make him content to believe God's word, that all things were created for man; if he can look more deeply, and see that this life does not end all; that it is necessary for God to furnish mental activity during all future time for His children; that the multiplication of animated forms on the earth-plane, may in fact be the expression of creative work on the spiritual plane,—work which beings like ourselves are even now engaged in, and which awaits us when our turn shall come to pass on;—if he can take so wide a view of human life and destiny as this, he will have no need to turn pessimist and take man's primacy in nature as accidental.

CHAPTER IX

THE DUAL EVOLUTION OF THE NATURAL WORLD

THOUGH perhaps inevitable, from the depths of superstition into which religion had sunk, it was nevertheless a profound pity that the great work of Darwin and his earliest followers should have proceeded by ignoring the spiritual basis of life. We should have had a vastly different arrangement of the body of scientific facts collected by them had these men paid attention to those intuitions which come from the infinite to all men who seek truth in a reverent spirit.

Consider in connection with this thought two important facts in the philosophy of Mormonism. The first relates to the purpose of existence, as set forth by our Saviour, namely, "Be ye perfect as your Father in heaven is perfect." If this means anything, it means an eternity of scientific investigation on the part of man; not only into the channels, but into the very well-springs of creation. How else should such perfection come?

The second relates to the obvious fact that life is the result of a dual creation—a creation of spirit and a creation of body. The second chapter of Genesis asserts that God "made every plant of the field before it was in the earth, and every herb before it grew." As first shaped by the hand of the Creator, the plant was a spiritual creation—perfectly tangible to him, but no doubt quite impalpable to finite minds. Man could know it only as it grew, *i. e.*, only as it took a body of earth-materials.

This same mystery has hung over life ever since the creation, leading the poet to exclaim:

> Flower in the crannied wall,
> I pluck you from the crannies.
> I hold you here, root and all, in my hand,
> Little flower; but if I could understand
> What you are, root and all, all in all,
> I should know what God is and man is.

Now while we cannot explain this mystery, something may perhaps be gained if we put it into the terms of science. What, then, probably took place in that first or spiritual creation of the plant?

Given creative intelligence, *i. e.*, the power to invent mentally toward a definite end; given next the "infinite and eternal energy" referred to by Spencer, or the universe of spirit in the terms of Scripture, as material to work upon; given lastly creative power, *i. e.*, power to impress will—probably in the form of motion—upon this universal medium, then this may be what took place in that first spiritual creation,—adopting the terms of molecular physics: A fraction of the universal spiritual medium was impressed by the Creator with a distinct vibration, both (let us say) as to quality, rotary or otherwise, and also as to rate, say, a fixed number of millions or billions per second. This—or some other manipulation of the life medium,—for it is beyond man to do aught else than speculate,—constituted the beginning of life. Into the whorl of spirit so set going, earth-matter shaped itself into definite form and outline by process of natural growth. This was the second creation. Scripture bears us out abundantly that the natural is ever shaped upon the spiritual.

But a greater marvel was involved after the union of the two: for at stated nodes in this evolution of spirit, the first creation reproduces itself. Every virile seed, whether of plant or of animal, is to be regarded as containing a repetition of that first or divinely-ordained spiritual vibration, coiled like a spring within its earthly matrix, and locked ready to be set free when the proper conditions surround it.

Now, whether God created but one such spiritual germ, and produced all the other forms by modifications afterward, or whether He created— creates, let us rather say—many such original organisms, who shall tell? In any event, why should there be bitterness about it? Whichever plan we assume, one thing is fixed: it is God's way of transmuting the formless and limitless into the formed and limited; and we shall not lack plausible speculations as to how he succeeds in doing it.

So also with respect to adaptations, which undeniably take place from age to age in almost every type of life: they are to be regarded as modifications — retardations, accelerations, or changes in quality—of the original spiritual vibrations constituting God's idea. But whether creative intelligence makes this change by acting on the seed of some individual organism, thus suddenly setting free a distinct variety, or by means of meteorological forces applied in mass, thus effecting changes scarcely perceptible save by centuries,—is matter for the investigation, but not for the religio-scientific rancor, of God's children. Here it need only be insisted that whichever way it shall be settled, it is God's way—not the way of chance.

Let us now bring these two facts together, namely (1) the necessity of an eternity of opportunity for investigation, if man is to become perfect as God is perfect, and (2) the obvious double aspect, mortal and spiritual, of all forms of life.

If in this, our second or earthly estate, we have untrammelled opportunity, so long as life shall last, for studying the *bodies* of things, is it unreasonable to hope that in some future estate, we shall have equally untrammelled access to study the *soul* of things? Indeed, is not such a change in the divine curriculum one of the necessities in the evolution of a child of God? How could he attain to the perfection of his Father without such an opportunity?

If the reader takes this step with me, then he is to conclude that even now, behind the veil which separates the natural and the spiritual world—a land very near to us, no doubt—are perhaps millions of "Workers" to whom God trusts problems in the economy of His creations. Such assistance is necessary to Him in working out His purposes respecting the earth;[1] to them it is essential as being the only means of attaining perfection.

Let us go one step further. Do we not see the inventive, that is to say, the creative faculty phenomenally active in man during this life? Shaping dead forms, forsooth—mechanical contrivances without the spiritual counterpart. These inventions we call art, and so they are—the highest art which the limitations of earth life permit us to attempt. But in that life to come, when we shall

---

[1] That God needs the help of intelligences lower than Himself, may seem startling to those who have been accustomed to characterize mankind as vile worms of the dust, which Omnipotence is shaping for heaven or hell, according to His divine pleasure. In a transcendent way, it is true enough that he does not need man's aid; but if He wants a world filled with men—His children; and if He desires those children to evolve in themselves the intelligence of their Father, He must have their aid; *i. e.*, they must do what He would have them do, otherwise they spoil on His hands, to use a homely phrase, in spite of everything He can do to save them. It is simply the necessity,—to which God as well as man must conform,—of doing a thing in the way it can be done, not in the way it can't.

investigate the very springs of creation, shall our inventions be limited to lifeless or mere mechanical forms? Is it not more reasonable to believe that as we approach the perfection of our Father, so we shall begin to do the things which He does?

But pause for a moment, to realize what this thought implies respecting those millions of advance workers of our race just referred to. Wherever God is at work shaping or modifying, or otherwise controlling, the operations of the natural world, there, no doubt, assisting Him in minor posts of duty, will be intelligent beings of our human type. And the results of their activity will doubtless appear in phenomena of the natural world. In my garden, for instance, are now blooming easily fifty varieties of the pansy, and on the face of any one of them are more subtly charming adjustments of color than the most exquisite artist of earth has been able to make in silk and satin. And all this, let it be remembered, is self-woven! What fair weaver among the immortals, I ask myself, is adjusting this marvellous loom of life?

Here, Dr. Loeb, will come your opportunity. To play with life as with a toy, has by your own admission, been the passion of all your years of investigation. You have even succeeded in fertilizing the egg of the sea-urchin without contact of the male germ. Shall you ever be able to poise, in delicate proportion, the chemical ingredients that make up the egg or the seed of a given form of life? No doubt about it—from a mechanical point of view. But will it hatch or sprout? Can you coil into it, and lock there, that other creation, the spiritual? We shall wait and see.

In the meanwhile, the whole aspect of our present plane of existence seems to deny such a possibility; seems to point out that God's secondary creation, the bodies of things, is peculiarly the subject-matter appointed for our study during this journeyman's course in his wonderful university. And surely there is material enough in this world of forms, even were our days prolonged to the combined life of all the antedeluvian patriarchs. From which consideration we may well conclude that our study of the shells of life will reach far over into the hereafter. But on the other hand, there must come a time, it seems to me, when life itself shall yield to man's power of analysis; and if to his power of analysis, then also to his power of synthesis.

As will thus be seen, becoming like God is, in the belief of Latter-day Saints, no mere fatuous dream of something to be accomplished by a passive compliance with ceremony or ritual; it implies an eternity of righteousness; that is, of right endeavor constantly heaven-directed. And we are now in the very midst of it. Let him who would understand the method of it, look about him, and take the most obvious, the most common-sense view of life. Let him realize that it is by means of our environment that we are shaped:

made God-like to the extent that we conquer and rise superior to it, but weakened and made craven to the extent that it overcomes us. Then let him reflect that as it is now, so it has been in the ages gone, and so will it be in the eons to come: God shapes our environment and points the way; we retrograde or advance according as we drift with the current or swim toward the goal.

And if environment is the means of educating us, then it must change according to our needs—quite as modern science has shown that it does change. Nor should we expect the changes to be cataclysmal, that is, of so violent a nature as to disrupt the vital and intellectual correspondences of the race. We should rather expect them to be evolutionary, changing as the intelligences dependent upon them shall advance; which is precisely again what science declares has taken place since the creation of the solar system.

Whence we conclude also: (1) that the environments of pre-existence were such as to grade naturally into earth-life—though the fact of our having forgotten that previous life, were it explicable in no other way, might imply a complete break in our correspondences; and (2) that the environments of the spirit-world, into which we are ushered by death, will be a logical, unbroken consequence of our present environments; of which two states I shall have more to say in later chapters.

And so also of those tremendous changes prefigured in Scripture "before the end shall come." Viewed, as the prophets probably viewed them, without the perspective of intermediate events, they no doubt looked cataclysmal; but there seems no good reason to believe that they will be more so than events already recorded in the geological record.

This must close my cursory glance at our interpretation of evolution as respects the earthly habitat of man, the child of God. If I have shown that so far from being at variance with evolution, or so far from being even in the attitude of waiting to take its cue from the investigations of science, Mormonism is in fact able to organize the truths of evolution into a larger whole, and supply intelligent motive, moreover, for the origin, trend, and final destiny of the cosmos,—then my purpose has been effected, and I am ready to take up the second aspect into which I divided my theme, viz., the evolution of the human race as modified by its past, present, and future environments. Happily, as was inevitable, this aspect has already received much incidental elucidation in connection with its correlative theme, whose treatment we must now close.

CHAPTER X

MAN'S SPIRITUAL LIFE A PROCESS OF EVOLUTION

IN a discourse, preached April 7, 1844, Joseph Smith takes occasion to answer the question: "The mind of man—the immortal spirit—where did it come from?" in the following manner:

All learned men and doctors of divinity say that God created it in the beginning. But this is not so; the very idea lessens man in my estimation. I do not believe the doctrine. I know better. Hear it, all ye ends of the world, for God has told me so. . . .

The mind or the intelligence which man possesses is co-eternal with God himself. . . . I am dwelling on the immortality [*i. e.*, the intelligence or immortal essence] of the spirit of man. Is it logical to say that the intelligence of spirits is immortal, and yet that it had a beginning? The intelligence of spirits had no beginning, neither will it have an end. That is good logic. That which has a beginning may have an end. . . . I take my ring from my finger and liken it to the mind of man,—the immortal part,—because it has no beginning. Suppose you cut it in two; then it has a beginning and an end. But join it again and it continues one eternal round. So with [the intelligence of] the spirit of man. As the Lord liveth, if it had a beginning it will have an end. All the fools and learned and wise men from the beginning of creation, who say that [the intelligence of] the spirit of man had a beginning, prove that it must have an end; and if that doctrine is true, then the doctrine of annihilation would be true.

But if I am right, I might with boldness proclaim from the house tops that God never had the power to create [the intelligence of] the spirit of man at all. God himself could not create himself. Intelligence is eternal, and exists upon a self-existent principle. . . . [The intelligence of] the spirit of man is not a created being; it existed from eternity and will exist to eternity.[1]

These are bold words; and the ideas they involve form the nucleus of a philosophy which is new to the world. Were you a Mormon, that is to say, were you in an attitude to exercise the requisite degree of faith, the truth they contain might be borne in upon you by the testimony of the same spirit which revealed them to him.

[1] The words in brackets are my own, and are inserted for two reasons: First, the context plainly requires them. It is easy to understand that "the intelligence of the spirit" would be shortened to "spirit" in a rapid discourse. Besides, Joseph Smith was not a technical scholar, at least, in the sense of a close, discriminative use of words; he spoke with a largeness of view and freedom of expression, which the general spirit of his teachings never fails to make clear. The other reason is that the prophet abundantly taught elsewhere that God is the father of our spirits; *i. e.*, of the spiritual bodies, into which the eternal mind or intelligence above referred to, was incarnated.

Even without that mental attitude, however, they are ideas which must challenge the respectful consideration of thinking men and women; and if they are so considered they will not fail of vindication.

But let us first try to understand the thought involved. Mormonism teaches that there is in each human being an ultimate principle of life, a *vis viva*, which is co-eternal with the universe. The word "intelligence" describes this principle somewhat ambiguously, since it has also other meanings; as, for instance, in the aphorism, "The glory of God is intelligence," where it stands for the sum total of the developed powers and attributes of Deity.

Had the Prophet been familiar with the concepts of modern psychology, he would probably have called this ultimate principle the ego, or principle of self-consciousness. Our Father in heaven evidently refers to this eternal principle in Himself when He describes His identity in the words: "I AM THAT I AM," and says to Moses, "Thus shalt thou say unto the children of Israel, I AM hath sent me to you" (Exodus iii., 14); and by Mormon philosophy, God could have no principle of existence in Himself the germ of which His children do not share.

I assume, then, that it is this principle,—the principle of self-consciousness, or ability to distinguish between the self and the not-self, which Joseph Smith declares to be eternal; and if he is right, then there never was a time when man could not say, "This is I, this is the universe." Nor will there ever come such a time, whatever be the exigencies of heaven or hell, since what was never created can never be destroyed.

Now, respecting the physical form of that ultimate principle—since form it must have had, being a reality—there is little to be gained by speculation. Judging by analogy, it was perhaps a fainter type of the spirit, as the spirit is a fainter type of the body. But respecting other attributes of the ego, we are on safer ground:

I. This ultimate uncreated being was a free agent. I reach that conclusion from the following reasoning: Being eternal, and therefore co-eternal with the universe, it was beholden to no power whatever for its existence; and being indestructible, it might, in a negative way, defy all the powers outside of itself combined. That is, if all the forces of the universe and of all other intelligent beings beside itself, should combine to make it say yes, it might still say no, and maintain its attitude. This evidently is the real meaning of free agency; without such ultimate negative power, no being can be said to be free.

Man still possesses this power, but a difference has sprung into being: he has now something to lose. He has the same right as ever to oppose the powers not himself; but he does so at the risk of being stripped of all that those powers have put upon him: his mortal body, his spiritual body, and all those correspondences with the universe which obedience to law has invested him with. But after being again reduced to the primal state of naked ego, he could maintain his negative attitude indefinitely and without fear of further changes.

II. This uncreated being, though negatively omnipotent, that is, able to resist the coercion of all other forces combined, was nevertheless devoid, perhaps, of all positive power. The reasons for this conclusion are not so immediately self-evident, still they seem to me entirely cogent and adequate. By positive power, I mean the ability to react upon spirit or upon matter so as to create what one may invent. In God we call this power omnipotence—the power by which He shapes the formed and limited universe out of the formless and limitless. Man is not without this power in minor degrees, as witness the triumph of our present civilization.

Now, if all forms of positive power be melted down in the crucible of analysis, we shall discover them to have invariably the same source—obedience to law, whereby, and whereby only, we can enter into correspondences with the universe. But law, let us not forget, is the will of God; and by the very terms of our conception, the ego has as yet obeyed no being outside of itself. It has therefore no creative power whatever. Again, if by analysis we seek the spring of all human endeavor, we shall discover it to be a desire for increase of power—a progressive approach toward the omnipotence of God—whatever other names we may give to our motives. If this, then, be the reason for man's—that is to say, the embodied ego's—eagerness to discover and comply with law during the present epoch of its being, it was evidently the reason also for its setting out upon or beginning the cycle of evolution which thus far has brought it here. But if it already had power, what motive could it have in thus coming into relations of subordination to God? There could be no reason. The ego was therefore a powerless being, in point of execution, whatever it may have been in point of conception.

III. The ego, or uncreated being, had the power of faith and repentance, or at least the capacity to receive these powers from God. What the extent of its knowledge (as a mere memorative collection of facts disassociated from power) was, we may not know. It could easily have been enormous, it must at least have been rudimentary. The very fact of self-consciousness involves, as a correlative, the consciousness of one's environment; it would also involve judgment, or the power to distinguish between the effect of this and that. Now, the essential characteristic of faith is the ability to recognize a power greater than one's self, and to trust that power; and the essential characteristic of repentance is to put oneself in harmony with the power so recognized and trusted. Whence I conclude that the ego had both these powers or the capacity to receive them from God, just as man has them now; for in consequence of its exercise of them it became man in fact and may become God.

Probably the first important occasion presented to the ego for saying, "I will," was that of being born into a spiritual tabernacle. Let us pause to consider its relative status after this tremendous event in its evolution.

First, by its own free will and consent, it had become subject to God. It had discovered the meaning of law and taken its first step in subordination thereto. It had learned to say, in the language of our Saviour, "Father, Thy will not mine be done." For what is this only creed of the Saviour but a concrete formula for coming into harmony with the universe?

In the next place, it had exchanged what must have been a limitless, untrammelled, but also aimless state of being,—a state in which it could react on nothing, nor could anything, without its consent, react on it,—for what was probably an environment circumscribed and presenting obstacles on every hand. The nature of this first spiritual environment I hope some day to find time to discuss under the title: "Lucifer, the Son of the Morning." Here it must suffice to point out in general what it must have been.

It seems self-evident, does it not, that without an environment presenting attrition to its native powers or germs of power, the soul would have nothing to overcome, and could therefore develop no strength or character. That law must have held in pre-existence as surely as it holds here. Now, to be ideally limited and circumscribed an environment must present just that range of difficulties which the powers of the spirit are fitted to surmount; phenomena of that complexity which the mind by the exertion of the will can comprehend and form correspondences with. Under no other circumstances can there be growth and development.

But as there actually have been growth and development, we may infer that God provided the requisite environment; not only for this first stage in pre-existence, but for every successive stage previous to earth life. It is also a legitimate inference, that however remotely different was that first environment, yet, as the ages rolled on which brought that life closer to this, so the environment grew more and more similar to our own. From another point of view we should say that the laws of nature were gradually changed, and these reacting on God's spiritual children modified them according to His infinite purposes. For after all, what are laws of any kind, natural or spiritual, but God's media for creating and adapting the environment to the growing intelligence of the race?

As for the rest, the spirit being free, forged ahead or lagged behind, during the millions of years of its pre-existence, quite in the same way that it does here,—and with precisely similar results. That is to say, if proper exercise, or, in other words, proper obedience to law, develops any power of the soul here, so it must have done there; whence we infer that these powers known as birth-traits are due only in a small degree to physical heredity. They are rather the results of work done or neglected during pre-mortal life; as much so, as traits we shall manifest in the hereafter will be results of this life plus that previous one.

As to the first appearance of man on this planet, we do not accept the theory of evolution. Not that there would be anything shocking in a simian ancestry on the physical side, for the ape, like man, is the work of God, and anything from God's hand is worthy our reverence. And if he had chosen the body of the highest mammal into which to incarnate an immortal, pre-existent soul,—thereby beginning on earth the race of man,—we should accept such an origin as altogether beautiful and good.

But Mormonism has a nobler conception. There never was a time in the universe when there was not a man and woman capable of physical generation, for, generically speaking, God is man, and man may become God. Adam and Eve were probably translated beings brought to this earth from another world for the express purpose of beginning the work of furnishing tabernacles for spirits awaiting a mortal career.

Our first parents were, indeed, created out of the dust of the earth, but in no sense differently from the way we ourselves are created out of it; save that it was perhaps the dust of some other earth! This dust, however, was refined and organized in nature's marvellous laboratory, ere it entered into the body of Adam and Eve. Through the medium of the grasses it first became milk and butter, or, as in the offering of Sarah to the heavenly visitors in Abraham's tent—"young calf, tender and good"; through the combined agencies of the growing wheat, the milk, and the oven, it turned up as well browned and steaming breakfast rolls; the flowers contributed dust to the growing Adam and Eve as honey, the orchards as rosy-cheeked apples and luscious grapes, and so on of all other natural—which is to say divine—contributory factors. Does it not infinitely dignify God to picture Him in this rôle of Creator, rather than in that other clumsy, mechanical trade of the potter fashioning a mud man, and breathing into him the breath of life?

Respecting the evolution of man in this life and the next, whether as an individual or as a race, the chapters which follow will speak somewhat more at length.

Suffice it here to point out in brief that Mormonism interprets, correlates, and thinks into one vast and progressive unity all the experiences that can come to the human family during the passage of the ages. And I can conclude this chapter in no fitter way than to refer to what I regard as the sublimest utterance of modern times, if not of all time; the dominant note of Mormonism, and an epitome of its philosophy; a climax in the trend of evolution, which even the bravest of evolutionists have not dared to utter; a truth which when understood in all its bearings, gives unity and perspective to life, and becomes a key to the meaning of the universe; an aphorism which resembles indeed and deserves to stand by the side of those immortal words with which Christ points out that the final purpose of life is to become perfect as our Father in heaven is perfect. This is the utterance: "AS MAN IS GOD ONCE WAS: AS GOD IS MAN MAY BECOME."

To men and women unacquainted with our religion, this sounds like blasphemy. But consider for a moment that mind is infinite, and time endless; besides "This is life eternal," said the Saviour, "to know thee, the only true God, and Jesus Christ whom thou hast sent." How can we truly know God, save as we become like Him? And if we are His children, does not all analogy proclaim it possible to become like Him? Admit this possibility and the aphorism above quoted follows; at any rate, let the reader hold the sublime thought in view, and see what comes of it in the discussion which follows.

CHAPTER XI

HOW GOD IS SHAPING THE DESTINY OF MANKIND

NEARLY three thousand years ago there lived in Asia a man in whom human egotism and arrogance had almost reached their apotheosis. As he walked one day in the "palace of the kingdom," the swelling pride of his heart found voice in this piece of vainglory: "Is not this great Babylon, which I have built for the royal dwelling place, by the might of my power and for the glory of my majesty?"

But hardly had the word left his mouth when there fell a voice from heaven saying, "O king Nebuchadnezzar, to thee it is spoken: The kingdom is departed from thee. And thou shalt be driven from men, and thy dwelling shall be with the beasts of the field; thou shalt be made to eat grass as oxen, and seven times shall pass over thee; until thou *know that the Most High ruleth in the kingdom of men.*" . . . "In the same hour was the thing fulfilled. . . . He was driven from men, and did eat grass as oxen, and his body was wet with the dew of heaven, till his hair was grown like eagles' feathers, and his nails like birds' claws."

The lesson proved effective. "At the end of the days," said the humbled monarch, "I lifted up mine eyes unto heaven, and my understanding returned unto me, and I blessed the Most High, and praised and honored him that liveth forever. . . . *He doeth according to his will . . . among the inhabitants of the earth;* . . . for all his works are truth, and his ways judgment: and those that walk in pride, he is able to abase." [1]

Thus was mankind given a striking object lesson of God's regnancy among even godless nations. And if He can so correlate environment as to bridge the extremes of human and brute life in a short "seven times" (years?), how much more easily can He shape the destiny of a people,—by forces ever persistent and yet so subtle that they

[1] Daniel, fourth chapter. It seems to me hardly a legitimate inference, from this single example, that every king or kingling holds his transitory supremacy by God's appointment or conscious sufferance. That would lead to the doctrine of divine rights of kings. God is no doubt aware of the social changes among men, since He notes the sparrow's fall; but His manner of ruling among the nations is rather that of letting people alone—leaving them free to work out their wills—but taking care of general results. Is it not a nobler conception to believe that He moulds a nation as He shapes a landscape—by the constant application of cosmic forces? I cannot believe that yonder tremendous cliff, which a waterfall is slowly wearing away, is an object of God's immediate concern. No more, then, is the ordinary princeling who gets really too much honor by this comparison. But just as this mighty gorge is being hollowed out of the solid mountain by natural forces, so both prince and people are yielding, generation after generation, to God's steadfast purposes.

shall never guess their trend and tendency! In a former chapter, it was maintained that the earth with all its furniture constitutes a divine university for the education of God's children. This conception would certainly imply His general control, not only of its mighty laboratories, but also of the students themselves; not, indeed, in that close, personal, not to say tyrannical supervision, which even *our* foremost schools are beginning to perceive is abortive and fruitless; but such a control as is consistent with complete individual freedom. If this view is well taken, such divine regnancy in the social affairs of mankind ought to be apparent in history. Let us therefore take a swift glance along the ages. Fortunately for us, our vistas are longer and more clearly defined than were those open to the eyes of Daniel.

In the comparisons to which I shall presently invite the attention of the reader, it will be well to have some criterion of judgment,—the noblest, most far-reaching ideal, if possible, which the race has yet conceived. I shall spend no time in arguing that this ideal is precisely that set forth in the Declaration of Independence: "We hold these truths to be self-evident, that all men are created equal, and endowed by their Creator with certain inalienable rights, among which are life, liberty, and the pursuit of happiness." The equal freedom, the equal dignity of the individual—an ideal perceived glimmeringly but not yet attained by the race—is then to be our criterion. It is part of the Gospel ideal, as I shall demonstrate in a later chapter,—"the perfect law of liberty."

Compare, then, in respect of this principle, the history of the first half of the world with that of the last half. They will be seen to be completely antipodal. The relationship may be compared to that of two recumbent pyramids, side by side, the bases at opposite ends. The pyramid pointing this way represents the old-world civilization—a civilization the outcome, not of right, but of might. Tyranny and sycophancy represent respectively the two phases of nearly every dominant Old World nation. Turn the coin over as many times as you will, and these qualities merely change places—tyranny above, sycophancy below. No amount of suffering could teach the slave leniency, when fate happened to make him master. The two qualities are in fact reciprocal: every tyrant is merely a dominant slave, every slave a fawning tyrant. The freeman at heart can be neither; for if fortune put him in chains, he will prefer to die rather than kiss the hand that bruises him; if it elevate him to power, he must give freedom to others, for freedom is in his heart.

The point to note is this: the tyrant and the slave are not the products of a certain kind of civilization. The opposite is more nearly true; the tyrant-slave social status is merely the expression of the universal slave-tyrant spirit of its peoples. No matter what age of the world they should have lived in, their civilization would have been the same. "Men do not gather figs from thorns nor grapes from thistles." That which constitutes the essence of the soul will inevitably bloom into act and ripen into institution.[1]

The general proof of this lies in the fact that individual liberty, as we are coming to understand it, is by no means an evolution of those ancient races, but of an entirely different race—whence the reader will note that my second pyramid, though alongside is yet separate from the first. Moreover, the modern descendants of those ancient world-powers, the hordes of Africa and Asia, do not differ to-day from their ancestors in the slave-tyrant spirit: they differ only in psychic puissance, being mere echoes of their mighty progenitors.

But let us come into closer quarters with these ancient peoples. Has it occurred to believers in

[1] I do not forget that environment never ceases to modify, and consequently that the slave-tyrant civilization here pointed out as a universal effect of pre-existent spiritual bias, becomes by reaction an active cause in the same direction. Relatively, however, this secondary bias is very small—just what we should expect when we measure the time of its operation with the almost infinite stretches during which the dominant bias accumulated. If a given fraction, say one per cent. only, of our present population, were belated spirits of the slave-tyrant type, we should perhaps materially modify them, so persistent and dynamic would be the influence of our free ideals. Conversely, if a single generation of the spirits now being born could have exchanged places with the ancients, each would in turn have attempted the overthrow of existing institutions; but at what cost of revolution and bloodshed!

the Mosaic account that the descendants of Cain the murderer, were perhaps incomparably superior to the descendants of Seth, in point of material civilization? I base this conclusion on three facts in the antedeluvian record. First, Cain's posterity were workers in brass and iron (Gen. iv., 22). It needs no argument to show that brass and iron imply a high state of mechanical development—cities, manufactures, trades, arts. Second, they were the makers and users of musical instruments (Gen. iv., 21), hence, by parity of reasoning, they had attained a social life of no mean artistic refinement. Third, it became necessary to forbid the sons of God—Seth's descendants—from intermarrying with the sons of men,—Cain's descendants.[1]

Yet in spite of the divine prohibition, "the sons of God saw the daughters of men, that they were fair; and they took them wives of all which they chose" (Gen. vi., 3). Is not this precisely what we should expect from the conclusion I have drawn as to the respective rank in civilization of the two races? For where a people attain a rela-

[1] That such a prohibition must have been made by the Lord is evident, not only from the fact that intermarriages of this kind are mentioned among the reasons for the Flood (Gen. vi., 2, 3, 12), but also from other passages, making similar intermarriages a sin. (See Ezra ix., 6; Nehemiah xiii , 26, 27; 2 Cor. vi., 14). New and wonderful light is thrown upon the relationships of the peoples before and after the Flood, by revelations to the Prophet Joseph Smith. Thence we learn that the expression "All flesh had corrupted his way upon the earth," signifies that the pure race of Seth, which alone

tively high status in material art and artistic refinement, there the daughters—and sons as well—will be "fair to look upon" and attractive, even though they bear the mark of Cain; so much so, that the sons and daughters of a race, higher perhaps in spiritual ideals, but lower in the trappings of this world's ideals, will inevitably be won over by them.

This civilization was continued after the Flood in Egypt and Babylon; a civilization tinctured through and through with the slave-tyrant conception of life. What are the remnants of its massive architecture, but monuments to the absolute supremacy of the monarch, the absolute subserviency of the people? The same tale is told by its sculpture and painting: the slave-tyrant spirit made these arts stand still, by national decree, ere their evolution had fairly begun. And so of their religions: salvation, the result of coming into harmony with universal law, was not dreamed of by them. It is divine vengeance—angered tyranny —that is always to be avoided, and divine favor—

could hold the Priesthood and therefore be the oracles of God, was all but extinct through transgressions of God's command not to intermarry with the cursed race; that, indeed, the Flood became necessary in order that the two races might start on more equal footing for posterity. Even as it was, Ham's wife was of Cain's seed. (Whence the real reason for Cain's curse being perpetuated through Canaan, Ham's son.) But this was no accident; it became necessary in order that a lineage might be continued on the earth for the rest of the spirits in heaven entitled to no better earth-life than that of Cain's posterity.

placated tyranny—that is always to be sought. And what but a race of slaves at heart could descend to the depths of superstition and degradation to which they fell, in their supposed attainment of these ends? Nor does their literature change this general estimate of them. As fast as it is recovered, it only echoes feebly what the monuments of their history have already proclaimed with a trumpet.

For convenience's sake—though a name is not of vital significance—this civilization may be called that of Ham. Its zenith was perhaps attained in the days of the Pyramid builders; unless indeed a greater was overwhelmed by the Flood. Slumbering in the dust is now the flower of that race once so mighty in intellect and will, but removed, in the cravenness of their souls, only a few degrees above their brethren, the Devil and his angels, who were cast out of heaven. Gone forever is the menace of their evil institutions, thanks to the God of heaven. For their descendants, though perhaps not materially diminished in numbers, crawl feebly about like ants among the columns of Karnac. No sadder commentary on their mental inferiority is possible than the hovels they sometimes build from the crumbling fragments of prince's palaces, and in the very halls of departed royalty!

Nor shall they ever again be factors in world-shaping. Education may put on them the veneer of the prevailing civilization, and here and there a belated spirit may rise to centre with pride the eyes of the race; but the ingrained attitude of their souls, biased by a million ages of pre-existent false ideals, will not be materially changed by superficial contact with nobler conceptions during the brief passage of time. Let us be grateful, then, for the feebleness in conception and will, which prevents them from combining to give expression to that bias in the resuscitation of their ancient institutions.

Let us next give attention to the other pyramid, under which figure I seek to indicate the gradual growth of our foremost modern ideal, the essential freedom and equality of the individual. This may be called the civilization of Shem. Its glory has already eclipsed the combined glories of ancient world powers and the end is not yet. The base of this pyramid shall indeed be supported by the Millennium itself, the Kingdom of God on the earth.

Its apex was Adam; the ideal for which it stands was kept alive to the days of Shem through the lineage of Seth and the antedeluvian patriarchs. Respecting the social institutions of this race there is no hint in the sacred record.[1] But in

---

[1] Save in the case of Enoch, the sixth from Adam. The enigmatical statement in Genesis (vi., 22, 24) that "Enoch walked with God for three hundred years . . . and was not, for God took him," is explained in a revelation to Joseph Smith, to signify that Enoch instituted a communistic order, on the lines of that set forth by Edward Bellamy in his *Looking Backward*, which developed such perfect social

the absence of evidence to the contrary, we are justified in believing it was similar to that of Abraham—a pastoral life, close to the heart of nature, and answering admirably to the dominant instinct of individual liberty. The very simplicity of such a life, free as it was from all the trappings of power, could excite only contempt in monarchs of the Hamitic type. Its obscurity was therefore its protection. All of the race that remained true to their spiritual ideals would, however, cling to it in spite of such contempt. The rest would inevitably be caught by the external glitter of the superior material civilization, and so be gradually absorbed by the dominant race. As this is precisely what happened, it is indirectly an evidence of the view above taken, that the individual-liberty ideal should date from the father of the race.

Trace now the gradual widening of our second pyramid throughout the history of Israel. Observe the individual-liberty ideal flash out: in Joseph tempted by Potiphar's wife; in the laws of Moses, securing justice to the most defenseless; in the reign of the Judges for over four hundred years; in most of the incidents in the life of David and in his writings; in the fearless denunciation by the ancient prophets; in Daniel refusing to bow

harmony that the founder and his city were taken from this earth as translated beings, even as was Elijah in a later day. This revelation only emphasizes, however, the attitude above taken; for what is such an order of society, but the complete triumph of individual liberty and equality?

down to Nebuchadnezzar's golden image; in the song of Hannah and Mary: "He hath brought down the mighty and exalted them of low degree."

Even when Israel swerved from this ideal, seduced by the example of neighboring nations, and set up a king, they never became basely subservient. This is especially apparent in the demand made by the Ten Tribes of Rehoboam, that he ease the yoke which Solomon had put upon them; and when this ill-advised young lion's whelp answered: "Whereas my father did lade you with a heavy yoke, I will add to your yoke: my father chastised you with whips, but I will chastise you with scorpions,"—an immediate cry went up: "To your tents, O Israel," and they all revolted in a day.

Is there not in this sturdy resistance to oppression something akin to the spirit of the Barons of England who won the Magna Charta from King John at Runymede; or the still more immortal Continental Congress which fashioned the Declaration of Independence? Nor are these mere coincidences in history, for when the links in the social evolution of the Semitic race shall all be taken up, it will be found that the Anglo-Saxon peoples are lineal descendants of that same Ten Tribes who defied the arrogancy of Solomon's successor.

But it remained for Jesus Christ to give the supreme and final expression to this law of human liberty, and so to interweave it with man's hope of eternal life that it shall never be improved upon throughout eternity. When He proclaimed the Golden Rule: "Do ye unto others, as ye would have others do unto you," He associated the law with perfect justice; but this was only an approach to its final expression. When He declared him greatest among mankind who most served mankind, He carried the law beyond mere justice. But when He taught mankind not to resent evil, but, on the contrary, to return good for evil; to love your enemies, and do good to them that despitefully use you, He associated it with the love of God, which passeth human understanding.

As these teachings shall become real and vital in the lives of men, so will the ills and wrongs of society disappear, and that perfect social equality dreamed of by poet, prophet, and philosopher as the Millennium,—that state foreshadowed in the Lord's Prayer: "Thy will be done on earth as it is done in heaven,"—take the place of the multiform social distractions which now divide and embitter mankind.

We have thus traced the sudden rise and gradual waning of the old-world or slave-tyrant ideal of human sovereignty, and contrasted it step by step with the gradual crescence of its antipodal ideal, that of individual liberty and equality; finding that the two are in no way related as cause and effect, but that, on the contrary, each is the spontaneous expression of a distinct class of

Shaping Man's Destiny

spirits, which, for convenience, have been named respectively after Ham and Shem. But as in all problems involving extremes, so here we have still to deal with the means,—a compromise civilization, which may be named after Japheth, the third son of Noah.

Call to mind first the prophetic blessing and cursing which the old patriarch pronounced upon his three sons, or rather upon his two eldest sons, and the son of his youngest: "Cursed be Canaan, a servant of servants shall he be unto his brethren. Blessed be the Lord God of Shem, and Canaan shall be his servant. God shall enlarge Japheth, and he shall dwell in the tents of Shem; and Canaan shall be his servant."

Whether all the future of Ham—who may have had other sons—was bound up in the curse of Canaan does not appear. History would say not; but that the latter end of Ham is thus decreed, the foregoing discussion will surely have made plain. In Shem's blessing, note the peculiar use of the phrase "Lord God"; prefiguring, what history has since demonstrated, that this race was to be the conservators of our great religious ideals: bequeathing to the world the Bible, the Book of Mormon, the Koran, and the Zend-Avesta. Japheth was to be "enlarged," and to "dwell in the tents of Shem." The first idea would imply that he was to be second to Shem in greatness; the second evidently that his ideals should be borrowed from Shem. What else than institutions and ideals could the figure "tent" stand for, applied in the large sense of racial evolution?

At any rate, the civilization of Greece and Rome presents just such a compromise relationship with the civilization of Shem. Here, indeed, was fraternity, but it lacked the deep spiritual source inculcated by the Nazarene, and actually forming the matrix of Anglo-Saxon democracy. It depended rather on birth and equality in martial prowess. Greeks to Greeks, and Romans to Romans, were freemen; but all other nations were barbarians, and were, in fact, made slaves without a trace of moral compunction. Moreover, there was a constant tendency to veer toward monarchy: Cæsars and Napoleons are, indeed, perilously dear to the race even to-day.

In religion the same compromise is visible. They consented here also to "dwell in the tents of Shem," but they impress one as being guests rather than natives. Unlike dwellers to the tent born, truth as an abstract entity has little significance to them. Though they accepted the tenets of Christ, they retained their pagan forms; for the race is dearly in love with pomp and circumstance. Whence also the propagation of their faith is rather by person-worship and fetich-worship than through the apperception of principle; by ritual and ceremonial rather than through the realization of divine law.

As respects industrial civilization, what inventions have they not borrowed from Shem?[1] In political institutions the tendency also is toward the free forms of the North; but does any student of political science seriously believe that republics can flourish south of the Alps and Carpathians? In Latin America we have a number of petty experiments in free government, nearly all proverbial for their instability. Mexico, the only real exception, is a republic only in name. Although its chief executive is by courtesy called President, there has been no national election for twenty-five years. Such a policy on the part of President Diaz has no doubt been the wisest compromise possible, considering the nature of the people over whom he presides; nevertheless, when compared with the fearless methods of America, Canada, and Australia, it serves only to emphasize the position of the Latin races as "dwellers in the tents of Shem."

In this very fact, however, lies the promise of safety to the social evolution of the world. Time was when the race dominated all the kingdoms of the earth; but it has evidently passed its zenith long ago; and mankind need therefore fear no future disturbance of world-wide consequence. That certain branches are farther gone in decadence than others was painfully manifested in the

[1] I have no desire to minimize the greatness of Japheth's contributions to civilization; these contributions are, however, such as spring out of a race genius for externalities—sculpture, painting, music, discipline—rather than out of such profound, spiritual ideals as those for which Shem is noted.

pusillanimity exhibited by the Spaniards in the late war with the United States; but that even the foremost branch could, as a nation, acquiesce in and maintain a lie in the Dreyfus trial, shows that the French themselves are headed downward.

The future of the Hamitic race is undoubtedly that pointed out by Noah: "A servant of servants shall he be to his brethren." Not in the sense of bondage,—for slavery debases the slave-holder more than it harms the slave,—but in the sense of the "hewer of wood and the drawer of water" for his brother. In other words, he will be the artisan of the world. The future of the Japhetic race will probably be that of gradual absorption and assimilation with the dominant civilization. The future of the Semitic race—who can paint its transcendent outcome! For the day-star of its greatness has but barely risen.

Thus has the "Most High ruled among the kingdoms of men." How He has brought about so marvellous an evolution of mankind will be discussed in the next chapter.

NOTE.—This edition being a reprint from the stereotyped plates of the Putnam edition; it is not easy to make changes, nevertheless, the above reference to our gallant Allies written at a time when all the world wondered at the Nation's attitude, seems now—fifteen years later—distinctly unfortunate; and the author therefore takes this somewhat unusual method of making amends. No one, after witnessing their heroic struggles and unparalleled sacrifices during four years of war, can doubt the innate strength and virtue of the French people, or that this branch of Japheth is entirely worthy "to dwell in the tents of Shem."—N. L. N.

CHAPTER XII

HOW GOD RULES AMONG THE NATIONS

AS will have been gathered by the thoughtful reader of the last chapter, God shapes the destiny of nations, during this middle epoch, or second estate of man, by the inevitable self-classification of spirits during their pre-mortal life. The doctrine of pre-existence, in so far as it is revealed by Scripture, is reserved for treatment in the Appendix (see A), since this exposition proceeds by scientific rather than by dogmatic arguments. Here the doctrine is put forward merely as an hypothesis, and no other warrant is claimed for its acceptance, than what obtains in other probable reasoning. If it explains phenomena otherwise inexplicable, or but faultily explicable by other theories, it will appeal to the searcher after final causes; if not, it may be passed by.

Not that I shall be able, in so brief and indirect a treatment as can be accorded it here, to exhaust the reasons for its acceptance; other reasons—notably those which theosophists marshall in support of reincarnation—will occur to the student who tries to account for the mysteries of life; especially those mysteries which are manifested in the phenomena clustering around heredity. I may add, furthermore, that, as in the case of many other tenets of religion, the final testimony of its truth must come, when it does come, rather by the inborn revelation of the Infinite to each individual soul, than upon the evidence either of Scripture or of reason.

Assuming, then, that all men who have functioned or will function on this earth had a pre-existence, in which the laws of psychic development were the same as here; and that, being free, such spirits must react on, and be shaped by environment according to their interpretation of phenomena—precisely also as in mortal life,—is it not more than probable that many—perhaps most—would locate Authority, or the compelling force of the universe, in personality, the concrete form, rather than in divine law, the abstract truth entity behind that form? Mortals do that, in spite of all God's efforts to make them love the truth rather than the dispenser of the truth. This would account for Lucifer's seducing, by the contagion of a persuasive personality, one third of the spirits in heaven into open rebellion against the impregnable forces of universal law. It would also account for the slave-tyrant bias out of which sprang the old civilization of the world: for the Alexander and Cæsar vortexes in ancient times and for the Napoleonic cyclones in our own day.

Apply now the simple law that like adheres to like, and we should inevitably have self-classification of spirits in heaven. Next take into account that in any vast aggregation of spirits brought together by concurrent conceptions as to the final location of authority, there must be all degrees of masterfulness—for this quality is based purely on intellectual weight. Approaches now the time, when the demands of psychic evolution require a more restricted environment, a new or mortal world, such as we are now in.

What will happen in that new world? It would hardly need the wisdom of God to foresee that there will be endless conflicts, where final authority is conceived to be located in persons rather than in law. Would not infinite justice demand, then, that these spirits be mortalized at such a time and in such an order, as least to upset God's plans; *i. e.*, as least to injure the evolution of souls who were beginning to perceive the true source of authority in law?

The flower of the Hamitic race were accordingly sent to earth when the world was young and empty; when, outside their own ranks, they must war upon rocks and trees and the wild beasts of the forest. It was surely wiser to bank their fury in pyramids of stone than in a Cæsar's column of human skulls.[1] Reflect for a moment how impossible would have been the present and future civilization of Shem if the Hamitic spirits had

[1] Vide *Cæsar's Column*, by Ignatius Donelly.

come to earth in reverse order, or even if Japheth's "enlargement" had been placed elsewhere than in the swelling tide of Greece and Rome. The lovers of freedom, who are to-day paving God's highways to the Millennium, would instead be grappling in death throes with the Pharaohs, the Nebuchadnezzars, and the Alexanders of slave-tyrant memory, and anarchy such as the world has never dreamed of would reign supreme.

Nor is it in the supreme perspective of history alone that God is shaping results; for while it is chiefly important that the world shall eventuate as He has planned, it is certainly a second consideration that peoples shall be thrown successively into such environment as to free them from the false bias of a previous environment. With such a principle of interpretation, the historical perspective of individual nations takes on a new significance. Space will permit of but a few examples illustrating this conception; but these, I believe, will be found strictly characteristic; that is to say, similar examples can be found in the history of every people.

Take, for instance, the confusion of tongues at the Tower of Babel. It is inconceivable that the reason for this event is that which is directly inferrable on the face of the divine record. The ultimate purpose of so scattering mankind must have been the good of the human race. And one need not look long before he discover that good. Had mankind remained one homogeneous whole, the very weight of what might be called the psychic dead level would have operated to prevent those differentiations of character and soul-expression, the reaction of which has been the source of the evolution of society.

Take from ancient history two examples, both resulting from this scattering. Let the first be that of Greece. Here, bounded by insignificant geographical limits, was incarnated a group of spirits so allied in psychic tendencies that they speedily became a light unto the world. Acted upon by a physical environment singularly propitious, and freed from the dullness of the world's dead level, as well as from the paralyzing effect of an absolute standard of art, such as hampered their neighbors, the Egyptians, they evolved ideals in literature, painting, and sculpture, from which the world still draws inspiration. Would this have been possible had these gifted spirits been distributed, say, throughout the humdrum hordes of China?

The converse conception is equally improbable. Take a similar quota of spirits segregated by divine justice for Chinese nationality, and let them be born successively in the isles of Greece, would they have produced the Iliad and Odyssey or built the Parthenon? But, says the objector, suppose they had been subjected to all the psychic influences that played upon the Greeks, would it not have made Greeks of them? The supposition is impossible. These psychic influences were nothing else than the spirit of the Greeks themselves made visible. Take away these people and you take away their whole social environment. There would, of course, have remained the same sun, but think you it would have been conceived as Phœbus Apollo driving daily across heaven's blue meadows in a golden chariot? There would have remained the same mountains, but would they have been peopled by that same glorious assemblage of gods and goddesses? There would have been the same groves and streams, the same sunlit waves bathing the golden shores; but fancy a group of Chinese spirits peopling them with nymphs and naiads, sirens and tritons!

The conclusion is almost inevitable that each segregated group of spirits expresses in earth-life primarily what they are, and only secondarily what they become; and since what is good and true and beautiful, being in harmony with the universe, has a tendency to live and spread; and what is intrinsically evil, to die and be stamped out, such groups can, by national momentum, benefit the world to a degree impossible were their virtues applied sporadically over vast areas; and at the same time they tend to do least harm to the general evolution of righteousness, since the vices and sins which constitute their weakness breathe out their ephemeral life for the most part at home.

Take next the Jewish nation as another conspicuous example illustrating this general law.

Here was a people fitted by the very quintessence of their soul-bias to keep alive the most important truths that man can know, the nature and attributes of the one true God, maker of heaven and earth, and the relationship of liberty which ought to subsist among all men. How could these truths have been upheld until they have all but overthrown idolatry and tyranny, if God had not segregated for a single nation the spirits imbued with them during pre-existence? And, note you, when this ideal had been fixed, these spirits were again scattered among the nations, unconscious missionaries, carrying with them their innate love of the one true God, and its reciprocal idea, the love of man, or the individual liberty ideal that is shaping modern institutions. Thus does the God of heaven seek to leaven the dull, heavy, cruel lump of humanity; thus fulfil His promise that in Abraham and in his seed shall all the nations of the earth be blessed.

Take now two modern instances. Do you think it purely accidental that the Western continent was hidden from the world for so many thousand years? Or that when discovered, the foremost peoples to seek refuge in it should be the Pilgrims and Quakers? Was it accidental that such a group of masterful spirits as the framers of our Declaration of Independence were born in the same age and thrown together by mutual sympathies? Could the spirits now banded together as Tammany Hall have conceived and launched this glorious nation, this new "Liberty enlightening the world"?

The ideals for which the American commonwealth stands would have been strangled at birth in any other land or at any other time in the world's history. And when mankind shall have the same reverence for the Book of Mormon that they have for the Bible, it will be recognized not only that all this was planned by the Almighty, ere Jacob blessed his sons or Moses smote the rock in the wilderness, but also that it was foretold by holy prophets over two thousand years ago.

The last example I shall adduce is that of the Mormon people themselves. Called by the voice of the Spirit "two of a family and one of a city," and led and driven alternately to the barren wastes of the Rocky Mountains, they are to-day holding up the highest standard of righteousness that the world has ever seen. Judged superficially they may, indeed, seem what their traducers call them, the poor, the unlettered, the despised of the world; for, in the language of Paul, "not many wise men, after the flesh, not many mighty, not many noble" have the moral courage to accept the real Gospel of Jesus Christ. As in the days of Christ, they have been chosen from the ranks of the fishermen, the farmers, the artisans of the world; but humble as they are, they are raised to the rank of true manhood and womanhood by a virtue which you that read, scholar and fine gentleman that you are, perchance may not possess—the moral courage to forsake houses and lands, break the dearest ties of kindred, face the obloquy of a surprised and outraged social circle, and cast in your lot with a people counted the "filth and offscourings of all things"—for the sake of an ideal.

Call them low-bred, if you will,—ignorant, uncouth, mistaken zealots, fanatics, anything that will relieve your sense of propriety,—your pitiful infatuation for sham and conventionality; but dare not call them cowards. For animating those ungraceful figures bent with toil; guiding the caresses of those calloused hands, unfit for palette or keyboard; strangely lighting those rugged countenances, when no apparent cause is visible, are the souls of heroes and heroines; not, indeed, of the kind that do and dare for the plaudits of the world; but of the kind utterly unconscious that they are brave; fearing only the eye of their Maker, and seeking solace of Him in secret places, with tears and broken sobs, when all the world spurns them!

Such are the foundation stones that Mormonism has dug from the mud and debris 'neath the feet of the gay and fashionable world. Such have been the Elders it has commissioned in the past to carry its message back to their fellows in bondage. Little wonder that they avoided the great and the learned and labored among the poor. But now their sons and daughters are here. These fear no comparison even by the world's standards. Tall and straight and comely, gifted with intellectual vigor and spiritual insight, they are among the flower of Shem reserved for this last conflict with falsehood and artificiality. Nor do they lack the courage of their fathers and mothers. At this very moment two thousand such young men are travelling throughout the world at the sacrifice of their own hard-earned means; preaching the message of the new dispensation to all who will listen; and finding ineffable joy even when a stone and bed of leaves by the wayside serves them for rest, and the infinite starry canopy is the only roof above their heads. And at home in the valleys, as the shades of night deepen, hundreds of young mothers are calling flocks of rosy-cheeked children into neat but unpretentious homes; and there in the little parlor they will kneel together and pray the Father that papa may be protected against mobs and evil designing men.

And there are fifty thousand other young men ready to go when the call shall come; and as many young women ready to do their part in keeping up the table, rearing their children to fear and love the Lord,—even sewing and washing, if need be, to send their husbands money with which to buy shoes. Nor is this fanaticism; it results from a dynamic realization of that reciprocal and indissoluble ideal—love of God and love of man; it is only a sane and rational approach toward that altruism which shall in time be world-wide,—a clear sensing of the law that he who would lose his life shall save it, he who would save his life shall lose it. And though the results measured in converts are meagre enough, yet measured in their reactions on the character of the Latter-day Saints as a people, they are above the price of rubies.

But it is precisely in this latter respect—the conservation of its own great religious ideals—that Mormonism will finally become a "light unto the nations": in its natural growth from within; in its standard of equal purity for both sexes; in its maintenance of the inviolable sacredness of the fountain of life—neither curtailing offspring, nor, in the phrase of Paul, "changing the natural use for that which is against nature"; in its recrudescence of the Bible ideal that "Children are the heritage of the Lord,—happy is the man that hath his quiver full of them"; in its insistence that every man, *and every woman*, has an inalienable right to this heritage; in its belief in continuous revelation, the reciprocal communication between man and God, as between personal beings,— Father and child; in short, in its mergence of life with religion as one conception, thereby bridging the gulf between profession and practice, and doing away with the shams and pretenses of an artificial holiness, to the end that the highest functions of religion may co-exist, if need were, with jumpers and overalls,—that is, with any necessary social status.

Such then is the very heart of Mormonism so

universally vilified and traduced among men. Need I point out that it, too, is one of the factors— a very important one—with which God is shaping the destiny of mankind? In this respect, therefore, it illustrates the general law that God segregates into groups the spirits to be born on earth, so that their reactions upon each other shall bring about His supreme purposes in the regeneration and salvation of mankind.

CHAPTER XIII

HOW GOD SHAPES THE DESTINY OF THE INDIVIDUAL

IN the two previous chapters I have shown respectively how the Lord is shaping the social destiny of the world, and also the social destinies of peoples. In this chapter I shall attempt to indicate how He also shapes the ends of individuals "rough hew them how we will."

If the thoughts and deeds of each day and hour pass immediate judgment on our souls, adding to or taking from the sum total of our power in the universe, how much more must the combined results of pre-existence fix the status which divine justice assigns to us in this new world. Being born, therefore, is being judged; for is it not a second opening of the book of life? There will be other openings in the hereafter, wherein the "deeds done in the body" will newly classify us, both as to companionship and habitat; but the point to note here is; that such a classification has already taken place, both in world-scope and in nation-scope as we have seen, and also in the scope of individuals, as I hope now to show.

"Thou shalt have no other gods before me,"

said Jehovah, and followed the commandment by what has always been regarded as a divine threat, in case of disobedience, viz., that He would "visit the iniquities of the fathers upon the children unto the third and fourth generations" of them that hate Him; which, however, is no threat at all, but merely a statement of the simple workings of eternal justice.

Consider all the bearings in the case. There is first the sin of idolatry,—the most grievous of all sins, since by it men are alienated from God, and so are cut off, like branches, from the very source of that spiritual life which constitutes the essential bond of their unity with the universe. A thousand evils follow in the wake of him who has thus strayed into darkness.

In the next place, the penalty for committing this sin must manifestly be upon them that commit it, not upon unborn generations. What should we think of a human law which hanged the grandson because his father's father escaped justice? Somehow, then, this *is* the penalty for turning away from God,—to be cursed with children of like proclivities. We are not yet able to see clearly in what way eternal bliss is bound up with the salvation of our posterity; but just as the supreme punishment brought upon himself by Judas was not so much his death, as that he should have no seed—that he should run out, as it were, like a stream in a desert,—so being cursed with Godless children is next to being cursed like

Judas; for as these children will, like the parents, probably not repent, and will therefore be lost to the generations of heaven, it is equivalent, from the eternal point of view, to having no seed whatever.

Consider next the aspect of the children to be born. Could divine justice consign to the parental care of idolators, spirits who had learned to love the Lord their God, or even spirits who were neutral on this foremost attitude of the soul; with the certainty that such souls would be biased during mortal life to their own undoing? Plainly not. Justice must seek out spirits deserving of no better parentage; spirits perilously near the border-line of those who fought against God and were cast out of heaven.

Being born under such parents would be no punishment to them,—merely justice; but it is a punishment to the parents, who, knowing God, and having made covenants with him, turn away to worship idols,—of wood or stone in the days gone by, and of wealth or social position, or whatever else in modern times takes the place of old-world idolatry.

But because justice consigns such spirits to godless parents, the love of God does not desert them. It is ever busy contriving environments that shall tend to save; sickness, sorrow, reverses in fortune, happiness, and prosperity, or the terrible knocks of fate,—anything either positive or negative that shall bring them face to face with the meaning of law, and from the teachings of law to faith in the Lawgiver. That is evidently the meaning of those other words, in the same divine fiat: "Showing mercy to thousands that love me and keep my commandments."

The immediate generalization to be drawn from this text is that parents will draw to themselves the kind of spirits they deserve,—the kind that their own psychic qualities shall have prepared the way for. The godless will perpetuate their godlessness in their offspring; the virtuous, the pious, the loving will attract like souls to themselves; and this law may be extended indefinitely.

It was no accident that Mozart came to a line of ancestors who had progressively prepared a body for him with a musical brain and an exquisite nervous organization. Would it have been justice to consign such a soul into the darkness of a tuneless mortal abode—a body admirably fitted perhaps for mounting clods, or felling trees, or hauling in a seine, but unable to respond to music more complex than the dinner horn? And so of the great poets, the great scientists, the great mechanics, the great inventors, the great statesmen. Obviously divine justice, in pronouncing judgment upon a soul's attainment during pre-existence, must work in harmony with, not in opposition to, the law of physical heredity. The new environment must be a continuation of the old, in so far as it shall conserve and accumulate a positive tendency. And justice may demand a similar sequence for negative tendencies; though here, whatever can be stripped from justice by love and mercy will surely be done.

While this may be counted the general law, it does not by any means explain the whole of God's providences for the evolution of the individual. Take that curious dilemma put by the disciples of Christ: "Master, who did sin, this man or his parents, that he was born blind?" (John ix., 2). Two possible causes for blindness are mooted in this question. The first has reference to spiritual heredity. If blindness came because of the man's sin, it could have been no other than a sin during pre-existence; a neglect to develop the psychic sub-basis of vision, or an abuse of this psychic attribute that should destroy its power during mortal life. The second points to physical heredity. Parents may so sin as to transmit an impaired nervous mechanism of sight. In our Saviour's answer a third possible cause presents itself: "Neither hath this man sinned, nor his parents: but that the works of God should be made manifest." The third alternative therefore is that the man was blind by God's providence.

Before developing these three possibilities in their relations to the phenomena of heredity, let us consider the nature of the change that takes place when spirits pass from their first to their second estate.

The prime characteristic is manifestly an occlusion of memory; not a complete shutting off, but almost so. The light from that previous life has ceased to be transparent, but still flickers in the memory of most men in a very subdued translucence, hardly above opacity. The dim sense of familiarity on meeting strangers, or hearing new truths; the vague sensation that a given situation has been perceived before,—constitute probably the lingering echoes of our first estate. Says the poet:

> Yet oft times a secret something,
>   Whispered, You're a stranger here;
> And I felt that I had wandered
>   From a more exalted sphere.

In the history of psychology are well authenticated cases of complete loss of memory; accompanied, however, with that same haunting sense of familiarity when the subjects were brought into contact with previous associations. The fact of our oblivion to pre-existence is therefore no evidence that we had no such previous life. It argues merely a deep and beneficent purpose on the part of Him who is shaping our destiny. What that purpose is in part we may guess from a consideration of the cases of lapsed memory above mentioned. In order to reacquire their lost knowledge, they were compelled to come into contact again with the elements of that knowledge; often with a decided advantage in the matter of thoroughness. Would not half the human race be benefited, from the standpoint of truth, if the hazy foundations of their mentality were entirely erased, and they were obliged to re-examine fundamental environment with more critical accuracy? So we may believe respecting the pupils of heaven advanced to this middle school: with all the objects of pre-existent environment in memory, much of earth-life would be merely guessed at from its inevitable familiarity; but with every object of comparison blotted out of mind, the charm of novelty would reinvest it. A deeper reason, however, for this veil of oblivion is associated with the very nature of repentance and forgiveness, and will be discussed later on.

How this veil was drawn down over humanity, need surely not disturb us in view of the fact that the hypnotist can induce the same blank in memory for a limited period of time. But certain facts connected with it will be pertinent to the discussion. Take the case of our Saviour. Either he was an exception in the matter of being oblivious to pre-existence, or else the veil was withdrawn on that memorable night preceding Calvary; for he prayed "Father, glorify thou me with the glory I had with thee, *before the world was.*"

Again, in respect of Christ, it is inconceivable that He who attained the fullness of Godhood should not be more perfect intellectually than any other man that has lived: a greater statesman than Moses, a sweeter singer than David, a profounder philosopher than Plato, a sublimer poet than Shakespeare. Where, then, were these traits of mental superiority? All hidden by the wisdom of God; eclipsed that the sun of His spiritual righteousness might alone shine out upon the darkened world.

Whence we may conclude that though the exercise of a sublime gift is proof that such a gift is in the soul, yet it is by no means certain that it is the only, or even the greatest, gift of the soul; nor that he who manifests no transcendent gift in mortal life has none in respect of eternity. For it is more than probable that all spirits are innately more glorious than they appear through the imperfect medium of earth-life; and that transcendent gifts are often hidden,—save when they are needed to give light to the world,—in order that some neglected, mediocre talent may have opportunity to grow.

Let no man therefore sit in harsh judgment on his fellow-man. Of positive qualities we may safely say, They are his because he earned them, either in this life or in a previous life; of some negative qualities also we may know the genesis, either through the man's sins or the sins of his parents; and that this man is born blind, that one deaf and dumb, the third one stupid, may indeed be—probably is—the result of doing or failing to do in pre-existence; but it may also be a dispensation of God, who, foreseeing the effect for evil of a certain attribute of the soul, mercifully veils its power to function during mortal life. "If thy right eye offend thee, pluck it out and cast it from thee; for it is profitable for thee that one of thy members should perish and not that thy whole body should be cast into hell."

With these three-fold antecedents, spiritual heredity, physical heredity, and foreordination by God, we shall be able to explain phenomena which are inexplicable by the data on which science now relies; as, for instance, the wide divergence in character and aptitudes of children from the same parents, where the physical antecedents are practically the same; and the marked diversity in gift and inclination often discernible in twins, whose prenatal environments were identical. We are also able to understand those apparent exceptions to all laws of heredity: a Moses cradled in the rushes of the Nile; a David, the most obscure son of an obscure man; a Mohammed, camel-driver in the great caravans of the desert; a Luther, one among a thousand half-buried monks; a Shakespeare, born ostensibly to comb wool and manufacture gloves; a Lincoln who by law of heredity should have remained a rail-splitter and tenth-rate farmer; a Joseph Smith, whose life opened as a hired hand in the backwoods of Vermont.

All these men, and thousands of others whose characters have been epoch-making either in great or in small degree, represent spirits the momentum of whose pre-existent lives was such that no mortal obstacles could stay its impact. Like John the Baptist, chosen before conception, and filled with the Holy Ghost from his birth (Luke i.); like Jeremiah, whom God foreknew and ordained a prophet unto the nations before he was formed in the womb (Jeremiah i., 5); like Christ, supremest of God's children, yet descending below the meanest in the lowliness of his birth, —all these mighty ones were foreordained by God to the missions of world-shaping that they so nobly fulfilled.

Such is also the explanation of all men and women who are born ahead of their time; prophets and seers whose voices, tuned to a higher, sublimer melody, ring out discordant on a dull contented world; harbingers of truths whose transcendent beauty only blinds and infuriates for the time being; heralds of a new and higher civilization, whose martyrs they willingly become.

And this thought leads to another: the physical tabernacles into which these spirits were born were perhaps not fitted, or but poorly fitted, for the lofty functions to which they were destined. What then? The royal tenants remodelled them to their own purposes; developed new brain cells; broke through the ancestral tendency to ossify at given stages of life; moulded the physical vehicle to the needs of the dominant intelligence. Whence we may reach the general conclusion that in every contest to decide which shall predominate the life, the physical or the spiritual heredity, it is always in the power of the latter to conquer.

Supremacy lies, I repeat, always potential in spiritual heredity;[1] but, alas, how rarely does it become dynamic. It is precisely in this contest that the soul has need of a teacher—some external companion more mature in the wisdom of experience, who shall foresee the battles, arouse the sleeping soul, and help buckle on its armor. Such a companion every man can be to his fellow-man; and if life lays upon us any supreme duty, it is this, of helping each generation to rise above the last. Such soul-guides are provided naturally in parents, brothers and sisters, preceptors and teachers; and, indirectly, it is for this end, too, that scientists investigate, mechanics invent, philosophers interpret, and poets write. All these forces may be reckoned as means by which God is shaping the destiny of the individual.

But all these combined would of themselves go but a little way in this battle between what Paul calls the flesh and the spirit; for the reason that they are too general; they form rather a favorable setting for victory, than aids toward cocking and priming the will in the day and hour that the individual contests come. A guide and monitor, such as the last exigency would require, God furnishes to each soul in the form of a guardian angel.

---

[1] Of the positive type, which type alone represents power. Negative spiritual tendencies, represent merely the absence of power.

Such is the revelation of Scripture, such the faith of Latter-day Saints.

It is to this representative of the Father that we owe nine tenths of those adjustments in our personal or individual environment, which in the sum total do most to shape our lives; His is the "Still small voice," which admonishes us to resist temptation; His the soothing companionship which comforts us in trial and tribulation. And yet even in this the most direct approach that the Father of lights can make toward influencing us for good, we can and do constantly resist; for amidst all the creatures of the universe, we—that is to say, spiritual beings—alone are free. Nor is that freedom alienable even by God himself; and therefore, although it remains true—to repeat that flash of insight by the immortal poet—that "a destiny shapes our ends rough hew them how we will," yet at the final analysis, we are saved or damned according as we consent to or resist the shaping.

CHAPTER XIV

THE SCIENTIFIC ASPECT OF FAITH IN GOD

IF the notion expressed in the phrase "survival of the fittest" represents essentially the spirit of evolution, then the outcome of mankind, as set forth in the three preceding chapters, must show that the conceptions of Mormonism respecting sociological evolution are in line with the foremost scientific thought of the age; not only in line, but leading the line, since its generalizations are wider and more far-reaching than those of any other hypotheses that have yet attempted to correlate and unify the progress of the race.

Hitherto, however, we have traced the evolution only as man has been, for the most part at least, unconsciously acted upon by the environment thrown around him by the Creator; in which respect, therefore, the history of his modification has differed from that of the non-psychic world—rocks, trees, and animals—only by the single factor of free-will on his part; which, though it has no doubt retarded the plans of the infinite Evolutor—if I may venture to coin a word—has not otherwise materially modified the outcome of those plans. As was inevitable, the futile rage of man's opposition during the ages to things as they are, could have no other effect than the retardation of his development, and collectively the retardation of the race; for to be ignorant of law is to be the toy, the plaything, the drift-wood of natural forces; just as to be acquainted with law, to live in harmony with law, which has measurably characterized the race in later times, has given him power and consequence,—armed him, as it were, with the omnipotence of God by so much.

But the unconscious evolution of the race cannot go on forever; a time comes when man must consent to be a conscious co-operator with God in his own psychic development; under penalty, should he refuse, of cutting short his eternal progress; in other words, of being damned. This is the irrefragable scientific truth on which the Gospel of Jesus Christ is based. For what is that Gospel but the definitely prescribed conditions under which man, in the exercise of his free will, may enter into covenant with God, and so become a co-worker with Jesus Christ in the perfecting of his own soul? Paul defines the Gospel as the "Power of God unto salvation." In the terms of scientific thought Paul's words would mean: the power which God places progressively into the hands of man for the working out of his psychic evolution.

On making such a compact man immediately

changes his status in the universe; for whereas he was before one of the class to be worked with, he passes over at once and takes rank among the "workers."[1] Here, for a million ages perhaps, under the supervision of Jesus Christ, he will fill posts of duty progressively suited to his growing powers; until by doing the works of God he eventually attains to the perfection of God. Such a change of status evidently underlies John's words (i. 12), wherein he says: "But as many as received him (*i. e.*, made covenant with God), to them gave he power to become the Sons of God," —"joint-heirs with Jesus Christ," as Paul puts it (Rom. viii., 17).

But are not men and women already children of God by right of birth in heaven? True enough; but they are not children of the covenant. They have not accepted the relationship of

[1] There are but three classes of intelligent beings in the universe; the workers, the worked-with, and the damned. The workers represent all who, by their own free will, have entered into covenant with God. The worked-with are spirits yet undetermined, whom divine love is reaching out for. Many of them are, according to their light, workers with a zeal that ought to put to shame the more slack of the covenant class; these must inevitably enroll themselves with the workers by definite compact when they shall finally learn to look up from law to the Source of Law. The damned are spirits who, having become irrevocable enemies of both workers and worked-with,—enemies in fact of the universe,—can have no further evolution, but are in process of sinking back to the state whence they began to evolve. The terms used in this classification are my own, and do not necessarily belong to the technical terminology of Mormonism.

subordination to the Father by act of choice, and no one can be enrolled among the workers who is not there by virtue of his own sovereign will; for all these have set out to become "perfect as their Father in heaven is perfect," and the foremost prerogative of that perfection is absolute freedom.

All men, therefore, if they would be "heirs of God, and joint-heirs with Christ" must enter the Kingdom by solemn covenant. "We believe," says one of our articles of faith, "that all men may be saved by obedience to the laws and ordinances of the Gospel. . . . We believe these laws and ordinances to be faith, repentance, baptism by immersion for the remission of sins, and the laying on of hands for the gift of the Holy Ghost." It shall be my purpose now to consider in sequence each of these conditions of adoption into the commonwealth of heaven, and show how simple and inevitable they are in the nature of thought itself, even without reference to the fiat of Jehovah.

Faith, the most obvious and universal of all the operations of mind, has been unnecessarily obscured by its association with the esoteric rites of religion, and by the profound attempts of theologians to explain its meaning. Even Paul's definition of it as the "Substance (assurance) of things hoped for, the evidence of things not seen," while logically true enough, is not unlike Dr. Johnson's famous explication of the word network as "anything reticulated or decussated at equal intervals with interstices between the intersections,"—more difficult to comprehend than the word itself.

Let us rather get at the vital significance of faith by noting its operation. "Without faith," says Paul, "it is impossible to please God." And then he proceeds to give the reasons, which are manifestly self-evident: "For he that cometh to God, must believe that he is, and that he is a rewarder of them that diligently seek him" (Heb. xi., 6). The reasoning is this: It is pleasing to God to have his children "seek Him," *i. e.*, enroll themselves as workers in the Kingdom of heaven. But they will not take the first step toward so pleasing Him, unless they feel assured of two things respecting Him: first that He actually exists and second that He will reward their seeking. What could be more conclusive?

It follows therefore that faith in God must be the fundamental principle of religion. But just how absolutely and fundamentally essential it is to the psychic unity of mankind, and therefore to man's salvation, does not appear on the surface. Most men consequently place the necessity of faith in God on a mere personal relation, the need of placating a Being supreme-by-will, who holds in his hands the threads of our destiny to snap in two or prolong according to His divine pleasure. No error of interpretation could be more egregious, nor more fatal in its effect upon the shaping of our lives.

Consider, by way of analogy, which supreme

fact it is that gives order, perspective, and ultimate relationship to all the diverse facts of physical science. Let me enumerate, from where I sit, a series of apparently unrelated phenomena, and then see how magically they fall into lines of sequence, when I shall name the controlling source of unity; that snow bank near the summit of Timpanogas, and the fact that it is slowly melting; yonder lightning-riven tree; the butterfly above me matching its wings with the sunlit maple leaves; that splendid slide of shale a half-mile long; the rotting of that fallen giant of the forest; the curling steam and smoke of that laboring locomotive; that charming series of waterfalls; the balsam-scented air that wafts its cadences to me;—and so of ten thousand other objects of sensation. To the ancients they were a heterogeneous mass of unrelated things, or related at best by an endless series of gods, goddesses, nymphs, gnomes, and fairies, and to a later day by astrology, necromancy, magic, what-not; but to us, even though we are but tyros in modern science, one supreme fact co-ordinates and subordinates them all—the influence of the sun. What a blessed sense of peace and finality has come to science with this perception, what gigantic strides in material civilization!

A similar peace, a similar unity, a similar sense of finality will bless mankind in the spiritual and social world, when they shall come to believe alike that "God is, and that he is a rewarder of them that diligently seek him." For, though the ages of mythology and idolatry are gone, how much nearer are we to a unity of faith in the God of Abraham, Isaac, and Jacob? Among the comparatively few who profess this faith there is endless variance, and the rest of mankind are either reverently agnostic or openly atheistic.

As long as these divisions shall remain, as long as this apathy respecting the Source of our psychic life shall benumb mankind, so long must the dream of the social reformer be deferred, so long must the Millennium remain a mirage. For race unity will depend upon something deeper than material well-being, however much the long-delayed equality in property rights may contribute to that end: the point where soul coalesces with soul is spirit, not flesh; least of all, then, the trappings of flesh.

Let us understand, then, once for all, that the reiterated passages in Holy Writ which enjoin faith in God as man's first duty, are not made insistent for the sake of God's glorification, but primarily, if not solely, for man's psychic evolution; for God is the Sun of the psychic world, the source of its life, the only possible bond of its unity; and not to come into unity with God is to be at variance with the universe, which means ultimately annihilation, so far as that is possible to man.

Let us next get some rational conception of what faith in God means. To believe that He is, implies vastly more than the passive acceptance of the dogma respecting His divine personality. "It is a fearful thing," says a text in scripture "to fall into the hands of the living God." If this be taken literally, that is, to imply merely physical contact, there need be little fear; but where "the living God" is understood to stand for law and order, whether as manifested in the natural world or in the ministrations of divine authority, it may well come home, freighted with dread and terror, to every soul. Faith in God as the Mohammetan holds it, means something; as the Christian holds it, it means more, including as it does, Jesus Christ; to the Mormon it means still more, including besides the objects of the Christian's faith the last dispensation of His will to man. It is not therefore a measureable quantity; to one man it may give power to look within the veil, as Joseph Smith did; to another, it may give only the first glimmerings of order and consistency in the universe. Certain it is that, in this wider sense, faith in God lies at the very basis of civilization; for what is civilization but the sum total of man's adjustments in accordance with his interpretations of law; and what is law but the living God— the only way in which He can live daily and hourly in our lives?

Let us next look at the quality of faith as variously manifested by mankind. Two of the most important types occurred in the ministry of the Saviour. The first was that manifested by Nathaniel (John i., 45–51): "Behold an Israelite indeed, in whom is no guile!" exclaimed the Saviour on seeing him approach.—"Whence knowest thou me?" asked Nathaniel. Jesus answered that He had seen him under the fig tree before Philip called him. "Rabbi," exclaimed Nathaniel, overcome by the swiftness of his spiritual intuitions, "thou art the Son of God; thou art the King of Israel."

Contrast now with this sudden, unreasoning, overwhelming conviction of Nathaniel, the slow, hesitating, investigating faith of Thomas. Eleven of the apostles had seen and conversed with the Lord after His resurrection, but their combined testimony did not affect Thomas. "Except I shall see in his hands the prints of the nails, and put my finger into the print of the nails, and thrust my hand into his side, I will not believe." Eight days later the sceptic's opportunity came. "Reach hither thy finger, and behold my hands," said the Saviour; "and reach hither thy hand and thrust it into my side: and be not faithless but believing." Then, and only then, did conviction reach the soul of Thomas, so that, like Nathaniel, he also exclaimed: "My Lord and my God!"

Note now our Saviour's comment on these two types of faith: "Thomas, because thou hast seen me, thou hast believed: blessed are they that have not seen and yet have believed." Nathaniel's was undoubtedly the superior, but both were positive forms of faith. What is the explanation of their differences? The first type is intuitional.

Nathaniel perceived the Kingship of Christ by percisely the same law that Christ perceived the guilelessness of Nathaniel. It was a perception not dependent upon external marks; it was rather a flowing out, as it were, and commingling of soul with soul. But Thomas's soul was too densely barred by its fleshly tabernacle thus to flow out and meet the Saviour. There was consequently no alternative but that Christ must flow into him; and that, too, by the only channels open to him,— the physical senses. It is characteristic of the sturdy integrity of the man, and therefore of his worthiness to be an apostle, that he did not feign a belief when the temptation to do so must have been overwhelming.

Faith of the quality necessary to produce conviction may be generalized as the native susceptibility or openness of the soul to the indwelling of truthness or the power that lights up and drives away the lurking shadows of doubt. I use the word truthness rather than truth, because the latter implies light accompanied with the images that emit the light; whereas the former implies pure light,—light abstracted from all definite relations. With truthness as the basis of your conviction you can give no reasons other than so it is, and it cannot be otherwise. Such was the nature of Nathaniel's testimony. He could not have told why he knew Jesus was the Christ, save only in the words of Peter at a later day, that God had revealed it to him. Such is the nature of every true testimony of the Gospel. It is the lighting up of our souls with truthness, the indwelling of that infinite Spirit which is saturated with and redolent of the mind and will of the Father.

On the other hand, where the basis of conviction is a definite series of truth-relations, as was the case with Thomas, reasons may be given back and forth tending more or less to modify the conviction. At bottom, however, this conviction rests on the same basis as the other; the degree of assurance, or truthness that lights up the soul; for just as the soul may be gloriously illumined by the inpouring of truthness or unconditioned light through the spiritual avenue of its being, so it may be dimly lighted by truthness, the abstraction of truth relations shining in upon it through the apertures of its natural plane of being.

Faith, truthness, and conviction will thus be seen to be a series of interrelated causes and effects. Faith is the prehensile power of the soul—the power by which it reaches out and coils its tendrils about truth; or, to vary the figure, it is the soul's absorptive power—the power by virtue of which it can be saturated with truth; or, to return to our first figure, it is the openness or susceptibility of the soul, whereby the light of truth can pour in and illumine its inner being. In either way of looking at it, faith results in truthness, and truthness as naturally results in conviction.

It is in the first, or immediate effect of faith, that all the phenomena of healing lie; for manifestly to the extent that the soul is lighted up with truthness, to that extent must all the spectres flee; and a goodly portion of the spectres lurking in every darkened mind are the ghosts or apparitions of physical ailments—diseases that exist only in the mind.[1] But even in real diseases or injuries—and Christian Science will scarcely succeed in persuading a man that a crushed skull, a broken leg, or a macerated hand is an illusion—faith is the best aid to nature in healing; for to the extent that truthness shall illumine the soul, to that extent will all negative tendencies—obstacles to nature's healing power—be in abeyance. Take the case of the man with a bullet hole in his breast. Life or death may hang entirely on his attitude of mind. Let him shrink and cower with fear and foreboding—in other words, rally round the wound all the hindrances to nature's recuperative power,—and he will probably die. But let him take the attitude: "It is nothing. Yes, a hole in the breast. What of it? I'll be out in a week. A little hole like that—not worth thinking about. I'll not think about it. I'm almost

---

[1] It is for the emphasizing of this supreme fact that Christian Scientists deserve credit. There was no need, however, to propagate, along with this truth, the monstrous error that phenomena, *i. e.*, the world and all things in it, are illusions of our senses. For manifestly even though they be not what crass materialists have held them to be,—even though they be insubstantial,—they are surely not to be ignored or despised. The very fact that they are, is evidence that God intended them to react on us to the development of eternal life.

well now. It simply can't get me down. I'm superior to it, and I don't yield." Let him think those things—let him keep back the ghosts—and nature's sole business is to close up the wound—a trifling matter. He will probably get well.

Nor is there apparently any time limit for the resurgence of nature's elastic forces, provided all weights are removed by faith. From the extreme instances in the ministry of Christ, wherein leprosy was instantly cleansed and a withered hand restored to its normal condition, even while the man held it out, down to the slow recovery from wasting diseases, healing is evidently accelerated or retarded according as the faith which assists nature is dynamic—full of will power, or static—full of resignation. "Faith without works is dead," says the apostle; and I cannot think of a more hopeless case of unburied deadness than the goody-good faith which gives up, and, with a limp and passive leaning on the Lord, prays and prays and prays, but makes no effort of will to assist the natural recuperative powers. How could the Lord respond to such contemptible inertness! What would the product be worth after it is healed? The grave is surely the proper place for a living thing so manifestly dead.

Reverting to the two types of faith, I may remark that mankind divides itself naturally into Nathaniels and Thomases; and according as either type predominates, so will the civilization of any epoch be spiritual or material. The faith which questions is peculiarly fitted to discover truth in the natural world; and consequently it is only a just tribute to say that our present unparalleled material civilization is due chiefly to those sturdy but cautious seekers after truth, the doubting Thomases of science. On the other hand, the high ideals which tend to shape our social life, the spirit which breathes from art and literature, the faith in God and the hope of a life hereafter, are as truly products of the intuitional type of faith.

The purpose of this paragraph is to point out the folly of either type's discrediting the other. Is Darwin to be damned because he had no testimony that Jesus is the Christ? What folly to think that God's providence, which was millions of years in preparing a habitat for man's earth-life, has no other place than this needle point in the cycle of being to influence a soul toward the true spiritual ideal! On the other hand, shall the man of science sneer at him who, with glowing countenance, sings: "I know that my Redeemer liveth?" Because his soul is closed and barred on the spiritual plane, does it follow that no other soul can commune directly with God? Let us rather strive to exemplify in our lives both these types of faith; exerting the fullest and most hesitating caution, when the truthness or soul-light sought can come only as an abstraction of truths apprehended through the physical senses; and on the other hand throwing open the skylight of our souls with the guileless trust of a child, when we would seek that purer source of truthness which leaves no room for doubt or fear. So shall the spiritual world illuminate the natural, and the natural make more real the spiritual.

Now, while faith is a native power of the soul—and is at the last analysis probably very closely allied to that power of will called attention in psychology,—it is by no means a fixed quantity. It is instantly subject to modification by act of will. No other attribute perhaps is susceptible to such swift enlargement, to such sudden occlusion. Let a man love and live by the truthness which faith ushers into his soul, and that very faith of truth-begetting capacity is enormously increased; but let him prove recreant to his truth-ideals, and presently they are gone; for darkness has taken their place—the man has no longer faith in the things he believed before.

Nor can faith remain as a passive attribute of the soul. The very condition of its existence is work. To cease striving is to be thrown into the limbos of doubt. The man who knows to-day that Jesus is the Christ may, in one short year, deny that he ever knew it; and he will speak truly. For this conviction is not based upon memory; it is the result of a stream of truthness, which remains constant as long as he is true to the obligations it involves. When he ceases to strive, his faith, closing in, shuts off the heavenly consciousness, and with it go his convictions. There can be no such thing as holding a truth in our souls and at the same time shirking its correlative responsibility. They who seem to do it may be set down for shams and hypocrites. It would not be a truth, that is to say, a living, vital relation; it would be only the shell or the echo of a truth.

And this thought brings me to the last topic in my theme,—the nature of false faith or superstition. This takes many forms, but they are all reducible to one aspect—a trust in personality, or something else concrete, rather than in law. Nor does one need to search far for the cause. Superstition has its source in spiritual inertia; or, to put my thought in Anglo-Saxon, in soul laziness. To fill the mind with truthness—the essence of law—requires no small effort of the will; since truthness, out of which grows the mental attitude, must be abstracted and generalized from many and widely divergent truths. Or if it be of the intuitional type, it requires no less of spiritual wrestling with the Lord. Consequently the man of indolent mind finds it much easier to base his mental attitude on that of another than to go to the bottom of things and know for himself.

Thus it is, for instance, that ten thousand young men and women in Zion lazily believe Mormonism is true because their parents know it is true. But this is only a small patch in the widespread weakness of society resulting from this bastard form of faith. Priestcraft thrives because of it; saint and relic worship are the very embodiment of it. Mobs usurp the functions of law, because their lives hold no abstract truth ideals. Corruption thrives in public office, because men's faith is centred in bosses, boodlers, and grafters rather than in that abstract thing, the will of the people.

But the subject widens in whatever direction one looks. What was it but this makeshift for true faith that enabled Satan to create a rebellion in heaven? What but the same subserviency to personality rather than to law that characterized the slave-tyrant civilization of the old world? From faith in persons, it is but one step downward to fetichism, or faith in charms and amulets; and to what hordes of cringing souls in the shadows of civilization, as well as in the fastnesses of barbarism, does not this aspect of faith take us?

Faith in law tends to unify mankind, since law being truth is universal and always consistent with itself; but faith in persons or fetiches tends to scatter and divide mankind, since personal leadership is a constantly and increasingly varying quantity. Thus all the inequalities, all the wrongs, all the miseries characterizing the social life of the world, spring directly or indirectly out of that interpretation which accepts the person—rather the authority wielded by the person—as the basis of subordination and homage. Even God himself is made no exception; but here no evil results—save as the tendency becomes confirmed in relation to lesser authority—for in God personality and law are one and inseparable.

True faith is that power which opens the soul to truthness—a quality abstracted and generalized both from persons and things; it lies at the basis of every advance in civilization, and is the true and only harbinger of the Millennium.

CHAPTER XV

TRUE EDUCATION AND TRUE REPENTANCE IDENTICAL OPERATIONS OF THE MIND

IT remains to be shown in a more definite way how the closing statement in the last chapter is true. As a preliminary, let me call attention to two parallel utterances, evidently intended to voice the same general truth. "Except ye repent," says Christ, "ye shall all likewise perish." Here is no equivocation. If His words are true, they are applicable to all mankind alike. Nor is it worth while to temporize with the word perish. It stands for the grim fact of damnation —our ultimate spiritual undoing. It is characteristic of the futility of dogmatic preaching, that this awful text no longer arouses fear and terror in the heart of the average listener. The reason evidently is that he cannot actively feel its truth.

Nearly two thousand years later in the world's history, Joseph Smith was led to utter the broad, unqualified assertion: "No man can be saved in ignorance"; re-emphasizing the fact in the explanation that "man is saved no faster than he gains intelligence." This attitude is apparently more cruel and relentless than that of our Saviour; especially as it seems to exclude from salvation a majority of those whom Christ's dictum includes; for is it not the lowly, the ignorant (according to the world's standard) that make up, for the most part, the hosts of the repentant? To be on the way to salvation by Christ's standard, and then to be side-tracked to damnation by the standard of Joseph Smith, seems to be spiritual confusion worse confounded.

To reconcile these apparent contradictions; to show that each standard of salvation is absolutely, irrevocably true; to demonstrate that the two expressions are identical in import,—being in fact only different points of view in relation to the same great truth,—shall be the immediate purpose of this chapter; whence, indirectly, it will be seen also that "faith—the power which opens the soul to truthness—lies at the basis of every advance in civilization, and is the true and only harbinger of the Millennium."

Manifestly our first business is with the concepts "ignorance" and "education." By the world's rating any man or woman would be ignorant who could not read and write; conversely, any man or woman would be educated who could read and write seven languages. But neither of these ratings might be just from God's point of view; for whereas man asks, "Has he been to school? What courses did he complete? Has he a degree?" God simply asks, "How has he made use of the world? Does he recognize and obey law? Is his life daily moulded and shaped by the harmonies of the universe that touch him on all sides? Does he tend to become perfect by suffering?"

We are sometimes very much puffed up by those artificial contrivances which we call our schools and colleges. What are they, in fact, but children's playhouses filled with toys, when compared with God's great university, the world itself, with its magnificent laboratories in sea and sky, in forest expanse and mountain deeps? Society will continue to demand scholarship as the badge of education ; life demands power. Men will still ask, "What does he know?" Social evolution enquires only, "What can he do?"

Note the fact that Joseph Smith said, "Man is saved no faster than he gains 'intelligence'." By the conceptions of Mormonism, therefore, man does not cease to be ignorant merely by acquiring knowledge; he becomes educated only as he gets intelligence. The college-bred man may or may not be intelligent. If the juices of life have been squeezed out of him; if his heart-powers—his love for God and love for man—have dried and withered in the arid barrennesses of mere intellectuality; if when he gets out he has lost the power, as well as the inclination, to "catch on"; if he is a confirmed bookworm, stopping only to contemplate occasionally the evidence, framed on the library wall, that he is an "educated gentleman," —a gentleman of leisure, thank God! and not one of the base proletariat ants that are crawling everywhere over the great globe, doing the menial work of the race: if this is the measure of the man, you may call him anything you like—a human exquisite—a rare exotic—worthy a golden frame or a crystal conservatory,—but do not imply that he is an intelligent being; for intelligence is power, not pride; character, not contempt for the destiny-shapers of the race. How, indeed, does this nondescript with a college degree affect the welfare of the world in a way differently from that of a mummy? Only in the fact that it eats, drinks, and otherwise lives upon the labor of beings it despises.

The only kind of education which squares with the ideals of Mormonism is that which trains a man to do. If it be asked, to do what, the answer is *to do the things that need to be done.* If it be further asked, who shall determine "the things needed to be done," the reply is that as respects the lower half of them they are self-evident. Man's first duty in life is to live, hence he must be taught to do along industrial lines. After securing a livelihood, his whole duty is to do the will of God. That means working for the salvation of his fellow-man; for there is only one way by which a man can save his own soul; that is by giving it for others. But this does not imply preaching only; it means anything that needs to be done for the uplifting of the race,—with God as director of what shall be done.[1]

True education is therefore training a man to do his part in the social world; in contradistinction to false education, which aims to polish him in certain conventional directions, so that he shall be able to pass muster before society as an "educated gentleman." Nor is intellectuality, though confessedly the basis of all forms of power, the crying need of true education. Relatively, indeed, this has already been overdone. Heart-power, with moral and spiritual force of character; the power that shall love men into the kingdom of God; the power pre-eminently manifested in the life of Christ,—this is what the world most needs, and what the schools of to-day are least fitted to give.

Let us now draw the lines a little closer between what I have denominated respectively the true and the false education. They will be made to stand out in minute and detailed contrast, if we trace the genesis and evolution of that power of the soul which the prophet mentions as intelligence.

Manifestly to the utterly ignorant being, if such a state were possible, all things—objects, forces, sensations—would have only the same transitory

[1] How this ideal is working out in the educational schemes of the Latter-day Saints cannot be discussed in the limits of this volume. It is reserved for a companion volume to be entitled, *Social Aspect of Mormonism*.

unrelated significance which we suppose them to have for the ox or any other member of the brute creation. And were his soul fitted with no other prehensile power than theirs, he must ever remain in a state of ignorance. But he has, as we have seen, the native power of gathering truthness from truths; also of getting truthness by direct inflow from the Source of all truths: in short, he has the power of faith, and therefore potentially the power of intelligence.

The first or immediate effect of the exercise of faith is to know; in other words, to perceive and feel that sense of consistency or harmony which we call truth. But knowledge is only half of intelligence. To stop here is to be falsely educated. If, however, the truth perceived becomes a dynamic fact in a man's character; if it is incorporated into his mental attitude, and reacts immediately upon his life; if, in short, it ceases to be something *in* a man, and becomes the man himself, changing the very color and texture of his soul, then knowledge has passed over into power—or character—or wisdom—or, to adopt the term used by Joseph Smith, has passed over into intelligence; and it is such a process alone that represents true education.

Thus are the two types of education put into sharp contrast: the false type,—represented alike by your college bookworm and your college tramp,—filling the mind of the student with truths which can never be his save to look at, and therefore so shaping his life as to make it resemble those vines which crawl in moist places and live by contact with the surface of things; the true type,—represented by the creators of food alike for your bookworm and your tramp,—helping the student to live progressively the truths he learns, and so shaping his life as to make it resemble, by comparison, the sturdy oak or majestic pine— symbols of character—which, gathering life by sunshine, incorporate it into strength by storm.

The two types might be classified in the terms of psychology as perceptives and apperceptives. The soul-energies of the first class,—the perceptives,—have, through constant abortions of sensation, come to spread themselves out on the surface of the body: lurking like insatiate demons at eye, and ear, and touch, and taste, and smell, and appetite; and producing nothing but increased desire for sensation from all they feed upon. Nine tenths of the human race belong wholly or in part to this class: the novel, the theatre, the excursion, and the globe-trotting fiends; the whiskey, the tobacco, the horse-racing, and the prize-fighting fiends; the roué, the prostitute, and their co-respondents,—sensation-mongers all to whom the pleasures of life mean surface contact with phenomena for excitation purposes alone. The second type, or apperceptives, are those to whom surface contact or perception is only a means to a nobler end—apperception. These latter incorporate into their lives the truths perceived through the senses, and so become the creators and moulders of civilization. The schools are fated by reason of fad and conventionality to turn out the former type: God's school, the university of strenuous effort accompanied with suffering, is ideally fitted to turn out the latter type. What, indeed, would the world come to, did we not all have a post-graduate course in this divine school of experience?

Now, before bringing these ideas relating to education into juxtaposition with Joseph Smith's standard of salvation, let us stop to get some rational conception of what salvation means.

No notion is held by the majority of mankind more luminously vague than this professed goal of all religious effort. From the rhapsodies of revivalism respecting heaven, the city celestial, pearly gates, golden harps, snowy wings, the beatific vision, the loving arms of Jesus, and so on, *ad gloriosam*, the thinker can only turn away with a feeling of metaphorical nausea. Let us therefore seize upon two elements latent in every conception of salvation, viz., the hope of eternal life, and the hope of eternal bliss, and see what comes of them.

As to the first idea, eternal life, we are thrown at once face to face with our ultimate conception of eternal existence, the universe itself. Manifestly anything formed and limited can have uninterrupted duration only on condition that it offer no friction to the universe; that is to say,

Education is Repentance

only as it is in harmony with the universe. But the universe means nothing to man save as it touches his being in the form of law, or rather the effect of law—phenomena. To the extent therefore that his life is at variance with law, to that extent is he in danger of forfeiting eternal life; and consequently to the extent that he values eternal life, will he seek to discover and put himself in harmony with law. But the differentiations involved in our smaller universe are the creations of God. He is the author of law as it touches us. Hence eternal life in an organized form is possible only as man learns and obeys His will.

No man, therefore, can be saved in ignorance; for what is ignorance but the very negative of law, the state antecedent even to the beginning of harmony with the universe. Unless the density of chaos,—ignorance as personified in man—be permeated by the vibration of law; unless it begins and continues to respond, how can it remain a formed and limited creation in the bosom of the uncreated? The forces of law and order must inevitably undo,—scatter—annihilate it, reduce it, to the primal, the formless, or uncreated state.

The discovery, therefore, of law (or truth), which involves the exercise of faith or the prehensile power of the soul; and the consequent obedience to law, which involves the exercise of an equally native power of the soul (assisted by the grace of God, of which more hereafter),—constitutes the progressive alternation which leads from ignorance to salvation. Nor need I stop to point out that it is owing to precisely such a series of psychic alternations that we have our present civilization.

But salvation involves eternal bliss as well as eternal life; and if we may judge from the sensations of our brief earth experience, bliss forms no part of that sensation which can lead to satiety; that is, to the gratification of desire. Pleasure, the ephemeral and bastard earth-cousin of joy, holds this place. Bliss (or joy) is inseparable from the discovery of truth,—the perception of how God creates; or the evolution of truth,—the revelation of man's own power to create. Eternal bliss is therefore impossible without endless opportunity for invention; indeed the absence of such opportunity could imply nothing else than monotony. But bliss in this sense is inseparable from power to do; and power to do is, as we have seen, an invariable accompaniment of the growth of intelligence. It follows, then, as Joseph Smith says: "Man is saved no faster than he gains intelligence."

Let us now turn to the correlative idea of repentance. Before a man can repent of his sins he must be made aware of them. But to be made aware of them implies that a higher standard of righteousness has entered his soul. The sequence then in the sinner's mind is this—first, a revelation of the righteousness of God; second, a comparison of his own life therewith, which results in a recognition or conviction of sin; third,—and this is the vital part of repentance,—the conforming of his life to the new standard.[1]

Let us next examine this phrase: righteousness of God. The suffix *ness* implies "the quality of being"; so also does the suffix *ous*. Righteousness therefore signifies the quality of being right. Now what is right but truth? What is truth but law? What is law but an expression of the harmony of the universe? And who but God has shaped our universe so that we can feel the harmonies of law? Righteousness is thus the will of God.

How does a man get a revelation of righteousness? By faith—precisely as he apprehends law. Such a revelation is nothing else in fact than the apprehending of law. But I need not go on. The reader has already perceived that the process of getting rid of sin and the process of getting rid

[1] Some one has cleverly arranged the following order of sequence in repentance: (1) Recognition of sin. (2) Remorse of conscience. (3) Restitution of the wrong done. (4) Resolution to sin no more. (5) Reformation of the sinner's life. It should have six R's instead of five, the first being recognition of righteousness. The second fact, which is made so much of in revivalism, is merely a fringe or incident of repentance; which, while it usually accompanies conviction of sin in the social, moral, or spiritual world, is often absent in repentance of intellectual sin, (*i. e.*, mistakes of judgment). The third condition is, for the most part, impossible; save as man offers to God a broken heart and a contrite spirit. The fourth is implied in the fifth. So that this classification may be boiled down to the three essential facts enumerated in the text.

of ignorance are identical, and that consequently it is no more possible to be saved without repentance than it is to be saved in ignorance. Education—of the kind which leads to intelligence—is therefore a means, if not the only means, of salvation.

Had this relationship of likeness between repentance, a dogma of the religious world, and the acquirement of intelligence, the central fact of every educational system, been perceived by ministers in the days of St. Augustine, and developed progressively as the world advanced, the clergy might have been at the head of all movements—secular and otherwise—for the propagation of truth and the spread of civilization; instead of being to-day the wardens—I was about to say the curators—of a cult more narrow and restricted than that of medicine, and less useful to the race by how much its dicta lack coherency and definite relationship to man's psychic needs.

But as they failed to perceive this supreme fact, it was preposterous on their part to expect that the momentum of progress could pause to be harnessed into a thousand man-made creeds: that the great stream of truth could cease plunging forward down the ages, because some of its incidental effects took shape as theological eddies; going round and round, each respectively with its fragmentary flotsam of confessional, proclaiming that it and it only represented the trend of the universe. God, who is "in all things, above all things, below all things, and through all things, the light of truth," could not be restricted in His revelations to man by papal bull or protestant heretic fires; faith, the angel with the key, could not delay throwing open to mankind his treasures of truth till labelled by pope and ear-marked by prelate; repentance swiftly sloughed his scriptural name rather than remain exclusively in cell and cloister, or even linger at chapel or mourner's bench; and eagerly did he go about the sceptical world, doing his glorious work under the simple guise of educational enthusiasm and integrity to ideal.

And so it was that full upon the track of these two morning stars burst civilization, the flood tide of God's benediction upon the world. Salvation shall need no other heralds.

CHAPTER XVI

LOGICAL NECESSITY OF REPENTANCE AND FORGIVENESS

"ETERNAL life shall need no other heralds," than alertness to the apprehension of truth and integrity to the ideals so apprehended; for these constitute the very means by which ignorance, which is only another name for sin, gives way progressively to intelligence and power. But ere eternal life shall have been attained, these heralds will have assumed again, for each advancing soul, their proper scriptural names of faith and repentance. And whenever that change of name shall take place, with it will come to each seeker after truth a strange, new emotion thrilling him to his soul's centre.

The last chapter was devoted to showing that true repentance and true education are synonymous, if not identical, operations; that in each case alike the beginning process is the reaching out of the soul's prehensile power (faith) after a new and higher ideal of truth or law; that so also, in each case alike, the closing process is the conforming of the life to the new ideal; and if, between the beginning and the closing, repentance often lingers in the field of remorse, while education hastens with gladness to slough the old life for the new, the sum total of effect on the soul was seen to be apparently the same.

Apparently; for it did not seem wise to obscure this great truth, concerning the similarity both in genesis and effect of secular and religious soul efforts, by distracting reservations and conditions.

The need of showing that it is the same divine love which reaches out to save both saint and sinner, must be my apology for leaving the chapter as I did. The time has now come, however, to show that the ultimate effects of the two operations are tremendously different; that repentance, while it includes all of true education, involves much besides.

Observe, first of all, that the soul-regeneration which comes from purely educational effort is nearly always indirect. That the learner is conforming to law, and therefore reaping power as a reward,—power the use of which he is responsible for to God,—is rarely recognized. It is rather some material motive that spurs him on; as, "If I attain to this qualification (say, bookkeeping), I shall be able to grasp that good," (say, a liberal salary). Thus too often an utterly selfish object is coupled with noble endeavor for power; with the result, that the power attained, while it adds to the sum total of efficiency in the material world cannot fail to react in a negative way upon the moral world; leading among other evil tendencies, to the cruel maxims of business which, summed up and generalized, constitute none other than that death-grip law of the ancient world: "Might makes right."

Against such reactionary tendencies as by-products of education, ethics, the religion without a God, is making a noble struggle, and not without visible results; for gradually mankind are beginning to see that every man is his brother's keeper; that to follow Cain in defiance of this law, is finally to be self-destructive; that injustice does not pay even as a business investment. And so from a thousand actions and reactions resulting from positive powers used in negative directions, there comes out of widespread social wrong, and pain, and suffering, a small increment of social right; which constitutes that fragment of the salt of civilization which has not lost the savor of God.

It is perhaps in this very circumstance, the failure to recognize the inevitableness of law in our educational efforts—the placing of motive in material rewards, such as riches, position, power, fame,—that all the mischief of misdirected power is wrought. If men were content to let virtue be its own reward; if after having climbed some summit of eternal truth, they should regard the increased power to climb as part of the reward, and the increased magnificence, almost the transformation, of all things from this new point of view, as the rest of the reward; instead of being blind to all this, and only stopping to ask, "What do they think of me below?" or perhaps taking advantage of their position, figuratively to roll rocks down on the heads of the more humble climbers,—if in short, men would recognize law as the criterion of their efforts, both for motive and reward, then the fruits of education, would not be so very far behind the fruits of repentance in saving power; for whereas in repentance God Himself is the unifying, directing force of character, in education with such a motive and such a reward law, or God indirect, would be the co-ordinating and subordinating power.

But rarely does educational effort attain to so high a motive, even in theory; which fact leads me to point out finally that the one aspect in which the results of repentance transcend the results of education is precisely this: that repentance takes a man out of the class fated to follow desultory motives, and brings him home to God; placing him among the workers, and giving his life an eternal perspective both in being and doing.

On the other side what, indeed, are the highest achievements of secular educational efforts, but the more or less feeble response of the race to the environments which God places around them? And as God's purpose in these environments is to induce men, of their own free will, to leave the worked-with class and join the workers, so we see that the two operations, education and repentance, though alike in method, are related to each other by subordination; for by the highest good of the one, the perception of law, a man may achieve only the lowest good of the other, the perception of the Author of law.[1] Thus the two merge into each other as dawning into perfect day.

Repentance, as here used in contrast with education, besides being both a perception of truth and a conforming of our life thereto, involves a deeply personal encounter with the Author of our being. We are, in fact, prodigals, awakening at last to realize how far we have strayed from home, and how we have wasted our opportunities. Something in our souls whispers at the same time how good is our Father in heaven; how watchful, how loving, how forgiving He has been; with what tenderness and sorrow His pure eyes have followed our downward course; and how His heart has yearned to call us home.

It is an awakening like this that breaks up the ice-floes in the deeps of our bosoms, and causes our hearts to overflow in sobs and tears. We see ourselves as God sees us, and are utterly abased. The agony piercing our souls in that moment of self-recognition cannot be described. How dare we call ourselves His children—we that are not worthy of the husks cast out to the swine! Oh, if we were but clean enough to call on His holy

---

[1] If indeed he can do that, which is doubtful; for, as the Scriptures say, no man can find out God. What he does get from the intelligent reaction of the world, is probably the earnest desire to find God; whence God, who always meets faith more than half way, reveals Himself.

name,—we whose lips would profane the word! If—but there is language no more. We have entered our Gethsemane, to learn the meaning of a broken heart and a contrite spirit.

Now for the first time does the life of Jesus the sinless One stand out for us, the "man of sorrows and acquainted with grief,"—our brother! How we pity His sufferings, how we love Him! For did He not die that such as we might live? Then we remember that He said: "Come unto me all ye that are heavy laden and I will give you rest." He, the man of sorrows, said it,—and Himself had pity for the weak and fallen. Our tears flow warmer—the black cloud is breaking. This new-found Friend will not turn away from us; and through Him our Father in heaven may receive us again.

And so eventually after days, and sometimes weeks, of soul-suffering, hope reigns in our hearts and joy ineffable.

Now, it is folly for the sceptic to pooh-pooh this experience as a mere neurotic state of the soul; for its recurrence in this or similar forms is so frequent among mankind that we are justified in considering it thoroughly characteristic and normal. Not that all must enter the kingdom of God through this dark gate,—for there are souls which, Nathaniel-like, have never strayed beyond the light of that kingdom; only those in whom selfishness has encrusted the soul and congealed the heart. To these, which constitute a very large majority of earth-spirits, what else but a violent tearing asunder of intrenched soul-habits, could be counted normal, in a movement involving a complete counter attitude in relation to God and the universe?

And if in the act of reconciliation with God,—the act by which man becomes a conscious co-worker with Christ, and without which his further psychic evolution is impossible: if, I repeat, in this necessary awakening, such soul-tragedies are not only normal but inevitable, then Christ as mediator and way of escape for such souls, is also a normal and inevitable expedient of divine mercy.

I do not attempt to explain here the esoteric doctrine that the equilibrium of heaven's perfect law having been broken by the fall of Adam, it could be restored only by the sacrifice of Christ. What, indeed, can man know concerning the necessity, looked at from heaven's point of view, of this awful tragedy? How presume to say whether it was eternal justice or earth-necessitated expediency that led to its divine predestination? That in some inscrutable way Christ's death was vital to the efficacy of the atonement, and reconciliation of man with God, we may well believe who have faith in the revelations of Scripture; for not only is He there prefigured as a "lamb slain from the foundations of the earth,"—an event also prophetically symbolized by all the sacrifices of the Mosaic covenant,—but the whole burden of the Gospel dispensation as recorded in the New Testament, turns upon the atonement so wrought out by His blood. Moreover, the sacrifices characteristic of all heathen religions from the beginning of time, become meaningless also if we deny the necessity and significance of the one great Sacrifice.

But while we cannot look from God's point of view at this pivotal event—and therefore it becomes us rather to hold the fact reverently than attempt futile explanations—we are not without a philosophical basis when we look at it from man's point of view. Should our faith in the atonement need bolstering, a sufficient rational explanation of Christ's passion is to be found in the fact that it needed among us a Being whose life and death should be such as to break through the stoniest heart in man down to the imprisoned love of God, even as Moses reached the water 'neath the Rock of Horeb.

How without Christ's life should we have known that God is a personal being, directly related to man as a divine Father? How without the voluntary sacrifice of His life should we have had an object lesson sufficiently striking to rescue us from the fatality of self-seeking and teach us love of God and love of man? For that He, the sinless One, who need not die, should willingly drain this bitter cup to demonstrate His love for man—what else than this could give birth to universal altruism? How without His resurrection should our faith in a hereafter have leaped that awful, that terrifying mystery—Death? How without his own attainment to the fulness of Godhood, dare man look forward to a psychic evolution involving nothing less than becoming "perfect as our Father in heaven is perfect?" Truly does the beloved apostle exclaim: "God so loved the world that he gave his only begotten son, that whosoever believeth in him should not perish, but have everlasting life."

Theosophists maintain that there was no need for Christ to die. Truly not—for their Christ, one of the Mahatmas, a diluted Buddha, not quite so far along toward the annihilation of Nirvana. But Christ the Saviour, the regenerator of the heart, not the mystifier of the head,—picture Him growing old and prosperous and famous and gray and decrepit, with bulletins posted every hour as to the last flickerings of His life: picture such a man, and ask yourself if a life and death so peaceful, so ordinary, could stir the heart-strings of millions yet unborn? Indeed, bring together from all the great teachers known to man ideal fragments of a life; and after you have combined them, how insignificant in spiritual dynamic power the whole would be, compared with the virile divinity stamped on even the smallest details in the earth-mission of the Messiah!

So much for His life as a regenerative object-lesson to His less perfect brethren and sisters. But it is not owing immediately to this fact that

His status with reference to man as King of kings and Lord of lords, is fixed for eternity. It is the more substantial fact, that upon Him rests by delegation of the Father the fulness of divine Authority. Divine law, which can no more execute itself than can human law, has made Him its executor. He is the harmony of the universe concreted for man. Without Him there is no approaching the Father, and consequently no salvation. In Him is the fulness of Priesthood or divine governing power, which therefore amounts to Godhood.

And this brings us back to a further consideration of the phenomena of repentance. All this display of emotion, this penance in the valley of remorse, and the final emergence therefrom with elastic step and glowing countenance—this is not the real fact of repentance; it is only the smoke and fire and noise of the conflict. The real fact lies precisely in this: that the soul has had a revelation of a new and supreme truth—a revelation of God. It has perceived that in Him, a personal being, inheres the authority of the universe. He is the adequate Cause of all things, and therefore the absolute and final Source of power: without Him is nothing but "utter darkness and the gnashing of teeth"—annihilation. If this vision has borne fruits—that is to say, if the repentance is genuine,—the soul will have taken the second step: it will absolutely have conformed its own attitude to this newly-perceived and supreme fact; will have learned to say, from the depths of its being: "Father, thy will be done."

Now the soul that has thus repented—howsoever contradictory it may seem—is absolved by the very fact of its repentance. It has complied with the law, and must therefore inevitably secure the reward. No power, not even God Himself, can rob it of the security of its newly-won relationship to the universe. It is inevitable in the nature of things that obedience to law carries with it absolution from former opposition to law. And this equilibrium is instant: we need fear no locked-up vengeance to be sprung upon us—no reprisals to satisfy an offended God.

Why then should the soul feel remorse, as we have seen that it does? Why should it yearn for forgiveness, as if the new status did not, after all, depend upon law, but upon divine caprice? Why is the soul not at rest, till assured of reconciliation with God? Why not be content in the conviction that in the very nature of things its repentance alone has absolved it?

This feeling of insecurity results from man's dual relationship to Deity; first, his relationship to God, which is essentially his relationship to Godhood, or the absolute power of the universe. This is purely an abstract, that is to say, a truth relation; to the extent that it has a concrete aspect at all, it is the relationship of a nascent or growing intelligence to a perfected Intelligence, and its only expression is therefore justice—the Karma of the Buddhists and the nemesis of the Greeks. Accordingly as the soul has conformed to law, so it is forgiven,—that is, absolved from all retroactive effects of its former disobedience; for such effects would be possible only from a God supreme-by-will, rather than supreme-by-law.

Man's second relationship is to the Father of spirits, which therefore is a purely personal relation—that of child to parent. As an inevitable consequence, the expression of this relationship is mercy, love, forbearance, long-suffering,—all the Christ-type of divine attributes. Herein then lies the source of the sinner's remorse: his awakened soul feels (rather than knows) how it has disgraced its divine ancestry, how it has spurned and outraged divine love. Confronted with a revelation of such baseness and ingratitude, how could it feel otherwise? But it perceives also that in the new relationship with God its life will be cast among the workers, Jesus Christ at their head; whose very bond of fellowship is love of God and love of man. It may not consciously reason to all this, but the truth-essence of it is there in the revelation which caused the soul-awakening. How can it enter this realm of the pure in heart, unless assured that it is forgiven?

Now, while absolution by divine justice is the very *sine qua non* of reconciliation with God, it alone could not avail for further progress unless the soul should also be assured of its absolution by love; for not to be so assured would be to carry a load of evil consciousness that would paralyze all efforts at improvement. It is this psychic fact, I think, that made the Lord take away all memory of pre-existence. He did not wish to load us down in a new world with the lock-step memories of a past one. No other status than this—of oblivion to the past—would comport with the category of innocence which the Scriptures attribute to the new-born babe; a status of forgiveness followed by a status of oblivion to things forgiven.

But forgiveness, be it noted, adds nothing positive to man's psychic evolution; it merely unloads the soul of remorse, thus freeing it for action, and tending to make it forget the scars of past transgression. In short, it restores innocence, which involves a consciousness of reciprocal love, but does not add power; consequently, and precisely as we should expect, children, though all born innocent alike, are by no means all gifted with power alike; and the same fact is true of souls restored to innocence by baptism.

CHAPTER XVII

THE LOGICAL NECESSITY OF BAPTISM

HOW can this assurance of forgiveness come to the troubled soul? "By the testimony of the spirit" will be the answer of all who have passed through the valley of the shadow of death; "by the peace of God which comes to give it rest—the peace which passeth all understanding." This is, of course, the final, the only answer; nothing short of such peace could give the assurance of reconciliation with God. But how does it come to man? Must he not do something in order to receive it?

In reasoning out this question, let us not depart from analogy. A and B, let us say, are dear friends. A in a moment of anger grievously wrongs B, but stung with remorse as sorely repents, resumes his amiable relations with B, but from a false sense of pride does not confess the wrong and ask forgiveness. B on his part has generously forgiven A, but out of delicacy cannot say so—indeed, would rather spare his friend further pain by burying the incident forever.

But that last is precisely what neither can do. The wrong is dead, truly enough, but it will not under. Oblivion cannot hide it till some token of forgiveness has passed between them. This token may be never so slight—a grasp of the hand, a moment of silence during which soul speaks to soul, or something even less tangible still; but unless there is a token, the ghost of wrong will not be laid. It haunts their every association, and more especially on occasions of mutual admiration. "And I could wrong such a friend—cur that I was," says the inner voice of A. "It was n't this noble, generous friend that did it," says the subconsciousness of B; "A's better self could never have stooped so low."

If these friends do not take heed, this ghost will estrange them—out of sheer desire on the part of each to be at ease. For the truth of this analogy, I appeal to the experience of every man and woman that reads this chapter.

It is precisely so with the greatest of all acts of reconciliation, that between God and man. Nor is it the part of man to choose what that peace-winged token shall be; for although a fugitive peace has come to thousands, through implicit faith in tokens of their own choosing, the ghost of unrest will rise again, whenever by the clearer dawning of truth it shall come to them that such tokens were neither of God's choosing, nor probably accepted by Him.[1] Nor can this false

---

[1] Among such fugitive peace expedients belong manifestly those pitiful tokens of absolution called indulgences, which so aroused the lions of the Reformation, but which are taken

security ever be made so subtile that God's light shall not discover it at last.

Now while God has invariably had a token of forgiveness in all His dealings with man, it has not always been the same thing. To Noah and his family it was the bow of promise; to the children of the Mosaic dispensation it took various forms according to the nature of the sin; sacrifices, burnt offerings, the scapegoat, the sprinkling of blood. In every Gospel dispensation the token of forgiveness has been baptism for him who is about to enter the kingdom, and prayer,—the confessional with God Himself, or perhaps represented by our guardian angel, as confessor,—for those who sin after entering the kingdom.

But baptism is more than a sign of reconciliation; it is the visible token of that covenant whereby man leaves the worked-with class, and is accepted among the workers. If the reader admits that the psychic evolution of the soul cannot go on forever in an indirect way,— the

tamely and quite as matters of fact in Spain to-day. And if these general forms of forgiveness—blanks of salvation to be filled in the name of John Doe, *et al*, bona-fide purchasers—are thus to be classed, how much better are the specific forms of the same thing—the absolutions of the auricular confessional? To self-chosen tokens of divine absolution, belong also all penances, pilgrimages, gifts to clergy, endowments of churches, etc., in so far as they are relied upon for the peace of heaven; also, all those facile adaptations of the ritual of Scripture now so common in modern Christian sects, to suit the prejudices, or æsthetic tastes of dilettante communicants.

unconscious result of environment; if he admits that the time must inevitably arrive when man must come face to face with his Master, and thereafter consent or refuse to become a conscious coöperator in his own salvation,—then it follows that man must make at last a definite contract or covenant with God, even as one personal being with another.

But such a contract is inconceivable without a token. Nor is man at liberty to choose that token; the greater of the two contracting parties always decides upon the terms. To ignore this fact is to be guided by the most childish form of self-stultification. How must we rate the intelligence of an immigrant who should choose a token of his own for becoming a citizen of the United States? Is the kingdom of God to be supposed less exacting in its order? How would the unity and harmony of heaven be reconcilable with such looseness in the laws of adoption?

Of course, if the supreme being with whom men make covenants be conceived as a universal, impalpable essence,—everywhere yet nowhere,— the covenants themselves may be vague and indefinite; the vaguer, the more indefinite, they are, the better; or at least the more consistent they would be with the nature of the chief contracting party. Indeed, no contract at all, is still better, or one made simply with one's self; for if God is such a universal essence, and the basis of all phenomena, man is as much God as that mountain, or this stream, or that star,—and therefore, as Theosophists say truly enough, the only God with whom he can ever come into psychic relation. But, on the other hand, if God is the prototype of man; if all man's ideas of order and harmony, as exhibited in governments and other social institutions, are in fact only the ragged echoes of the infinite order of heaven's institutions,—then surely the token of admission into that higher social order cannot be less definite, less exacting than similar tokens in earthly governments.

With this brief outline of explanation, I assume the two following series of facts to be irrefragable: first, man's psychic evolution becomes at length impossible without conscious co-operation with God; second, that co-operation, involving as it does the eternal responsibility resulting from accepting God as final and absolute authority in all his future being and doing, cannot begin save by an untrammelled act of free will on man's part,—in other words, a definite compact with God; third, such a compact between personal beings is impossible without a token; fourth, it being God's kingdom of workers into which man seeks to enter, God alone can determine what the token of admission shall be. Or, from another point of view: first, deliverance from the bondage of sin is possible only through repentance; second, such deliverance is effective for further progress only as the sinner is also freed from the consciousness of his sins, *i. e.*, only as he feels himself forgiven; but, third, such an act of reconciliation between personal beings is impossible without a token; fourth, God only has a right to determine that token.

Thus by each series the same conclusion is reached: a token between God and man is essential to salvation; and no other token than that chosen by God is effective; either as the seal of God's peace to the wracked soul of the sinner, or as the badge of his citizenship in the kingdom of heaven. In order, then, to establish in the domain of probable reasoning,—and that without reference to the fiat of Jehovah, though that fiat alone should be conclusive,—the logical necessity of baptism, it remains only for me to show that this token alike of forgiveness and of citizenship is actually the token chosen by God. At first it would seem that the only evidence of this latter fact is the overwhelming, the uncontradicted testimony of Scripture; but on second thought, it must occur to all that a token chosen by God would exhibit evidences of the wisdom of God. Let us then look at the question from this point of view.

To exhibit such divine evidences, a token must, in my humble opinion, be characterized by three general facts: (1) it must be uniformly intelligible, so as to conduce to the unity of mankind; (2) it must be widely, if not uniformly, applicable, so as to be within reach of all mankind; and (3) besides doing its essential work as a token, it must be rich in soul suggestions.

If it be objected in respect of the first condition that baptism, as interpreted by Christian sects, has tended to scatter mankind, the reply is, that there is nothing difficult whatever in the scriptural idea itself; and the proof of this is that the simplest mind turned loose upon the sacred pages and untrammelled by sect prejudice can come to no other than the one right conclusion. The fact that certain texts are tortured past recognition in support of other forms of baptism is no proof that those other forms sprang originally from interpretations of the Bible; it only shows to what desperate lengths men will go, after having gratuitously changed the divine token, to find color and sanction for their substitution. Besides, baptism counts for nothing save as administered by divine authority; and when such authority is upon the earth, there is unbroken communication with heaven, to settle questions of this kind, which, if left unsettled, would tend to divide mankind,—just, in fact, as there was in the days of the apostles. God never intended baptism should be administered under any other circumstances.

As to the second condition, there can be no question of the almost uniform accessibility of baptism to the human race. Had the token been a pilgrimage to Jerusalem, it must have excluded the majority of mankind; had it been even so simple a thing as recording allegiance to God in the Bible, it would not have been within the reach of all; but water is everywhere, and, like air, is one of the gifts of God uniformly free,—at least for such purposes,—to rich and poor alike.

As to the third condition, the first rich soul suggestion I find is that baptism typifies or symbolizes our mortal birth [1] and parallels all its implications. Does the spirit in being born leave an old world—pre-existence—to enter a new? So does the person baptized. Does the fact of a spirit's mortal birth restore his innocence? So does baptism. Does birth bring a spirit to the protecting arms of a loving father (and mother)? So does baptism. Does birth start a spirit upon a new and wonderful life, under the guidance of loving parentage? So does baptism. Is birth the universally recognized badge of relationship to that parentage? So by baptism, are sons and daughters born to God, of their own free will.

As a second example of rich suggestion, I may mention that baptism is compared by Paul to a planting (Rom. vi., 5). What happens when a seed is placed in proper soil? Its soul energies are stirred; a new life within it is set free, which springs upward, seeking to become like its parent. Is not this precisely a parallel of that spiritual potentiality in us which, set free by baptism, seeks to become perfect as its Father is perfect?

Let us next consider the fact that baptism is

---

[1] It was Christ Himself who pointed out this parallel: "Except a man be born of the water and of the spirit," said he to Nicodemus, "he cannot enter the kingdom of heaven."—John iii., 5.

compared to a cleansing. "And now why tarriest thou?" said Ananias to Paul, "Arise and be baptized and wash away thy sins." Surely the parallel here pointed out is obvious. "The like figure whereunto baptism doth now save us," says Peter (I. iii., 21). "Not the putting away of the filth of the flesh"—for that would be merely the natural effect of the water; "but the answer of a good conscience toward God"; in other words, a parallel cleansing of the soul by the act for which baptism is a token.

We have seen then that baptism symbolizes birth, and growth, and regeneration or cleansing; now we are to see that it also typifies two other tremendous facts in the soul's evolution, viz., death and resurrection. "We are buried with Christ by baptism unto death," says Paul, "that like as Christ was raised from the dead by the glory of the Father, even so we also should walk in newness of life" (Rom. vi., 4). Draw out the parallel as far as you like here, the effect is only intensified. What can be more horrible than the body which mortifies and decomposes in the earth? Well, sin, which figuratively is left in the watery grave, is no less repulsive to God. Again, what can be more radiantly pure than a resurrected being, whom even the sun's rays could not further purify? Such by comparison is the change wrought, or made possible, by a life of regeneration to which baptism is the door.

Where, then, in the whole range of natural

objects touching man, could another phenomenon be chosen which, besides being a token, should exhibit, in a flash, man's whole psychic life and destiny? Let the sceptic sit down and ponder this question, then try object after object, and at last confess that immersion in water is a token the choice of which is worthy the wisdom of God Himself. And let those proud prelates of the Middle Ages who sought, by substituting sprinkling, to improve upon God's token—and all their defenders in our day,—be forever ashamed of their vain presumption. And let mankind, who have been led astray by these presumptuous teachers, awake from the fugitive peace into which this false token has lulled them, and seek the God of Abraham, Isaac, and Jacob, with whom only is salvation.

Baptism is thus seen to be a logical necessity in the psychic evolution of the soul,—a condition essential to salvation. In this day, when the tendency is to dismantle the ship of salvation of every characteristic thing by which it can take hold of wind or wave on its own account, leaving the crew only a floating hulk in which to sing, and pray, and groan, and gaze heavenward for help—a spectacle of infinite comedy to the Devil on a neighboring peak; a day, in which the tendency is toward a so-called unity so utterly emasculated and characterless, that it is disturbed by coughing aloud,—this doctrine (and others like it), the reassertion by logic of the thundertones of revelation, ought to try men's faith like a trip hammer; to test whether there is yet any virile rebound in it, or whether it has degenerated into a mere jelly-like mass of sentimental sham and pretense.

Mormons desire Christian unity also; but not at the sacrifice of the trunk and limbs of the tree, and the holding of a love feast around the piled-up leaves.[1] Real unity is possible only on the basis of truth—grim, unrelenting, uncompromising truth. Better a thousand times the tonic bitterness of division, than the insipid sweet of a boneless, sinewless, nerveless affectation of universal brotherly love.

This must close my discussion of the first or external epoch in the psychic evolution of the soul. From pre-existence up till the time it "found itself,"—that is, up till the time it recognized God as God, and entered into covenant with Him, the forces shaping it were for the most part

[1] In this figure the trunk stands for God,—that is to say divine authority as represented by the Priesthood; the limbs and branches stand therefore for the expression of that authority in Church organization and social forms; the leaves would thus be the response in faith-profession of the members; and the fruit would be the reaction of that faith-profession in works of repentance. Now, it is precisely this faith-profession (not works or Church forms) that is proposed as a basis for Christian unity; and as leaves cut from their branches are dead, so such profession can never be anything else than sham or maudlin sentiment. I append this note to defend the justness of my analogy; also, lest it might be thought a better figure to have the innocuous universal love-feast happen around the stripped and barren pole (of mere confession that Jesus is the Christ).

indirect; the nearest approach to direct or self-conscious evolution being at those periods when law was recognized as criterion both for inspiration and reward. Following the course of this evolution, we have seen how, responding little by little to a thousand adjustments of environment involving time, place, and general condition of birth such as parentage, associates, occupation; and involving also all the individual vicissitudes of life, as these are shaped by Providence, ever without violating its free agency,—the soul at last "comes to God"—must come to God, if its evolution is to continue forever.

I like the phrase of Paul's "coming to God"; it implies not only psychic unity with God, but progressive approach to His perfection and power. From the time of baptism onward, an internal or self-conscious epoch of evolution will begin: the man has been born again. And while evolution will go on also by indirect forces to the end of time, it will take on a new significance by reason of being interpreted from a spiritual point of view.

CHAPTER XVIII

THE NATURE OF SPIRITUAL EVOLUTION

NATURAL as the language of imagery is to the oriental mind, it is doubtful whether the Jews, learned though they were in esoteric exegesis, grasped even faintly the significance of Christ's definition of the kingdom of God. Indeed, the Apostles themselves, who were daily with the Master, did not fully understand it, till after the Resurrection when they were endued with power from on high; and Judas, who did not live till the day of Pentecost, probably never knew, unless perhaps it was the sudden revelation of it that overwhelmed him into his own death.

The occasion for the definition was this: The Pharisees, chafing under the bondage of Rome, and reading for consolation the prophetic scrolls concerning Israel's deliverance and final triumph, were especially eager for the advent of the kingdom of God, which they naturally regarded as the day of their salvation. But when Jesus was approached on the subject He made this enigmatical answer: "The kingdom of God cometh not with outward show: neither shall they say 'Lo here!'

or ' Lo there!' for, behold, the kingdom of God is within you."

Here was a conception of power and supremacy utterly new to the old-world civilization, and coming as it did in the very mid-day radiance of the Hamitic ideal that might makes right, small wonder if it was incomprehensible. The idea that a something latent in the human heart was powerful enough to destroy the legions of Rome, and break in pieces the iron kingdom, would be the last thought to come into their minds. Theirs was the notion of an external kingdom, the restoration of Solomon's empire. "Lo here!"—the army of deliverance terrible in its panoply of war; "Lo there!"—the pomp and circumstance of an oriental monarch, the dynasty of David come again to power,—such were the visions that filled the Jewish imagination. And when a few days later Christ, as had been prophesied of their deliverer, rode into Jerusalem on an ass, it was the hope of such a kingdom that made the multitude strew garments and palm branches in his way, and shout: "Hosanna to the son of David: Blessed is he that cometh in the name of the Lord!"

"The kingdom of God is within you." We have lived to see the triumph of this power which steals among mankind in the darkness of the night, as it were, and not with outward show. Simply a truth-ideal, microscopic in its first faint flutterings of life; a faint and far-away song awakened in the soul of man wherever faith has opened the door to

Spiritual Evolution 187

the angel of light. We have seen the great and the mighty of Ham and Japheth fall before this invisible yet invincible host of Shem. Nor has the triumph of this inner kingdom more than fairly begun: its glory shall yet encompass the earth and eventually baptize her with a new name—heaven.

How remarkably this spiritual awakening, this beginning of the psychic evolution of the soul is repeated by analogy in almost every living thing! Take the oak as a simple example. Out on the tips of its branches is born—by flowering and fertilization—first a husk, or body of tough, fibrous material, next a soul of meat, and lastly, hidden away somewhere in the latter, a microscopic oak—the one potentiality that shall enable it to become perfect, as its parent oak is perfect. Likewise is hidden away in the soul of man a miniature kingdom of God; or, to be more exact, the potentiality of becoming perfect as his Father in heaven is perfect.

Man's outer husk has been slowly growing since his birth in heaven; so has his soul been filling out with the meat of almost endless experiences. Is this husk of body, filled with its meat of soul, to begin *e*volving, even as it has for ages been *in*volving? Or is it destined to rot on the rock of doubt, barely covered with the blackening leaves of mere physical or earth-experiences? That depends entirely on whether it falls in good soil, and then whether its germ-potentiality, the kingdom of God within it, begins to grow and come out of it.

But let us at this point of the analogy note an important difference. The acorn rests where it falls; unlike man, therefore, a chance determines largely whether it shall become an oak. Nor has it more than one brief season in which to succeed or fail. Were I a revivalist, I should perhaps insist most strongly on the likeness of this last aspect. But I am not. Like Paul, I feel to say: "If in this life only we have hope in Christ, we are of all men most miserable." Soul evolution may begin hereafter in the spirit world; yet no doubt the longer it is delayed the more perilous will be the outcome. Nevertheless, it holds finally true that unless evolution does begin, there happens to the soul what happens to the acorn that fails to sprout: it goes back to the elements whence it was created.

Let us next look at some other significant parallels. In the first place, while the acorn holds within itself the potentiality of an oak, it is absolutely dependent on an external power, the sun, not only to set free that miniature life within it, but to nurture and protect it, season after season, until it actually attains its complete evolution. So also without the grace of God to awaken it and the constant providence of God to fortify and develop it, the heaven-potentiality in man must equally remain dormant, to the soul's final undoing.

But here again comes in a difference. The conditions being favorable, it is not given to the soul of the oak to resist the forces of its evolution. It is, or it is not, by the will of God alone. Not so with the soul of man. Not only must he will to co-operate with grace, both in the awakening and in the development of the God-ideal within him, if these operations are to go on at all; but, should he choose to do so, he can cease assisting and effectually oppose and destroy this divine power at any point in his evolution. For man is free,—free as God in a negative sense; potentially as free in a positive sense; and dynamically as free, to the extent that his psychic evolution has been completed.

In the light of these simple analogies, let us compare some passages of Scripture which, like baptism, have been the means of splitting Christianity up into the wrangle and jangle of sectism.

"For by grace," says Paul, "are ye saved through faith, and that not of yourselves,—it is the gift of God: not of works, lest any man should boast." (Eph. ii., 8, 9). In this passage four important concepts occur: grace, salvation, faith, and works. The question is, How are they related? Manifestly the order of sequence is this: (1) faith, the exercise of that native power which opens the soul to truth; (2) grace or the inpouring of the spirit of God, in consequence of the opening of man's soul to truthness; (3) salvation, involving two things, the awakening of the God-ideal in man, and the progressive evolution of that ideal under the fostering power of grace; (4) works. In the sense of the exertion of man's will, these are implied in two of the previous operations: in the faith that opens the door to grace, and in the progressive soul-adjustments which are involved in the evolution of the God-ideal. Works in this latter sense are distinctly pointed out by Paul as necessary, in the verse next to those above quoted. "For we are his workmanship, created in Jesus Christ unto good works,"—the works being, as indicated above, those which flow out of grace, *i. e.*, those which we "are created into Christ Jesus" to perform.

Which, then, are the works set in opposition to grace—the works Paul seems to condemn? We shall see presently.

The apostle James contends, and I think irrefragably, that only by works is faith made perfect. "What doth it profit, though a man say he have faith, and have not works? Can faith save him? If a brother or sister be naked, and destitute of daily food, and one of you say unto them: 'Depart in peace, be ye warmed and filled'—nevertheless ye give them not those things which are needful to the body: what doth it profit? Even so faith, if it hath not works is dead, being alone."

Truly enough, Brother James; but dead things are not always buried; for to this order of corpses belong all the shams and artificialities that curse the world to-day. Indeed, dead faith,—the kind that can be galvanized into just enough life to sing and pray and groan and profess that it can do nothing for itself, but must rely solely on the merits of Jesus—is by far the most popular species of deadly self-delusion that the race has ever yet stumbled upon; developing forms of religion which are in the nature of specialized cults, quite separate and apart from life itself.

Recollect for a moment how absolutely true the apostles' words are. If we agree even that the faith be real to the extent that it results in grace, that is, in the awakening or planting of a truth ideal, how shall that ideal become effectual for salvation unless the soul conforms its order of life to it? A thing impossible without strenuous soul-effort in the nature either of self-sacrifice, if it be an evil habit that must be cut away, or self-advancement, if it be some power of righteousness to be attained.

Suppose the acorn to be endowed with volition, that its growth and development, like man's, depend not upon God's will, but its own; and that as soon as it has passed through the ecstacy of sprouting, it should lie back with a languid affectation of loving helplessness and say: "I can do nothing for myself, I must rely solely on the blessed power of the sun." How far would such a programme advance its evolution? Why, supineness of that kind would not suffice for the backbone of a mushroom, let alone the strength of an oak.

How can it be otherwise with man? If he has received grace, what is it but a trumpet call to work? And if he lies down under the delusion that such effeminacy is pleasing to God, what becomes of His grace? Just as the warmth of the sun, which serves to develop the growing acorn, becomes the very means of its destruction, should it cease to grow, so grace, which continues to bless and build a living faith, becomes damnation to a dead one.

Nor can a manly self-reliance be offensive to God, as the morbid sentimentalists among Christians would have us believe. The acorn can never become an oak without the help of the sun, truly enough. On the other hand, the sun can never produce an oak without the help of an acorn. And if such reciprocal relationship holds with non-volitional beings, how much more with beings of equally free will? Can man become perfect without the help of God? Manifestly not. Can God make a perfect man without that man's active co-operation? No; for if He could evolve him physically and mentally by His will, as He does the birds and fishes, the man would at last be only an automaton, lacking the essential glory of a psychic being,—a perfected free will.

Both reason and the common experience of the race therefore stand behind the declaration of James that grace (or faith) without works is dead. Nor does any other text in Scripture contradict it. Paul's words, above quoted, while often interpreted so as to contradict James, do in fact only emphasize the same truth turned round. Paul's attitude is this: "Works without grace (or faith) are dead"—a truth no less important, as I shall now proceed to show.

The work of sending roots earthward, and trunk, limbs, branches, and twigs skyward—if that may be called work which is without volition—is a typical example of organic vegetable growth; in other words, of evolution. The analogous case of man receiving grace upon grace from God, and successively harmonizing his life thereto, presents no less an instance of organic human growth or soul-evolution, since idealization and expression are indissolubly locked as cause and effect. But consider now that a tolerable imitation of a growing oak can be made by a skilful artificer by sheer means of hammer and glue. But it would not be alive, however much it might deceive the beholder; for the reason—if it is not utterly ridiculous to give a reason,—that its parts would not be related by organic evolution.

In like manner there may be, in religion, works without faith; works growing purely out of the head, not out of the heart of hearts, which is the altar of grace. Take two men, one of whom by fervent devotion receives the grace of God, and in obedience thereto is baptized and begins to readjust his habits so as to live a godly life: doing whatever the Lord reveals to be right as naturally as stem follows leaf on the oak. The other man imitates—for various reasons: just to be doing; or for worldly advantage; or for fear of hell-fire; or because he thinks his friend a good man, and it is best to be on the safe side if there should happen to be anything in religion.

Thus during the course of a life-time the works of these two men are so nearly alike as to deceive their fellow-communicants; and while the life of the first counts everything for salvation, the life of the other counts nothing. It is the case of the natural and the artificial oak over again. In spite of a life full of good deeds, the soul of the latter has not yet begun to sprout. Of what avail is it for purposes of salvation to have branches or twigs of righteousness nailed onto the soul? "For by grace are ye saved through faith . . . not by works, lest any man should boast."

There can be no salvation that does not begin by cementing the union between God and man. But this man who imitates has not yet found God; how then could the life of God flow into his life? Nor do his many good deeds flow out of his own soul, as flows the life of a tree from trunk to branches, leaves, and fruit. In a word, his religion has consisted of a series of mechanical adjustments, while that of his brother has been a series of related acts all tied together as one organic evolution of the soul. There is only death in the one while there is life eternal in the other.

Nor need we look far to discover Paul's reason for taking an attitude so uncompromising toward righteousness of the mechanical order; for was it not this very species of lifeless works that characterized the religion of the Jews? Paul's words are in fact but a very faint echo of Christ's denunciation of this barren religion of the head. Listen to His awful words:

Woe unto you, Scribes and Pharisees, hypocrites! For ye pay tithe of mint and anise, and cummin, and have omitted the weightier matters of the law, judgment, mercy, faith; these ought ye to have done, and not left the others undone. Ye blind guides! which strain at a gnat and swallow a camel. . . . Woe unto you, Scribes and Pharisees, hypocrites! for ye are like unto whited sepulchres, which indeed appear beautiful outward but are within full of dead men's bones and all uncleanness.

Nothing could be more searchingly true of religions which, losing the power of Godliness, continue punctiliously to observe the forms of Godliness, making the latter, indeed, a screen for the diablerie of hell; or, as Christ puts it, a painted sarcophagus to hide the festering corruption of their dead hearts. Nor is this hypocrisy peculiar to old-world religions. The tendency to mechanical forms is always directly in the ratio of the fickleness of man's purpose; for, while natural forms of life, such as the trees of a forest, are dependent upon God's will, and are consequently kept green and growing, psychic forms, such as those of religious societies, are dependent primarily upon the will of man; not only for the faith which leads to the outpouring of grace, but for that progressive repentance on which condition alone grace can continue. What wonder then that religions present to God the aspect of dried-up forests oftener than otherwise along down the ages! That there are many such psychic forests now waiting the torch of God's justice, who can doubt, that has made any comparisons between form and substance in the numerous sects of the day?

Coming back to Christ's declaration that the kingdom of God is potentially within man, even as the oak is in the acorn, we may first note in respect of causes that the law of evolution holds as well in the spiritual as in the natural world; that as the sun is the source of the natural, so the spirit of God, or grace, is the source of the spiritual evolution; but that, while God's will as expressed in natural law acts without reference to the consent of any form of life subject to it, His will as expressed in grace is operative only as earnestly desired by man, and may be in fact made of no effect toward spiritual evolution if opposed by man; that as natural evolution is but the unfolding of God's ideal into the eternal harmony of things, so spiritual evolution is but the unfolding of His ideals in the eternal social relationships of psychic beings; that in fact the kingdom of God within man, is nothing else than God's prophecy of a kingdom to be evolved external to man;

Spiritual Evolution

whence the consistency of Christ's definition with that other conception of Paul and the apostles, which involves a perfect church organization of apostles, prophets, bishops, elders, pastors, teachers, deacons, helps, governments,—all the machinery necessary to carry out God's will in the social evolution of the race.

We may next note, in respect of effects, that two dangers stand between the inner kingdom, or God's ideal, and its evolution to an outer kingdom, or expression of God's ideal. The first danger is pointed out by James: Faith without works is dead. The operation of this danger tends to produce those religions characterized by mere maudlin sentimentalism: like some green thing which, refusing to grow upward in the strength and symmetry of a tree, merely spreads and sprawls over the ground in useless leaves. The second danger is pointed out by Paul: Works without faith (or grace) are dead,—a danger characterized by all merely mechanical forms, rites, and ceremonies of religion, and well represented by a tree the limbs and branches of which are nailed on, painted, and furnished with artificial leaves,—the incarnation of sham and hypocrisy.

The Church of God steers clear of both these dangers; recognizing the grace of God as the only source of spiritual ideals, and daily and hourly repentance as the only means of evolving those ideals to their full function of salvation.

CHAPTER XIX

SPIRITUAL FORCES ONLY HIGHER POWERS OF FORCES KNOWN TO PHYSICS

THERE remains then the concept "grace" to be further explained. In the foregoing chapter it was used to signify that inpouring of truthness or the spirit of God into the soul of man, whereby he is enabled to know, without doubt, that God lives, that Jesus is the Christ, or any other eternal truth necessary to the beginning of his conscious psychic evolution. As used there it involves also the nurture and development of the truth-ideals so revealed; whence the analogy was drawn between the sun's relationship to the germination and development of plant life, and God's relationship, through the medium of grace, to the conversion and ultimate salvation of man. Were I writing an exposition on purely religious grounds, I should let the term go at that; but the scientist may well ask: What is this thing called grace or the Spirit of God? How is it related to the known forces of physics? How is it apprehensible by man?

By the conception of Mormonism, all the processes which go on, whether in the natural or in the spiritual world, are God's processes. If man has discovered the nature of these processes in the natural world, he has a basis for reasoning to the nature of those in the spiritual world. For the line between the two is evidently no chasm: it represents to man merely the present boundary of the known—the point where science ends and faith begins; but as this line has been receding from the known into the unknown world by every new and important discovery, who shall say that, to God at least, there is such a line at all? Is it not more rational to believe that the natural world grades into the spiritual, as darkness into day?

Science has reached the conclusion that all forces are but variously tensed forms of one final, supreme spiritual energy filling the universe. Differentiation in this "infinite and eternal energy," whereby are manifested the progressively related phenomena of heat, light, actinism, chemism, and so on, proceeds on the basis of a relative increase in the rate of vibration per second. Beginning with sound, which is a wave motion of the air, we receive the first psychic impression when the beats are about sixteen to the second, and continue to hear, in a gradually increasing pitch, until the vibrations attain to about 41,000 per second, when they are lost to the ear. Nor do they reach the consciousness through any other channel, until they increase to a rate of one billion wave-beats per second,—not of the air, but of that finer, universal medium,—when a second psychic sensation is recorded as electricity.

The next gap occurs beyond the billion mark. After leaving electrical phenomena we get no other sensation till we reach heat, at a lowest limit perhaps of three hundred trillion wave-beats per second. The unknown region between involves therefore an interval represented by 299,999,000,000,000, silent or unregistered vibrations per second!

From 300 trillion vibrations per second, the lowest point of heat, to 400 trillions, the lowest point of light (the red ray), the scale is continuous. So also it passes by a progressive increase of rate through orange, yellow, green, blue, and indigo, reaching again a limit of psychic interpretation in violet, which has 756 trillion vibrations per second. But the sun's energy does not cease at the highest point of light. By delicate instruments the dark rays above violet have been explored over a range sixteen times as wide as the zone of light! It is in this region that actinism and chemism work their marvels in the natural world.

But there comes next another gap of total psychic darkness, in spite of the fact that man's natural senses have been so marvellously multiplied in effectiveness by scientific inventions. This gap is represented by the vibrations occurring in the interval between 1 quadrillion and about 250 quadrillions per second. Then come the X-rays, beginning at 288 quadrillions per second and ending at four and a half quintillion (4,500,000,-000,000,000,000!) After that, nothing is known to science; but the inference is obvious that there may be waves of the eternal medium of still higher vibratory power.[1]

Let us realize clearly what all this means. These avenues of insight into the harmony of the universe are not open or closed to mortal senses by chance; God arranged them so. Why He lifts the curtain only at places, leaving vast gaps of darkness,—where beings differently organized might perceive wonderful things,—we can only surmise at best; perhaps because man's energies are not great enough to adjust his life to a wider range of truthness than what the natural world affords.

At any rate, so it is; and he is wise who lets God,—that is to say, Nature or things as they are,—decide his range of investigation; just as he is foolish who, in cell or cloister or hermit's cave, tortures his psychic powers into dim perceptions along avenues not yet lighted up by infinite Wisdom. A few glimpses into ghostland are but a poor recompense for marvellous opportunities in the natural world neglected. A religion which encourages such stolen peeps at things locked and barred to ordinary psychic powers is, on the face

---

[1] These figures are taken from a table arranged recently by Sir William Crookes and quoted by Camille Flamarion in his late book entitled *The Unknown*, pages 15 and 16.

of it, a false religion. What should we think of teachers who would encourage pupils to neglect their primary studies and waste time prying through key-holes into the class-work of the high school? On the other hand, what value should we place on the scraps of advanced knowledge so purloined? And yet there are people who stand in awe of mahatmas, clairvoyants, and spirit mediums.

Of course where a general knowledge of the past or of the future is necessary to balance properly our life pursuits in the present, God will raise the curtains for seers and prophets; whose visions thus become our guides, in so far as guides of that kind are necessary. For the rest, if the nature and constitution of things as they are stand for anything, then they proclaim this truth: that mortal experiences are peculiarly the present duty of mortal beings; to the end that by their proper reaction they shall further the psychic advancement of the soul.

But in order that there may be such a true reaction, it is necessary that there be a true interpretation: one must know what is right before one can do what is right. Here then precisely comes in the need of grace, or that continuous stream of truthness from God, in the light of which mortal experiences take a true relative value and perspective; whence rises again the question, whether such an addition to the normal consciousness of man is possible.

From *a posteriori* grounds the case would be simple enough, if men would accept that kind of evidence. That any one can refuse credence to the testimony of ten thousand times ten thousand witnesses, who declare they know God lives, that Jesus is the Christ, that the Gospel is true, or that any given action or requirement is from God,—may seem astounding enough, but so it is. Unfortunately—perhaps fortunately—we are not fitted to know because others know; the faith engendered by such testimony is at best but cold and apathetic. It may incline us to believe that grace is possible, without making us wish to share the blessing; or it may simply lead us to pity what we, in our arrogation of superior mental strength, may regard as merely the self-hypnosis of religious enthusiasm. Let us see, then, what support is offered on *a priori* grounds.

If God can so tense the eternal medium as to touch our psychic life in the aspects of gravitation, sound, heat, light, actinism, chemism, and so on, is it to be thought incredible that He can impress it with a rate of vibration which shall carry assurances of Himself or of His mind and will to our souls? The energy of the universe so impressed by the mind and will of the Father is the Holy Ghost of Scripture. That it does not respond to the laboratory tests for lower differentiations of the eternal medium,—what of it? Does not each of these require its own peculiar test? Because one form is discoverable by an electrometer, is another form to be discredited because it responds only in the human soul?

But the Holy Ghost has differentiations within itself, which appeal respectively to different aspects of the soul, as these shall be in need of light or sustenance: As the Spirit of God, it is colored or suffused with the Father's personality; as the Spirit of Christ (Rom. viii., 9; I Peter i.), it bears to man the warm love of the Saviour; as the Comforter (John xiv., 16, 26), it carries balm to the bruised heart; as the Spirit of truth (John xv., 26; also xvi., 13), it may be defined as the pure white light of intellectuality; so also it is called the Spirit of holiness, of grace, of wisdom, of might, of counsel, of promise and of prophecy; and named by its fruits, it is called a spirit of love, joy, peace, long-suffering, gentleness, goodness, faith, meekness, temperance (Gal. v., 22, 23). "But all these worketh that one and the self-same spirit, dividing to every man severally as he will."

What could be more natural than to look upon grace, or the inpouring of truthness, as a higher, perhaps the highest, power of that same infinite energy whose lower powers constitute the subject-matter of physics? But lest it be thought that Mormonism reached this conclusion from a further generalization of scientific research, it needs to be said that Joseph Smith came first with his doctrine; nor was he ever sufficiently acquainted with the discoveries of physics to have reached it in any other way. The law of the conservation of energy, on which the interrelation of cosmic forces is predicated, was announced by F. K. Mohr in 1837; the revelation on which the above conclusion is based was given to Joseph Smith in 1833.[1] Furthermore, it is doubtful whether one Latter-day Saint in ten is aware to-day of the coincidence between science and revelation above pointed out.

But we may come into yet closer touch with the nature of the Spirit of God in its operation on the heart and mind of man. As our Father in heaven, who conditions this medium of grace so that it shall transmit His mind and will, is a personal being; and as man, whose soul is touched and stirred by grace, is equally a personal being, it will be seen that coming into communion with God is purely a case of divine telepathy,—if I may use a scientific term for so sacred a relation. And if, now, we enlarge our executive conception of God so as to include not only our Father in heaven but Jesus Christ and all the hosts that make up the working organization of Divine Authority,—including also our guardian angels, as representatives of God nearest to man,—all using the Holy Ghost as a medium; and then consider man *en rapport* with whatever part of this divine executive personnel that his life may need,—we shall be ready to conceive a system of heavenly communication beside which all

[1] See *Doctrine and Covenants*, Section 88: 7–13.

telegraphic systems, wireless or otherwise, are crude in the extreme.

For whereas these latter, being mere mechanical contrivances, can convey only the signs of ideas; the other system, being organically related to spiritually organized intelligences, and having for receiver and transmitter the quivering soul itself, can send through the eternal ether, not mere clumsy symbols, which may or may not yield their content, but the naked, unclothed thoughts and emotions themselves, — truthness both in idea and in feeling,—which shall leave no room for the spectres of doubt, nor fail to give joy, peace, long-suffering, patience, fortitude, or whatever other virtue or power the soul may be in need of.

Such is the capability of the system, and such is probably the use made of it in the commonwealth of heaven; man, however, partakes of its perfect communion only to the extent that he can, through faith and diligence, elevate his life into the sphere of its influence. Theoretically it is a perfect guide to every man who has made covenants with God; practically it can guide him only as his mind is in harmony with the mind of God. Faith must consequently open the door to it, and faith, be it remembered, is dependent upon will. Moreover, a life of undeviating truth,—that is, a life of repentance, a life devoted to carrying out the ideals which grace progressively brings to man,—is the only condition on which it will remain with him. It is therefore at once the means and the reward of perfect individual freedom.

It is at this point, perhaps, that we shall best be able to understand the philosophy of prayer. The notion that divine worship is for the glorification of God has for its correlative the idea that God is supreme-by-will, rather than supreme-by-law; also that he loves flattery and adulation, like some vain earthly monarch of the Alexander-type. If now we remember,—what must surely be the truth,—that selfishness is at a minimum and altruism at a maximum with God, we must readjust this notion respecting the object of divine worship. Somehow, all the good of it, all the glory of it, must accrue to him who worships; while the joy experienced by Him who is worshipped, can be nothing else than the pure joy of knowing that His children are doing the one thing that shall most quickly advance them toward their salvation. For it is by prayer that we come into communion with God, and so open the channel of that divine telepathy whence the riches of grace can flow into our souls to the full extent of their capacity; and as the grace of God is the only means of our progressive spiritual evolution, so accordingly should we value prayer, the means whereby we may attain it.

But is it enough merely to feel the spirit of worship and keep silent, as some Christian liberalists teach? The acorn no doubt swells with ecstatic sensations of life, but still it goes on to sprout; the rosebud may feel, instinct within it, a spirit of beauty and fragrance, but it does not for that reason fail to bloom. Should either of these organisms refuse to express itself, it must die ere it is born. So also of the spirit of prayer: he who will not voice his love of God and love of man, must inevitably smother the noble impulse in the darkness of his own bosom; for, like the plants, man is a creature of evolution, and his psychic life, being the main part of the man himself, must evolve—come out from the darkness of his inner being—in word and deed, if it is to live at all.

Divine worship, being thus a condition of grace, is consequently a conditon of salvation; but such worship is far from being adoration, which centres in and is addressed merely to persons. On the contrary, the components of true worship are reverence for law, as incarnated in God; love for our Father in heaven, as a divine Parent; fraternal sympathy and companionship with the workers; and loyalty to the leadership of Jesus Christ. To feel these emotions is to have the spirit of prayer; to express them in word, or song, or deed, or tears of joy, is to place oneself *en rapport* with God and the workers, and so be fitted to receive grace upon grace, until the soul shall become perfect as its Father in heaven is perfect.

It is only by virtue of man's being able so to get into communion with God, that we have the holy Scriptures. It becomes interesting, therefore, to consider the various effects of this superior light as reflected in the words and works of mankind. That is a very narrow conception of God's providence which denies inspiration to any other than the sacred writings. These are expressions of God's truth in the social, moral, and spiritual world, truly enough; but is it thinkable that the equal Father of all would confine the light of His word to one narrow people?

If the Bible is more perfectly a revelation of God than is the Koran, it is not because God was partial to the Jews; it was doubtless owing to the fact that Israel was fitted for purer light, no less also than that its prophets were purer mediums. But the Bible, in its turn, is less perfectly a revelation of the divine word than are the *Book of Mormon* and *Doctrine and Covenants;* representing as these later scriptures do, the revelations of God to a dispensation capable of more exacting truth ideals.

The mystifying element in holy writ disappears largely when we bear in mind that Scripture is at best a compromise between the pure white light of absolute truth, and the more or less colored personal medium through which, perforce, it must shine for man. Sometimes the personal element all but predominates, as when Paul confessed, on one or two occasions, that it was he, not the spirit, which wrote a particular doctrine. Again, passages occur in which the medium seems almost completely in abeyance; as when, after "Thus saith the Lord," the words are directly those of

God or Jesus Christ. Between these extremes all Scripture evidently oscillates.

But we need definite terms to describe degrees of infallibility in Scripture. When grace gives merely that sensation of truthness which satisfies for conviction, it ought to be called inspiration; but when the divine telepathy brings into consciousness, not only the truth effluence, but the very objects giving off that effluence (*i. e.*, as when the mind has an open vision, or hears the voice of its divine correspondent), it ought to be called revelation. Scripture is made up of both these forms of truth-expression; from the crude product of mere human judgment, faintly tinged —or perhaps untinged at all—with the light of heaven, up through the varying translucency of inspiration to the transparency of revelation; a translucency and transparency which, however, do not necessarily appear, save to him whose soul is lighted by grace.

But to modify in such a way as this the cast-iron mediæval doctrine of the absolute infallibility of Scripture—will it not overthrow one of the very pillars of religion? Perhaps—if the religion be of a kind supported by pillars; that is to say, if it be of a mechanical order. But the social evolution of the race is hastened in the ratio that such religions fall; for it is this very dogma of scriptural finality, this absolutism of interpretation, this notion that revelation is all in and cured, once for all,—that has stranded modern Christian sects just where Egyptian art was stranded for a similar reason.

Let us realize that God never intended the life and light of inspiration to be conserved by means of the dovetailing, glue-jointing interpretations of theological carpentry,—such as make up the manifold creeds and confessions of modern sectism. Scriptural texts are rather to be regarded in the light of things planted and growing: capable of indefinite organic expansion and application, but sure to lose their spirit the moment you cut and fit them into a mechanical theology.

"The things of God," says Paul, "knoweth no man but the spirit of God." Grace is the only possible interpreter of grace,—but it is a very safe interpreter. "If thine eye be single," says our Saviour, "thy body shall be full of light." To the extent that this light of grace is within us, to that extent shall we be able to assimilate the light of revelation, whether in nature or in Scripture; and if we attempt to build a theological system by any other impulse than this light gives, the structure will be a mere mechanical contrivance, —a wooden something made up of dead works,— not a living, growing organism.

Nor need we feel called upon to stultify ourselves by assuming that any Scripture, coming as it does from God, must necessarily be perfect. For if the revelation of vegetable life in yonder tree, in the fashioning of which God has had untrammelled sway, is nevertheless, by the interaction of natural forces, far from perfect, why should we expect a revelation of psychic life to be faultless, trammelled as it must be, by the inertia of a will negatively as free as God's own, and reflected from a mind very rudimentary in its development? Nevertheless, as we perceive the principle of life in the tree to be perfect, so by the eye of grace shall we be able to catch glimpses of the perfect mind of God, behind and beneath the imperfect form of its expression in Scripture.

Coming back now to the central theme of this chapter, that grace or unbroken communion with God is the only means of psychic evolution, the question arises, In what avenues of life may we expect grace to be our guide? This, as will be seen, is only a restatement of the question raised in the second chapter, viz., as to how far man must be guided by relative truth, the result of his own generalizations, and how far he may expect guidance by absolute truth, the result of God's generalizations. Will grace or absolute truth assist him in prospecting for gold and silver? In winning an election? In building a railroad? In settling the question whether Bacon wrote Shakespeare's plays?

The answer, though necessarily general, is unequivocal. Since after making covenants with God, grace is the medium of man's evolution, he will have an unbroken stream of it to the extent that he responds successively to what God would have him do next; in other words, to the extent that he acts on Christ's maxim: "Thy will not mine be done." This may often be so primitive a thing as building a log school-house, or digging a canal, or even so unspiritual a thing as running for Congress,—for God is in all the affairs of men, whether great or small, which have to do with the evolution of the human race. On the other hand, grace will fail him, and he will have to move forward by mere human light, to the extent that he switches off—as he is free to do—on schemes not in the direct line of God's purposes,—schemes not necessarily wrong—simply desultory, out of place, and therefore wasteful.

By what other policy than this could God bring into one grand, final, consummate unity, all the centrifugal tendencies of His children? Christ's mission is an example of a life guided at all points by absolute truth, or the mind of God; but it is easy to conceive, though hard to believe, Him turning aside for mere earthly fame; in which case He would have been left to His own innate powers and on equal footing with other men of similar talent.

As to knowing when one is on the individual quest and when on the Lord's quest, it is not a matter that can be settled by rules of procedure. Grace is the sole interpreter of grace. He who lives so near to heaven that his life is enveloped in heaven's halo, will know when he leaves the Master's service for his own; and no sophistry, however specious, about end and means, will succeed in blinding his soul to the withdrawal of the divine light, and as a consequence leaving unillumined his mere earth-born wisdom. However, the object of departure,—wealth, position, fame,—may throw around itself such a glamour of goodness and justification that for a time,—perhaps, alas! for all time—the quest will be followed to the very *cul de sac* of its barren inconsequence.

If, when that point has been reached, the soul has any truth integrity left, it will exclaim with Solomon, "Vanity, vanity," and return to God's service; if not, it will continue following its earth-ideals, and, in lieu of real joy, go on flaunting its apples of Sodom in order to squeeze out a little counterfeit happiness from the envy and greed excited in the eyes outside the wall of its own mundane achievement.

There remains then the question of how man comes into possession of grace; not as of a light loaned him previous to conversion, to guide him into the path of truth; but as of a lamp, his very own, to keep filled, to trim, and to use wherever the service of the Master shall lead him. Manifestly such a dispensation of the gift and power of the Holy Ghost would be a conscious dispensation, and must, therefore, like forgiveness and the covenant of baptism, involve a token. That token is the laying on of hands and the conferring of the Holy Ghost in the name of Jesus Christ; for so has God ordained.

Note that here, too, symbolism plays an important part. The person receiving this ordinance, indicates by his attitude that he has subordinated his will to the authority of the kingdom of God, of which presently he shall become a free citizen; the person laying on hands acts the part of God, who alone has authority to confer the right to receive the gift of grace. He must therefore be a man divinely commissioned, if the ordinance is to be anything else than a solemn mockery. The Holy Ghost so conferred upon man becomes the servant of his will to the extent that he is the servant of God's will. It is the medium by which he shall work out his own salvation.

CHAPTER XX

WHAT INTELLIGENT BEINGS WILL DO IN THE HEREAFTER

THE first and chief element in the happiness of heaven [says a Catholic writer][1] will consist in the beatific vision; that is, in seeing God face to face, unveiled as He really is. The "face to face," however, is literally true only of our blessed Saviour, who ascended into heaven with His sacred body. Otherwise, as God is a spirit, He has no body and consequently no face. In paradise, spirits (angels and our souls) see spirits. We shall see God and angels, not with the eye of the body, nor by the vibration of cosmic light, but with the spiritual eye, with the soul's intellectual perception, elevated by a supernatural influx from God. As in ordinary vision the image of an object is impressed on the retina, so in the beatific vision, the perfect image of God will be reflected on the soul, impressing on it a vivid representation of Him. We shall thus enjoy an intellectual possession of Him, very different from our possession of earthly things.

This doctrine of the beatific vision is by no means confined to the Catholic Church. Here is

[1] The Rev. C. Van Der Donckt of Pocatello, Idaho, in the *Improvement Era*, August, 1902, Deseret News Co., Salt Lake City.

the way in which a noted Presbyterian delivered himself on this theme:

> The question is often asked, "What shall we do when we get to heaven? Wherein will consist our happiness?" I shall answer this question for myself. When I get to heaven, I shall spend the first five million years of my life in gazing upon the face of God; then if my wife is near I shall turn and look at her for five minutes. Then I shall gaze upon the glory of God again for a million million years; and when the longing of my eyes shall have been satisfied, and my soul is suffused with the beatific vision, I shall snatch up my harp and begin playing.

Will this reverend gentleman go on playing during the rest of eternity? Or will he occasionally take a breathing spell, to gaze again for a few odd hundred million years? Perhaps, too, his wife will have become relatively dearer by that time, and so will furnish another means of relieving the eternal *ennui*. I fully understand, as did the audience, no doubt, that he meant no personal slight nor any undervaluation of the conjugal tie; it was merely a case of not loving his wife less, but of loving the Lord more.

I realize, too, that this extravagant forecast of heaven is not to be taken as the best and most rational exposition that could be made of the "beatific-vision" idea of eternal bliss. But after all allowance has been made for hyperbole and religious hallucination, what is there in the notion to commend it even faintly to common-sense? Wherein does it touch the experience of the race, even by the remotest analogy? Is there anything in life to suggest that one can gaze with rapture even for a single hour? How then dare we commit our hope of eternity to such a chimera of fancy?

On the other hand, what kind of being must God be, if we suppose Him to get pleasure from having a billion billion eyes,—the animated periphery of a hollow glory sphere with God as its centre,—glued upon Him from all sides for millions of years at a stretch? And then to have a certain quadrant of the enraptured gazers suddenly seized with harp-madness for other millions of years! Surely He will need the full measure of His infinite patience and long suffering!

Such a notion of heavenly bliss on the one side, and of God on the other, are the outcome of the mediæval conceptions of the earth as a place cursed, of mortal life as penal servitude, of work as the penalty of sin, and of God as a supreme-by-will Being who was to be placated by much praying and singing. Naturally, therefore, heaven would be figured in a manner antipodal to all experiences here below. Instead of the earth cursed, an ethereal heaven is imagined somewhere in space, to which the soul flies at death; instead of the toil and labor of earth-life, "there is sweet rest in heaven,"—an eternity of idleness; and for the

Man's Future Occupation 219

praying and singing exacted in the world, there is substituted the eternal program of gazing and harping in the world to come.

How these iridescent soap-bubbles blown by religion-makers break and vanish with the first ray of common sense! "This is life eternal" said the Saviour, truly enough, "that they might know thee, the only true God, and Jesus Christ whom thou hast sent." But what a piece of fatuous reasoning, to conclude that knowing God and Christ is a matter of idle gazing upon them for eternity. As well expect a clam to comprehend the unity of the solar system by opening its mud-valve to the sun's rays!

What the Saviour said is absolutely and philosophically true: eternal life is in us to the extent that we know God and Jesus Christ. But knowing our Father in heaven is nothing less than becoming like Him. Knowing law is knowing God objectively; living in harmony with law is knowing God subjectively. The first gives knowledge, the second, power; and the end of such a course of successive knowing and doing is nothing less than omniscience, or perfect power to know, and omnipotence, or perfect power to do. Could anything less than these powers comprehend God? Grace is thus seen to be the progressive medium of knowing God: the light by which we see law, the power by which our feeble wills are re-enforced to the living of law.

Now, as man enters the spirit world knowing

God no further than he knew Him when he said good-by to mortality, it follows that he has no time to idle away with the "beatific vision," if he values eternal life; or even if he could see God objectively, he would be able to assimilate Him only to the extent that he has Godliness within him; or, to use the phrase of psychology, only to the extent of his apperceptive material. So far, therefore, from escaping work by escaping from the world, he must greatly increase his diligence, if he desires to be saved.

It is on the basis of this thought that Mormonism predicates an eternity of scientific endeavor for man; a future life devoted progressively to the apprehension of and obedience to law, till all the secrets of creation are known, and the untrammelled power to create has been attained. Such is the glorious career that lies before the workers.

The nature of this future work, as also the order in which it will come, will of course be determined by divine wisdom. Some speculations in relation to it may, however, be indulged in with profit. Since God is in all the processes of nature, it is more than probable that there are unnumbered posts of minor responsibility where intelligence such as ours can serve His purposes, and, by serving, help to attain creative perfection. The mere naming of such a possibility flashes before the mind opportunities in the natural world,—or, rather, in the workshop out of which the natural world grows—that millions of years could not exhaust! What nobler conception of future existence could there possibly be than this? What life more filled with truth-surprises, and therefore with the very essence of eternal bliss?

Next, contemplate the world of art,—the possibilities yet undreamed of in literature, music, painting, sculpture, architecture, and similar lines of creation. It is not likely, however, that such studies will be carried on there as here—widely divorced from investigations of the natural forms whence alone they can draw true life and inspiration. Our souls will probably find, in these expressions of art, a happy means of overflow for the excess harmonies attained in the study of God's world and works. Nor is it likely that we shall ever evolve beyond the susceptibilities out of which art grows, and to which it ministers; for our life there must necessarily resemble our life here. The "many mansions" mentioned by our Saviour is suggestive of this, as is also the Eternal City described by John the Revelator. It must be self-evident also that the art products which shall be part of our environment in heaven will be the work of our own hands, just as they are here. To suppose our souls unrelated to them by creation is nothing less than to say we are equally unrelated to them by appreciation: for he who does not make, is but poorly fitted to enjoy.

There is next the social world, involving the problem of learning to live in perfect harmony with our superiors, our equals, and our inferiors; a problem that has hardly approached solution as yet among mankind. It is a question that involves the co-ordination and subordination of the individual in a thousand complex relationships, and always along lines both of justice and of love. Surely there is work of the highest order of sociology in the hereafter; for what is our noblest conception of heaven but that of a place of perfect social harmony?

And we must create the heaven we expect to enjoy—else how could we enjoy it? God can aid us in this all-important work, but He cannot do it for us; for if He should arbitrarily co-ordinate and subordinate us, would the result be a state of bliss without alloy? Or should we chafe, as we do here, under God's appointment? And, being free, how long should we stay in the niche prepared for us by infinite wisdom? The fact is, heaven becomes impossible on any other lines than the social co-ordinating and subordinating evolution of its inhabitants under the influence of grace.

It is for this reason, no doubt, that the first serious work demanded of him who has entered into covenant with God, is to accustom himself to the broad lines of heavenly government as foreshadowed in the organization of the Church; and he who cannot curb his propensity to fly off at tangents in respect of divine authority upon the earth, demonstrates, above all things, his unfitness to be placed among the workers in heaven.

Nor would I have the reader believe that in the Church government, which thus marks out crudely the order of heaven, there is coercion of any man's free will. Such a policy would defeat itself,—making at once both tyrants and slaves, neither of whom could exist a day in heaven. This fact will be made entirely clear in a companion volume, *The Social Aspect of Mormonism*, wherein I hope to show forth a system of divine government entirely worthy the authorship of God who revealed it.

Now, while Latter-day Saints thus look forward to a thoroughly socialized future, a future made up of physical, mental, moral, and spiritual activities along lines the beginnings of which are already laid in life, they do not by any means surrender the idea of coming into the presence of holy angels, the Saviour, and the eternal Father. But they expect to meet these exalted beings, not in idle, deadlock, convention-ecstacies protracted to millions of years, but in the sensible, rational way in which workers meet leaders. Moreover, the presence of the Father and the Son with any man does not depend upon sight nor any other physical sense; for the Holy Ghost is instinct with the glory of their personalities, and whoever lives so pure a life as to be filled with this spirit, dwells in the divine presence in a much more real sense, than if he jostled with a million-million other souls in the endeavor to get an ocular vision. Indeed, it is pretty safe to say that he who has not thus lived in their presence on earth, need never expect to get the face-to-face vision in heaven.

As to the natural epochs in the future life, two only have been indicated by revelation. The first is that of the spirit-world, occupying the time between death and the resurrection; the second is the life after the resurrection. Perhaps it will not be out of place to discuss briefly these two states and the transitions which lead to them.

To understand the nature of the world of spirits, it is necessary to remember the dual nature of all animated beings. God first created things spiritually, and then naturally, so we are told in Genesis. The negative testimony of all experience lends credence to this view of life; negative because we must infer the presence of spirit or life in the living from the fact of its absence in the dead. The bird in yonder tree, for instance, is just now singing and flitting about by reason of a power beyond reach of analysis. Anon the gun of the collector will bring it fluttering to the ground; only half of it, however, to be quite exact; for that which enabled it to sing and flit will be gone forever. So of all living things: we are ever in the presence of spirit, and recognize it by a thousand happenings to be inseparably associated with life; but isolated from its earthly counterpart, it eludes every known scientific power of investigation.

Assuming then that everything which lives,—plant, animal, man—does so by reason of a spirit which is either life itself or the vehicle of life, we reach the conclusion that the spirit-world is right here, bound up with the natural world,—hidden away in it as sugar is in water. That is to say, life has two aspects, an outer, which is mortal, and an inner, which is spiritual. This conception is well illustrated by the instantaneous appearances and disappearances of our Saviour after His resurrection; showing that he could function now in the spiritual, now in the natural, world without essential change of location.

If it be accepted, then, that the spirit world is, in flora, fauna, and natural topography, the spiritual counterpart of the natural world, differing only perhaps in being a more perfect expression of the divine idea, it must follow that the psychic life of the individual will go on uninterrupted by death. Indeed, it is doubtful whether, on awakening in that next world, the spirit will at first be aware of the change, so familiar will the environments seem. Nor is there reason to believe that contact with objects in the new world will produce reactions relatively different from those on the natural plane. It will only be by a certain ease and swiftness of movement, and perhaps by the absence of shams and make-believes, that the fact of death, or transition from mortal life, will become most pronounced.

Some years ago I had occasion to admire a clump of cedars growing under the spray of the Shoshone Falls. They were as straight as sunbeams and as symmetrical as angels' spears. At first I wondered how the Oregon timber cedar could get to such a place; but as the trees graded upward from that awful chasm by natural transitions on the mountain side, till they ended in the low, crooked, and gnarled species so common to the American desert, I made a more careful examination and found them to be all of one family. Here was food for reflection. Who could have dreamed that God's idea of the scrub cedar was so beautiful! Those perfect specimens, perennially tipped with the rainbow, represent spirit cedars completely expressed. This, then, is what every scrub cedar would be were its inner life fully evolved. And so of all other dwarfed vegetable or animal forms.

Then I thought of scrub human beings—the crippled, the stunted, the deformed, in mind and body, the crooked, gnarled, half-cured specimens that cumber the deserts of life. These, too, have fallen short of God's idea—short of the full expression of their spiritual stature. What then? When they return to the spirit world, will their deformities go with them? Will the deaf, the dumb, the lame, be deaf, dumb, and lame there as here?

Hardly. The measure of truthness in their souls, the sum total of their spiritual likeness to God, will be neither increased nor decreased by the fact of death; but there seems to be no reason why defects peculiar to earth-life—defects only incidentally related to psychic evolution—should be perpetuated there. The spirit counterpart of the withered arm will not be withered and shrunken. In form and outline it will perhaps resemble the other; only in texture will the educated spiritual arm be superior to that which has hung limp and idle during earth-life. But eternity will present opportunities without end for the adjustment of all such inequalities.

One other difference of man's next estate has already been suggested. If there is one more distinctively characteristic of the present world than any other, it is perhaps the opportunities it affords for shams and artificialities. It is as if the Lord gave man a covering for hypocrisy, just to make love of truth a cosmic virtue,—the doing of right purely for right's sake. But there is reason to believe that this world's multiform refuge of lies will be left among the grim trophies of death and hell; souls that pass on will be as naked to truth as when they were born. As Paul says: "Here we see through a glass darkly, there face to face."

In virtue of what principle, then, will it become impossible to hide "under Gospel colors," or any other colors, "just for a screen?" In virtue of the principle of soul-radiancy, I think. The glory of God's person is represented as brighter than that of the sun,—and "the glory of God is intelligence." When the angel Moroni appeared in the darkness to Joseph Smith, the light emanating from his person was sufficient to illumine the boy's humble chamber as brightly as at noon-day. Accordingly, we may infer that as is the intelligence of any being, so is the radiancy of his soul. "Shining raiment" is evidently no figure of speech in descriptions of heaven. By contrast what must be the opacity of souls doomed to hell!

This fact—that our souls will be radiant according to the righteousness of God in them—will inevitably lead to voluntary classifications; for "Light cleaveth unto light, darkness unto darkness." Even in earth-life this tendency is already well-marked, in spite of our facilities for shams and make-believes. There it will be pronounced. The Scriptures name two localities in the spirit-world: paradise, where spirits dwell that have accepted Christ; and hades, a prison for spirits still in darkness. "To-day shalt thou be with me in paradise," said Jesus to the repentant thief; He could just as truly have said to the other malefactor, "To-day shalt thou be with me in hades," for he visited both places during the time his body lay in the tomb; moreover, from the latter place, so it is recorded, He "led captivity captive"—out of purgatory into paradise.

Hades is not to be pictured as a dungeon where shrinking, terror-stricken souls are shut in by bolts and bars; on the contrary, spirits go there by choice,—on the principle that men choose darkness rather than light because their deeds are evil. Nor could you drag one of these dark or tawny ones into paradise; any more than you can drive bats into the glare of daylight. If Christ led souls out, it was because the light of repentance had first given them the radiancy of paradise. Light is the only power that can release from the bondage of sin. Accordingly, part of that future life of altruism which awaits the workers will be to carry the Gospel light into these benighted regions; "till every knee shall bow, and every tongue confess, that Jesus is the Christ."

A few words now respecting the resurrection and this chapter must close. Very little that is definite has been revealed on this subject; other than the assurance that our spirits shall eventually be clothed with glorious bodies of flesh and bone; bodies as palpable to the sense of touch as was that of Christ, when he bade Thomas feel the print of the nails and thrust his hand into his Master's side. "For a spirit hath not flesh and bones as ye see me have."

How is it to be accomplished? Just as we set aside the mechanical conception of creation, so we may safely spiritualize the mechanical notion that graves will yawn at the sound of a trumpet. Unlike man, God does not work by any other than organic processes; and when that tremendous event shall have been accomplished, we shall see that the principle was one of evolution, and as inevitable as that which from a mere microscopic cell formed the natural body. Indeed, could the growth of a resurrected body well be more marvellous than this?

Such was evidently the conception of Paul when he compared death and the resurrection to a seed planted and reproducing itself. In the seed was the inherent possibility of a new body, but it had to die in order to get it. It was not the old body that was resuscitated. This gave merely the potentiality to draw from the storehouse of nature a new body. The drawing of the new body was the process of changing potentiality into fact.

It will probably be the same with man. The fact of having lived a mortal life, if only for an instant, gives the spirit the potentiality of drawing to itself a resurrected body when the time shall be ripe for it; and I use the word ripe because, the resurrection being a potentiality, the time for its realization will manifestly vary according to the fitness of the spirit to live the advanced life which the new estate brings. "First Christ, then they who are Christ's, at his coming," is the way this thought is put in Scripture.

Whether the body so organically drawn from the storehouse of the universe will be composed of matter newly compounded, or be made up of atoms so definitely individualized by the old body during mortal life that they can fit into no other organism, is a question I leave to men who love disputations better than I do. The Bible would seem to favor the latter idea; but the subject is practically beyond scientific investigation, and therefore so far from affecting the present truth-status of our souls, that it has really no vital significance whatever.

Putting resurrection as a potentiality of the spirit, disposes of that multitude of perplexing questions, as to whether the cripple will have his deformed body again, the aged their decrepit frames, the young their immaturity, and so on. Manifestly, if it is in the spirit to draw a body, then the body drawn will be of the exact texture of the spirit itself—glorious or otherwise according to its own radiancy; but there seems no good reason why the imperfect expressions—the congestions—of earth-life should be repeated. Perhaps in the case of infants, the bodies resurrected, or drawn from the materials of the universe, will resemble in dimensions those laid down; since it was here an organic process which death interrupted; but these bodies would thereafter as surely grow to maturity as if they were still living on the earth-plane.

Another thought, unavoidable from such a conception, is that resurrection is now going on, and probably has been since the days of the Saviour; the question of time being as inevitably subject to law as any other event in God's providence. Such, at any rate, is a common-sense view of what is at best an extremely speculative subject; and no serious disturbance can come into the order of our lives when we keep within hailing distance of common sense.

CHAPTER XXI

PHILOSOPHICAL DIFFICULTIES TO THE CONCEPT OF A PERSONAL GOD

IN a previous chapter the proposition was laid down that Mormonism is a transcendent system of evolution; transcendent because it not only includes and thinks into line the facts of scientific evolution, but organizes them into an endless perspective, both as to the past and as to the future. This claim, it is hoped, has been fully justified by the foregoing discussion. For the rest, Mormonism has no favors to ask, no concessions to make, in respect of any other system of thought; and this for the simple reason that it is an organic not a mechanical religion. Its doctrines do not hang together by virtue of the decrees of ecclesiastical councils. On the contrary, they grow out of each other as naturally as the branches and leaves of a tree; for, as becomes a living, growing organism, religion is not conceived by Latter-day Saints as something superimposed upon life, nor even as something integrated with life, but as life itself, from God's point of view.

Moreover, Mormonism has no cut-and-dried

limitations of social growth and development to defend; so far from this being the case, it is pledged by one of its articles of faith to accept all truth, irrespective of who may bring it. As basic or fundamental doctrine it insists on only one tenet, viz., —in the words of Paul—"Let God be true, even though it make every man a liar." This is only a concrete way of placing Truth above conventionality; for the "living God" to each man is the measure of truthness within him, however it came there, whether from sifting nature or opening his soul to revelation. How else can God live in our lives? And God can be true for each man only as that man resolutely lives his ideals, even, if need be, at the cost of his life.

A distinguished writer has said, in respect of the conventions and institutions of men, that the very fact of their having existed for thousands of years is the foremost reason for demanding that they demonstrate their right to exist longer. Each life, so far from being shaped and moulded by what men have been before, should be the immediate expression of the kingdom of God within it,—an evolution of the truth ideals implanted within it by its perception and generalization of Law or divine harmony. "Come out of Babylon" is the burden of Scripture. This is possible only by shortening the train of sequences in our lives. If a man would cut loose from the world, his acts must spring directly out of his interpretation of nature and the intuitions he gets direct from nature's God, and not from the shams and artificialities of convention. Let God indeed be true for every man, be the social consequences what they may! Let history's grim claws be kept off the human race.

The statement of this basic tenet serves also to narrow the discussion again to the question, What is God? Now, it is inconceivable that any lover of truth reading the foregoing discussion respecting the psychic evolution of man should not wish with all his heart that it might be true. Unfortunately, he perceives that the whole beautiful system depends on one primal fact, that God is what the Bible reveals Him to be, a personal being, the perfected man. Destroy this concept, and Mormonism goes down, leaving mankind again in spiritual chaos; amid a wilderness of facts without perspective; knowing neither whence we came, why we are here, nor whither we tend,—save perhaps as we place credence in the speculations of Buddha; for whatever in Christianity definitely answers any of these categories in a way differently from the answer of the Hindoo sage, is based upon that same ultimate premise, however much concealed or ignored or repudiated,—the premise of a personal God.

Elsewhere I have taken the ground that a great mistake was made when science overthrew the personal or Christ-type of God; that the demands of philosophy for the Buddhistic type—that of a universal spiritual essence—were mistaken demands. I did not intend, by any means, to beg this question; the need of discussing aspects more immediately urgent, however, led me to dismiss the subject with the remark, that experience being the criterion of judgment in science, mankind are not really justified in postulating any other type of creative intelligence than the man-type; for what other type have they ever, or can they ever, come into relation with?

This did not settle the question, however, as I fully realized at the time; and the opportunity has now come for entering fully and frankly into the logical difficulties which led theologians to give up the "God of Abraham, Isaac, and Jacob" for a sort of Christianized form of the God of Buddha.

These difficulties at first sight seem all but overwhelming; nevertheless, I shall proceed to put them in as strong and vital a form as my antagonist could possibly wish—satisfied, as I am, that they are not insuperable. But my antagonist ought, by the by, never to be anyone attributing Godhood to Jesus Christ; for if the Father cannot hold his place throughout eternity in the character of a personal being, no more can the Son; and if the Son cannot, how can we, who depend upon the Son for our salvation? Every Christian ought therefore to be glad, if the thesis of God's personality can be sustained. So also ought every scientist; for it would demonstrate, even in analogies relating to this highest generalization in the realm of intelligence, that the law of experience is the safest guide to correct reasoning.

The first difficulty relates to the infinitude of God. The Scriptures reveal the fact that God is infinite, and even did they not, a moment's reflection must make the fact self-evident; for if the universe is infinite,—and we cannot think it otherwise,—and God be figured even as simply co-equal with it, He also must be infinite; by how much more then must He be possessed of infinitude when we postulate Him as superior to the universe.

But to be infinite is to be unbounded, unlimited, unconditioned. How then can infinitude be predicated of Jesus Christ, who, as we know, is limited as to form, and who was conditioned by birth, death, and resurrection? And if not to the Son, how to the Father, whom we postulate to be the exact prototype of the Son? It would seem impossible.

Our next difficulty turns on the predication that God is eternal. This fact is revealed in many passages of Scripture, but it is also self-evident—being only another statement, indeed, of the notion of infinitude; for if the universe is boundless, it must be so equally as regards both time and space; and therefore God, who must be thought of as superior to the universe, cannot be less boundless in time than in space. In other words, He must be eternal.

But to be eternal is to have neither beginning

nor end. Christ evidently had a beginning in His capacity as God, for the relationship of Son itself implies not only a beginning of organized life, but a limitation of power; and although He could pray, "Father, glorify thou me with the glory I had with thee before the world was," and Paul gives evidence of this same pre-eminence in heaven, by declaring that by Him and through Him the worlds were made,—yet had He things to learn in mortal life: He grew in stature and in wisdom, was made perfect through suffering, and finally took His place on the right hand of the Majesty on high. If anything therefore seems fixed and certain from our apprehension of His life and the revelations concerning Him, it is that His Godhood had a beginning. But since God is an eternal being, how could Jesus Christ be God?

The difficulty applies equally to the Father; for is it to be supposed that He belongs to a race which gives birth to sons, yet He Himself was unborn; that He existed from out the depths of eternity creating galaxies of worlds without number, supremely alone, until He came to our insignificant planet and to the year A.D. 1, when He caused to be born a being like Himself, who became co-equal in divine power and glory? Mormonism is more modest: it believes that the Father, like the Son, is a perfected man; or, to quote again its supreme aphorism of psychic evolution, "As man is, God once was; as God is, man may become."

But note now the dilemma when we oppose to this aphorism the absolute and irrevocable demand of reason, that God must be eternal. For, if this aphorism be true, there was a time when our Father was not God. Who then was God? His Father, do you say? We l, by the same necessity, there must have been a time when He, too, was not God. Who then?

This brings us face to face with another difficulty: there is but one God. Reason and revelation alike dec are this fact; for not to be God and Lord alone is to be limited and conditioned by some other power, and is therefore not to be infinite. As the universe is one, so God, the psychic power of the universe, must be one. But if the aphorism above quoted be true, there must be an infinite number of beings related to each other by sequence, yet all reigning co-ordinately as Gods.

Let not the Christian be too swift, however, in disclaiming belief in a doctrine apparently so preposterous, for his own system involves at least two such Gods, the Father and the Son; and whatever reasoning can reconcile the unity of God with the Christian's limited polytheism, can equally reconcile it with the Mormon's unlimited polytheism.

But pointing out, in mere terms of infinity, the apparent discrepancy between Jehovah, the "God of Abraham, Isaac, and Jacob," and that infinite, eternal One, that Being without bounds, without limits, without conditions,—

Objections Met

Whom none can comprehend and none explore,
Who fills existence with himself alone,
Embracing all, supporting, ruling o'er
Being whom we call God, and know no more.

—a mere enumeration, I repeat, in abstract terms, of the apparent contradictions between the God of the Bible and that ultimate source of being and power which must be postulated in conceptions involving the universe as a whole,—gives the reader but very faint and inadequate notions of the real difficulty which this discussion aims to bridge over. Let us therefore be brave enough to approach these apparent contradictions in a more concrete fashion.

We shall do well to examine first our conception of the world on which we live. It is a real, solid earth, is it not? The stupendous cliffs rising, terrace above terrace, on three sides of me as I write, and leaving me only a triangular skyline, are no delusions of my senses. The capstone of yonder peak two thousand feet above me has weight, and should it come crashing down the gorge, would crush all living things in its path. The pines that half hide the seams and scars on the terrace butments and make a sombre fringe against yonder sunlit cloud; the cascades that thunder down three separate canyons uniting within a stone's throw of me, after making a hundred waterfalls and filling the gorge with music; the woodpecker hammering into yonder rotting stump; the badger lazily crawling up that dusty trail, the chipmonks chattering in that pine tree; the spider that is just now spinning the rope by which it lowers itself from the roof of my cave; the snowbanks on the opposite mountain slope; the July breeze from somewhere above that makes me put on my overcoat; and Provo River, a half mile almost perpendicularly below me, flowing contentedly at last after its million years of titanic labor,—all these things are realities, if I who write and you to whom I write are realities. And if we are not, then nothing matters; Christian Scientists may have their way, for then, like the rest of creation, they, too, would be delusions.

The point I wish to make is that this world and all things in it that appeal to the senses of man are real, tangible creations. There may be spiritual spheres, astral planes, and what not, in the universe, for its mysteries are many and unfathomable. What we should not forget is, that there *is*, —it is ridiculous to say there may be,—a real, solid, tangible world, one which it is entirely safe to take as a sample of God's work as Creator. Here, right around us, not in metaphysical creations, lies then the making or marring of our eternal lives. Is our world such a one as the Buddhistic- or Christian-Science type of God would create for the perfecting of psychic beings?

Our next consideration must be the relationship

Objections Met

of our world to the rest of creation. There was a time when our forefathers,—pardonably, let us say,—regarded the earth as the solid centre of all things, and all the rest of the universe—sun, moon, stars, and sky—as only a feathery canopy. Since then science has humbled us. Now we recognize our earth as only one of the smaller planets of the solar system, and our sun as only one of the inferior stars. So, also, we have learned that there are millions of these shining orbs, even to our poor, finite vision,—a million millions therefore in the spaces beyond our telescopes, which only our imagination can explore. Each of these myriad blazing suns, to reason by analogy, controls its retinue of worlds. It is not impossible, therefore, that there may be a billion earths far greater and more glorious than ours, each filled with beings of our own race, but inconceivably advanced beyond us in divine intelligence.

How then have we fallen and been humbled to the dust, poor benighted earth-spirits that we are! But the saddest part of our abasement is in this fact: that in the ratio that the world has shrunk to insignificance, its Creator has become vague and shadowy. Once He walked and talked with men in the gardens and on the rugged mountains of the earth; now He traverses only the Milky Way. Then He conversed with prophets and holy men, as a father might counsel with his sons; now He is become, in the words of the poet, a conception—

Whom none can comprehend and none explore,
Being whom we call God and know no more.

The gulf which Mormonism seeks to bridge is that between the demands of a vital, living faith, such as a child may have in its father, and the demands of reason as its eye sweeps the stellar universe. The first is soothed and cheered by the history of God's manifestations unto man: by the voice of the "Lord God walking in the garden in the cool of the evening"; or admonishing Moses to take off his shoes because he was on holy ground; or calling in the darkness of the night to the boy Samuel, during the days when the "word of the Lord was precious in the land"; or answering the stricken Job out of the whirlwind; or bearing witness to John the Baptist, "This is my beloved Son in whom I am well pleased." But how do these special manifestations comport with the demands of reason for a being infinite, eternal, unconditioned—

Whose presence bright
All space doth occupy, all motions guide?

To limit such a being even to so wondrous a galaxy of allied solar systems as the Pleiades seem to present, would be to withdraw Him from the universe and confine Him to what by comparison would be less than a grain of sand to the bulk of the sun; what, then, of the conception which limits Him to the rôle of Jehovah in connection with the history of the earth? Is the God depicted in Derzhaven's poem, from which I have quoted above, the same Being that gave directions to Noah for making an ark out of gopher wood; or that wrote with His finger the Ten Commandments on the tablet of stone; or that instructed Moses how to build the Tabernacle in the wilderness; or that spoke to the high priest once a year out of the Ark of the Covenant; or that figured in the visions of Isaiah and Daniel, Paul, and John the Revelator? If faith must give up these objects, how barren and perfunctory would religion become! Yet if reason must square its concepts by them, what (apparent) confusion would immediately enter into science!

And so of all the concepts relating to Jesus Christ as Saviour of mankind. His atonement is spoken of as an infinite sacrifice. Are we to suppose that nowhere in the universe was salvation possible till brought about by the tragedy on Mount Calvary? That on no sphere in space could beings pass that psychic epoch known as resurrection, till Christ led the way on our earth?

Such, then, is an outline of the apparent contradictions between the God of the Bible and the God demanded by reason. Of the two sides to this controversy, the men of science are the more honest; for, while they are feign to admit the necessity of an ultimate Source of psychic being, they cannot reconcile the unity, eternity, and infinitude of such a Being with the limitations demanded by the personal Creator and controller of our earth, or by a being who can act the rôle of Providence, and be influenced by prayer; and so they do not try, preferring to derive the earth and all things in it from what they are pleased to call the persistence and transmutation of energy. Modern Christians, on the other hand, while agreeing to the scientific conception of God, are continually, yet very illogically, quoting the Biblical manifestations before referred to as evidence of His existence; either not perceiving or else wilfully disregarding the fact that every example so adduced, of special providence or intervention in behalf of things earthly, is a fact immediately limiting or conditioning Him, and therefore opposed to His infinitude.[1]

Mormonism is under no such pressure toward soul-stultification as that of accepting the philosophic aspect of Deity, and then of promulgating subordinate doctrines in direct contradiction thereto, in order to have a religion at all; for Mormonism sees the essential truth of both these conceptions, and has no difficulty in reconciling them, as I shall attempt to show in the chapters which follow.

[1] Christian ministers are quick, however, to perceive and point out this fact, when modern instances of God's manifestations, such as those claimed by Joseph Smith, are in question.

CHAPTER XXII

GODHOOD AS INCARNATED

WHILE I was laboring, [writes the Prophet Joseph Smith,] under these extreme difficulties caused by the contests of religionists, [as to which sect was right], I was one day reading the Epistle of James, first chapter, and fifth verse, which says, "If any of you lack wisdom let him ask of God, that giveth unto all men liberally and upbraideth not, and it shall be given him." Never did any passage of Scripture come with more power to the heart of man than did this to mine. It seemed to enter into every feeling of my heart. I reflected on it again and again, knowing that if any person needed wisdom from God, I did; for how to act, I did not know, and unless I could get more wisdom than I then had, I should never know; for religious teachers of the various sects understood the same passage so differently as to destroy all confidence in settling the question by an appeal to the Bible.

At length I came to the conclusion that I must either remain in darkness and confusion or else I must do as James directs, that is, ask of God. At length I determined to ask of God; concluding that if He gives wisdom to them that lack wisdom,—gives liberally and does not upbraid,—I might venture.

In accordance with this determination I retired to the woods.

It was on the morning of a beautiful clear day, early in the spring of eighteen hundred and twenty, and the first time in my life that I had made such an attempt; for amidst all my anxieties, I had never as yet made the attempt to pray vocally. After I had reached the place previously chosen, and looked around to be sure that I was alone, I kneeled down and began to offer up the desires of my heart to God.

I had scarcely done so, when suddenly I was seized by some power which entirely overcame me, even exerting such astonishing influence over me as to bind my tongue so that I could not speak. Thick darkness gathered around me, and for a time it seemed as if I were doomed to sudden destruction.

But, exerting all my powers in calling on God to deliver me, and at the very moment when I was ready to sink into despair, and abandon myself to destruction,—not to an imaginary ruin, but to the grasp of some actual being from the unseen world who had power over me such as I had never felt before,—I saw exactly over my head a pillar of light above the brightness of the sun, which descended gradually until it fell upon me.

It no sooner appeared than I found myself delivered from the enemy which had held me bound. *When the light rested upon me, I saw two personages, whose brightness and glory defy all description, standing above me in the air. One of them spoke unto me, calling me by name, and said pointing to the other, "This is my beloved son, hear him."*

By the truth or falsity of this vision, Mormonism rises or falls. The Prophet, at the time of receiving it, was scarcely more mature in years than was Samuel of old when the Lord called to him in the darkness of the night. But mere child that he was, there was in him a spirit such as always marks the beginning of an epoch in the affairs of men. What fourteen-year boy of your acquaintance was ever profoundly agitated as to the true way of eternal life? Measure him by the mental traits of your own sons. What boy in his early teens ever before had the acumen to weigh the conflicting messages of his religious teachers, the resolution to cut loose from them, and the simple faith to go direct to the fountain head of wisdom for his inspiration?

Nor must it be imagined that this vision was reshaped during later years. Contemporaneous accounts of it agree exactly with the simple narrative above recorded; for, with the innocent trust of childhood, Joseph had gone to a certain minister of the Gospel, who was a friend to the family, and related what he had seen and heard. He was not prepared for the storm of denunciation which immediately broke from half-a-dozen pulpits in the neighborhood. But he soon learned what pains of travail must accompany the birth of Truth. From that day till his martyrdom in 1844, he was a marked and persecuted man.

It will be noted that in this vision are involved, directly or indirectly, the doctrine of special providence or answer to prayer; the active opposition of negative spiritual powers to the salvation of men; the supremacy of the positive forces of the universe; the personal or anthropomorphic form of both the Father and Son; the authority of Jesus Christ in the affairs of this earth by the delegation of the Father.

But the essential fact of the vision was the explication of Christ's words to Nathaniel, "Who hath seen me, hath seen the Father,"—the reaffirmation of Paul's explanation of these words, when he spoke of Jesus as being the "brightness of his Father's glory, the express image of his person." There was nothing in the religious teachings of the day that could have given Joseph Smith the conception that appears in this vision. Had he been a conscious impostor he would have chosen figures in keeping with the ideas of his time. He could not have known, as we know now, the vital significance of this new revelation of the Father and the Son. He could not have realized that this open vision was the one thing needed to overthrow a thousand years of vain attempts to merge the speculations of Buddha and Plato with the teachings of the Bible. It is significant, however, of the simple but sturdy integrity of the boy that no amount of wheedling, ridicule, or denunciation could swerve him one iota from the reality of what he had seen and heard.[1]

---

[1] "I soon found," writes the Prophet, "that my telling the story had excited a great deal of prejudice against me among

Godhood as Incarnated 249

And for the earnest seeker after truth,—for the man or woman whose soul's salvation has become the foremost question of life,—I should be willing to rest this discussion by simply referring him, for the truth of Joseph Smith's first vision, to that same passage in James: "If any man lack wisdom let him ask of God that giveth to all men liberally and upbraideth not, and it shall be given him"; especially in view of the fact that complete and final conviction on this point, when it does come, must come from God, and from Him

professors of religion, and was the cause of great persecution, which continued to increase. And though I was an obscure boy, only between fourteen and fifteen years of age, and my circumstances in life such as to make a boy of no consequence in the world, yet men of high standing would take notice sufficient to excite the public mind against me, and create a hot persecution; and this was common among all the sects—all united to persecute me. . . . It was nevertheless a fact that I had seen a vision. I have thought since that I felt much like Paul when he made his defense before king Agrippa. . . . Some said he was dishonest, others that he was mad, and so he was ridiculed and reviled; but all this did not destroy the reality of his vision. He had seen a light and heard a voice,—he knew he had; and all the persecution under heaven could not make it otherwise. . . . So it was with me; I had actually seen a light, and in the midst of that light I saw two personages, and they did in reality speak to me; and though I was hated and persecuted for saying so, yet it was true: and . . . I was led to say in my heart, Why persecute for telling the truth? I have actually seen a vision, and who am I that I can withstand God? Or why does the world think to make me deny what I have actually seen? For I had seen a vision. I knew it, and I knew that God knew it, and I could not deny it, neither dare I do it, lest I offend God and come under condemnation."

only. But as this book is an attempt to look at the tenets of Mormonism from a scientific point of view, I shall proceed with my argument and attempt to show, by a course of probable reasoning, that a Being so limited and circumscribed is not inconsistent with the demands of reason that the Ruler of the universe must be a power absolute, infinite, and eternal.

CHAPTER XXIII

THE REAL MEANING OF GODHOOD

IT is an old saying in monarchies that the king can never die. The incumbent of the kingly office is subject to all the vicissitudes of other mortals; nevertheless, so long as the kingdom holds intact, the aphorism is undoubtedly true.

So in our own country we might say the President cannot be assassinated, although three of our fellow-citizens, while holding that exalted office, have been taken away by the bullet of the assassin. The President, or, to be more exact, the Presidency, is not a power subject to the fluctuations of the individual. It is a something formed out of the combined psychic life of the nation. As long as the nation endures, it endures. Were the nation eternal, it would be eternal; were the nation infinite, it would be infinite.

This simple analogy ought to make clear in what sense God is infinite, eternal, self-existent, and absolute or alone. These ultimate categories are predicable of God, because they are predicable of that which makes Him God, viz., of Godhood. Take Godhood from Jehovah, and He might still (theoretically) remain our Father in heaven, but He would not be God; any more than Roosevelt, stripped of the power delegated by the suffrages of this nation, would remain President.

It is somewhat remarkable that an explanation so obvious has not before been made use of to reconcile the contradictions between God as creator and providence and God as the supreme and final conception of power. The failure to do so only emphasizes, however, the all but universal extent to which mankind has been imbued with the autocratic notion of Deity. This notion stands pronounced even in the terms expressing God's divinity. God*head*, not God*hood*—the supreme-by-will, rather than the supreme-by-law—has been the interpretation of His omnipotence by mankind. As a consequence He has for the most part been viewed in the light of a tyrant to be feared and placated, rather than as the supreme executive of law and order, to be revered and loved; and religion, instead of being a natural social system based on the interpretation of the harmony of the universe—man's interpretation constantly corrected by God's—has degenerated into a ridiculously artificial system of rites and ceremonies, prayers and genuflections; which, if not correlated in thought with a supreme, but vain and whimsical autocrat, on whose sceptre alone hangs salvation or damnation, have no meaning whatever. To bring this thought home, suppose one of your own species elevated to the rank of recipient of this homage, and endowed with the qualities of mind necessary to find pleasure in it. What kind of being should you have? Is God such a being?

Godhood, then, in the sense of ordainer and executor of law,—not Godhead, in the sense of Head-god, or tyrant by right of supreme will,—is what makes a "just man made perfect" God (*e. g.*, Jesus Christ); and when he has attained to this supreme rank of intelligence he is God omnipotent, omniscient, omnipresent, eternal, infinite, absolute—for all these powers are the powers of Godhood with which he has been invested.

I am quite willing that this explanation shall be taken with a proper reservation, till all its implications and corollaries be examined.

The first implication necessarily relates to the nature of Godhood itself. Philosophers from time out of mind have been busy trying to construct a final cause—always with pitiable results, either in circle-arguments, or downright self-stultification.[1] Is it not time that mankind recognized the innate absurdity of such attempts? Is it because Causation is apprehensible by segments, while Time and Space are seen to be continuous, that it is not immediately perceived, even as they are, to be an eternal relation?

Reflect upon this question for a moment. How could there possibly be a first cause? The moment

---

[1] For an example of the inextricable dilemmas resulting from such efforts, see Appendix B.

we try to single out any cause as first, we perceive it to be either the effect of some antecedent cause —in which case it is not first—or an act of will of some intelligent being. But an intelligent being must be a personal being, innately eternal and free, as an ego, and superior to the universe by reason of initiative and the mastery of universal forces—in short a being like unto God.[1] As such, his omnipotence or power to create would be a product of psychic evolution (see Chapters VIII, IX, and X), and consequently not a first cause. There is therefore no first cause. Causation is an eternal constituent of the universe—the central fact of Godhood itself.

If this conclusion is not immediately self-evident, it may be strengthened by supposing the universe reduced to the uncreated or formless state—the state of chaos or homogeneous nothingness[2]—and then considering Causation absent as an eternal relation. How would creation begin?

---

[1] That he could not be the impalpable essence of Buddhism and Creator at the same time, see Chapters IV. and V., also appendix B, where this question is argued out.

[2] Buddhism actually postulates such a state, which it calls *Pralaya* or universal night, alternating with a state of Creation, called *Manvantana*, or universal day, at intervals represented in terms of our years, by a period of fifteen digits respectively; but of course the creative principle or God, which is represented by the universe itself, is postulated as the efficient cause of both states. What possible purpose infinite being could have in these monotonous appearances and disappearances throughout eternity, theosophists do not inform us.

It could not. But the universe exhibits on every hand the actual evidences of creation. Godhood, or the power to create, must therefore have been eternally present.

It follows from this conception that there is only one such supreme power in the universe; in other words, there can be but one true God (in the sense of Godhood) who is absolute and alone. The forces in opposition to God, known as sin and the Devil, are retrograde movements incidental to, and made possible only by some tremendous psychic evolution set going by Omnipotence Himself. They are to God's purposes what the backward rush of water up some bayou of the Mississippi is to the onward sweep of that stream. Not only would such backward movements be impossible without the correlative forward movement, but in their very nature they must be transitory; for just as the Mississippi will in the course of a few geologic years wipe out the stench and miasma along its course, by filling up the breeding holes, so must all negative forces that poison the moral and spiritual atmosphere of life, be finally obliterated by the resistless onward sweep of God's purposes.

But while the Devil and his cohorts of evil, together with those forms of sin which are incidental to unperfected human nature—sins which would exist even if there were no tempter—will thus ultimately be swept out of existence, even as the Scriptures foretell, this is not saying that there will not be similar reactionary forces in any future scheme of psychic evolution like that exhibited by our present world. Indeed, a little reflection must make it seem probable that negative forces like those with which we are familiar, are inseparable from, not to say necessary to, all such world projects of Deity.

To realize that this must be so, consider for a moment how such negative forces arise. A countless number of self-conscious beings, innately eternal and free, but powerless in their primal state to condition the universe around them, begin that course of psychic evolution the outcome of which is the progressive accumulation of power (see Chapters VIII, IX, and X). After millions of ages devoted to the apprehension of and compliance with law—in other words, of obedience to the will of God—they have reached a stage not unfairly represented by ourselves on this earth; a stage, not indeed of omnipotence, but of varying degrees of conscious power; a power which they are free to exert just as the bias of their prevailing ideas shall suggest.

Now is it not more than probable that in every such aggregate of intelligent beings some proud Lucifer will arise, and, forgetting the source of the power which swells his bosom, seek again to establish his throne above that of the Almighty? And should he do so, will he not also get a third—or a fifth, or a tenth—of the hosts of heaven to follow him in the forlorn cause? And would they not equally be cast down into hell? Such a world would thus have its quota of devils precisely as we have ours: spirits who have forever lost the power to say, "Father, thy will be done," and consequently have no other alternative than to expend their power in opposition to God, to the final and inevitable undoing of themselves.

So much for the effect of the sin unpardonable (because unrepentable); but what of the two-thirds—or three-fourths, nine-tenths, or whatever the proportion might be—of the spirits who would remain loyal in such a supreme conflict? Is it not altogether likely that they would do as we are doing—take a zig-zag course, occasionally living up to the truth impressed upon them directly (by God) or indirectly (by nature), but ready at the slightest whim of self-gratification, to spend the power accumulated during cycles of slow evolution in opposition to the very Source and origin of it all? Who can doubt that such will always be the case—making that Scripture an eternal axiom which says: "Many are called but few are chosen."

But, to come back to our point of departure, while such reactionary forces may seem formidable obstacles to the doctrine that God is absolute, they can seem so only to mortals, who, being in the midst of them, cannot see them in eternal perspective; to Godhood itself, viewing with infinite eye the trend of the universe, they must seem less potent even than the very shadows of trifles.

CHAPTER XXIV

GODHOOD INOPERATIVE UNLESS INCARNATED

REVERTING now to my analogy of the previous chapter, I may remark that while the President is beyond the reach of the assassin—since he is not born of woman but is begotten directly by the will of a mighty people—this is what the murderer's bullet can do: it can suspend the executive will of the nation, till its power can be relocated; for magnificent as is this power,—the combined will of eighty millions of people,—it is practically *nil*, a thing inoperative,—suspended, as it were, in the air,—unless it be invested in a man.

In like manner Godhood, our supreme concept of power, carrying with it omnipotence, omniscience, omnipresence—all the categories which reason correlates with the universe—is incapable of the simplest creative act, save as it is exercised by a being like our Father in heaven or His son Jesus Christ. For by our very manner of conceiving it as separate and distinct from an organized psychic being, we imply, as in the case of Presidency, a power potential but lacking the first re-

Godhood Incarnated

quisites of creative power—the capacity to invent, and the ability so to co-ordinate and differentiate the application of power as to bring into being the thing invented.

Godhood alone is therefore not God, any more than Presidency alone is President. Without Godhood a psychic being might invent a solar system, but it could never be projected beyond his own mind; without a psychic being to rest upon, Godhood must remain inoperative, a mere static or potential power, throughout eternity. Strictly speaking, therefore, the categories above named, omnipotence, omniscience, etc., are predicable of Godhood only when invested upon a perfected man; in other words, they are predicable only of God.

We have thus explained how Jesus Christ could become God. For though Catholics insist that He was always God, we cannot so reconcile the fact that He was first the Son of God, the only begotten of the Father, the first-born among many brethren—all which terms imply a time when He was not God; and therefore, instead of the prevalent idea which is read into the first verse of John's Gospel, viz., "In the beginning was Christ, and Christ was with God, and Christ was God,"—I prefer to render the mystery which John hid in the word *logos*, and which has been translated "the Word," by a term which shall not impugn the passages just quoted relating to his birth, and which shall, moreover, be consistent with his manner of becoming God, viz., "In the beginning (*i. e.*, always, eternally) was Godhood, and Godhood was with (*i. e.*, part of) God . . . and Godhood was made flesh (*i. e.*, was conferred upon man), and dwelt among us, full of grace and truth." [1]

Note the fact that the words "full of grace and truth" favor my interpretation; for where else than in Godhood or Godliness do these attributes inhere? Even the parenthetical expression, "and we beheld his glory, the glory as of that of the only begotten of the Father," indicates the reception of divine attributes as the very heart of the mystery. At any rate the fact that Christ's organized spiritual life began with the Father—at which time He was consequently not God—is to be reconciled with this other fact proclaimed by Paul that now, "In him dwelleth bodily (*i. e.*, in bodily form) the fulness of Godhood" (Col. ii., 9). My explanation reconciles these apparent contradic-

[1] I do not put this interpretation forward as authoritative,—that would be extremely foolish in any one save God Himself, through the medium of His inspired oracles. I merely wish to suggest that the Beloved Disciple, who was perhaps more deeply versed in the mysteries of God's economy than any other of the Apostles, designed, by the mysterious use of the word *logos*, to indicate something more than the mere personality of the Son. My interpretation does not preclude the idea that He was with the Father—as indeed we all were—in the beginning, before the world was. But it does make the passage consistent with the fact that our Elder Brother, though he stands foremost among God's children and is the first to receive Godhood, does not differ essentially in the course of His psychic life from that of Peter, Paul, Isaiah, or any other of His brothers or sisters.

tories; and that, too, without the need of that soft palliation for religious self-stultification—mystery. So, too, we can now understand how Jesus Christ may be referred to as the eternal God—eternal being one of the categories of the power that makes him God.

Having made plain how one man born of woman became God, I have justified our Saviour's supreme injunction: "Be ye perfect as your Father in heaven is perfect"; also the supreme aphorism of Mormonism: "As man is, God once was; as God is, man may become." I have, moreover, indicated how there may be an infinite number of psychic beings who have attained this supreme rank, and yet, in the sense of the power which ranks them, how there can be only one true God everlasting—"without body, parts, or passions," if you will; how beings yet unborn may, through attaining to the "fullness of Godhood bodily," in future ages be spoken of respectively as "God everlasting—from eternity to eternity."

Many interesting questions spring up at this point which it will be profitable to consider somewhat at length.

In a previous part of this discussion it was pointed out that the Mormon aphorism as to the sequential relations of man and God, implies the possibility of an infinite number of divine beings, related to each other by sequence, and reigning co-ordinately (at least in time if not in authority) as Gods in the universe. The same idea is implied in the opening paragraphs of this chapter; for if the power to create is an eternal relation, and yet no creative act can issue, save as this power is united with a psychic being perfected enough to wield it, it follows that the universe was never without a perfected psychic being; but as "perfected" implies a course of psychic evolution such as we are passing through now, it follows that there must be an infinite line of such psychic beings.

A line of beings related by sequence—such an idea experience enables us to understand; but an infinite line—that is beyond comprehension. A succession without a beginning absolutely staggers the human mind. How could there *not* be a first! we exclaim. The only answer is the echo of how. But the contradictory alternative, How *could* there be a first? is equally incomprehensible. For the moment we assume a first God, we immediately ask, What God enabled this being to attain to the rank of Godhood?

It was the mistaken notion that the human mind absolutely demands a resting place, that led philosophers to postulate as final cause, an infinitely extended, uncaused, unconditioned, or Necessary Being—not *a* being, however, for that would imply limitation, but being unqualified. Now if it were possible to believe such being could invent and execute a creation—an hypothesis transcending all experience,—the moment it succeeded, it would cease to be necessary being, for it would be conditioned in relation to its creation as cause to effect; but the fact that such a condition was inherent in it shows that it never was necessary being. For the tangle of contradictions involved in such a scheme of deriving the visible universe, see Dean Mansel's exposition of the Necessary Being as Creator (Appendix B).

But supposing that such a notion could be made to seem rational, the practical question is, What would our ideals gain thereby? Conceive a time when Creation began. Well, what was before that? Darkness—chaos. A million years before? Darkness—chaos. A million million—not years—but ages? Darkness—chaos. A billion billion cycle of ages? Darkness—chaos. Deity sleeps—*he has not yet stirred from all eternity!*

The Buddhist notion is at least a trifle better. It gives us a rhythmic, albeit a senseless, purposeless, motion in the universe: a night of 100,000,000,000,000 years, during which Deity inbreathes, drawing into the universal darkness of Chaos men and worlds alike; then a day of equal length during which He breathes them out again!

Compare either of these notions with the Mormon conception of infinitely extending galaxies of worlds peopled by intelligent beings in process of psychic evolution! Granting that all three notions are incomprehensible, which is the nobler conception? Again, which agrees with our experience, limited though it be?

But coming back, the idea that the human mind

demands a resting place in the series of causation is a mistaken notion. Are we troubled because our ideas of space and time are necessarily infinite? Yet these present exactly the analogues of the disturbing elements in Causation. For instance, How can there *not* be a beginning to space (or time)? Unanswerable. Well, let us try it. Let us go in a straight line eastward on the wings of light (185,000 miles per second). After a million million years we rest. Surely, this is the beginning of space. Well, if it is, what is just beyond? Try again,—this time a billion ages. Again we rest, and look eastward. No eternal wall here, no evidence yet of a beginning. We increase our speed a million-fold, and fly for a billion billion ages. *We are not an inch nearer the beginning than when we started; nor have we taken one second of time from the beginning and added it to the end; for there is neither beginning nor end to space and time.*

What then? Simply this: there is space immediately around us to breathe God's air, build the home nest, and draw from mother earth our simple subsistence; what care we then that the same space extends infinitely in all directions around us? There is time each day to do the simple tasks required of us by our Creator: let the infinite past and future then take care of themselves.

So also harvest follows seed-time—effect follows cause by law inevitable. Why should we be disturbed that the chain extends infinitely both behind and in front of us? *Our only concern need be that the links we forge be of steel and not of grass.*

One more question in this illimitable excursion we have been taking, and this chapter must close. If, as seems possible, there should be an infinite number of beings like Christ exercising co-ordinately, perhaps independently, the functions of Godhood, what is to preserve unity among them —what to prevent the clash of power which association with human sovereignties has taught us to expect?

If our judgment in the matter were based solely on human analogy, then the question might well be asked. Fancy half a dozen Presidents governing co-ordinately in these United States! Even where sovereignties have well-defined lines of demarkation, a generation rarely passes without imbroglios. But the analogies between governments human and divine hold only in superficial relations. In human governments, the right to rule is rarely, save in republics, based on fitness to rule. In divine governments it is based on no other qualification; and not on relative but absolute fitness. What, indeed, is the essential fact of Godhood, if it is not absolute oneness with the universe? He, therefore, who attains to this power must so have subdued or co-ordinated his own personality, as to offer no friction to the universal constitution of things. Of such a being, it may be said, "He is a God of Truth and cannot lie." Such is the relation which constitutes the unity of the Father, Son, and Holy Ghost. There might be a million—or an infinite number—of such beings, so far as individual initiative in creation is concerned, and yet essentially only one true God in the universe. For if each shaped his creations in accordance with absolute truth, how could the universal unity be broken—how could a clash in sovereignty occur?

As to the minor question of the ways and means, it need not be entered into here. Sufficient to point out, that where space for world-building is infinite, and materials inexhaustible, and time eternal, there need arise no question of precedence or subordination. As a simple instance of what might be done in our own part of the universe, it is enough to say that within the hollow sphere formed on the radius between our sun and the nearest fixed star, there is ample room for a million solar systems like our own—and creative power has not yet ceased its activity with that.

CHAPTER XXV

JEHOVAH, GOD OF ABRAHAM, ISAAC, AND JACOB

"WE know," says Paul in his first epistle to the Corinthians (viii., 4, 5, and 6), "that no idol is anything in this world, and that there is no God but one; for though there be that are called Gods, *whether in heaven* or on earth,—*as there are Gods many and Lords many,*—yet to us there is but one God, the Father, of whom are all things and we unto him, and one Lord, Jesus Christ, through whom are all things and we through him."

It is a decided relief to feel one's self back again in our own immediate regions of the universe. For although the arguments in the last chapter became necessary because of the *ignis fatuus* chase which philosophers have led the world, yet, the mind of man being incapable, at this stage of its psychic evolution, to apprehend infinite relations, all such discussions are intrinsically profitless, and may, indeed, be harmful: for to pursue a proposition which at one moment assumes the form, "It must be," and the next, "It can't be," is to invite insanity. Most wisely therefore did the

Apostle restrict our philosophizing to God the Father as the *immediate* cause of all things, and to Jesus Christ as the immediate intelligent agency through which God's will becomes effective.

For it is evident by the expression "one God" that Paul did not have in mind the abstract notion of divine unity, such as forms the concept of the philosopher and the scientist; his notion was restricted to the one, individual being—Jehovah, the God of Abraham, Isaac, and Jacob, limited in form, infinite only as the executive of Godhood—to whom alone mankind owes allegiance: else why should he couple His personality with that of Jesus Christ, whom elsewhere he describes as the "brightness of the Father's glory, the express image of His person?"

I have taken the liberty of placing in italics certain words in this passage, in order to call attention to an idea often overlooked. That Paul meant to include among the beings that "are called Gods" all the idols worshipped by ancient nations, is plain on the surface; on the other hand, his tacit admission that there are Gods many and Lords many, *as well in heaven* as upon the earth, shows that he had in view the very possibility discussed in the last chapter; and took occasion, moreover, to exclude even such perfected divine beings from any part in our homage.

Mankind of to-day, therefore, with all their superior knowledge of the physical universe, are restricted to the same divine allegiance as were the peoples mentioned in the Old Testament (whom, by the by, it is becoming quite the fashion, in certain advanced (?) churches, to speak slightingly of as decidedly anthropomorphic and local in their ideas of Deity). It is a blessed restriction—one which I, at least, shall never be tempted to transcend; for that our Father's relations to the greater universe are founded on the rock of truth, I am willing to believe on the evidence that His creations endure; plainly, therefore, *my* whole duty in life consists in making my relations with Him equally fixed and steadfast, until Christ's injunction shall, if possible, be fulfilled, and I become "perfect as He is perfect." This supreme motive must dominate my life—become the guiding principle of my religion: life and religion being by this very fact merged into one. In my acting upon it day by day, every object, every experience, will have for me a definite meaning: I shall ever tread upon *terra firma*, for I have cast aside the cloud-gauze and phantasmagoria of metaphysical speculation.

There remains the question of testing so restricted an idea of God by the revelations which He has given of Himself in the holy Scriptures.

That God is infinite, eternal, omnipotent, omniscient, omnipresent, absolute or alone, in the universe, I have already reconciled with His personality by showing that these attributes are true of the power which makes Him God,—incidentally showing therefore, in the only way it can be shown, how these same categories are also true of Christ. Let us therefore pass to other revelations, more directly affecting the Father as a personal being.

"God is a spirit," says John, "and they that worship him must worship in spirit and in truth."

Well, is not Christ also a spirit—are we not all spirits—in the same sense? Because a spirit becomes incarnated in a body, does he cease to be a spirit? Again, if we are to worship Him "in spirit," does that imply we are to cease being organized personalities? The fact which the Apostle wished to convey was merely this: As it is the eternal, spiritual essence which constitutes the life and mind of God, so we must approach. Him by that same spiritual essence in ourselves, and not by the purely corporal or physical rites so common among idolators.[1] This passage therefore does not overthrow the personal idea of

---

[1] "I am well aware," says a Catholic writer, "that the Latterday Saints interpret this text as meaning a spirit clothed with a body; but what nearly the whole of mankind, Christians, Jews, Mohammedans, have believed for ages cannot be upset by the gratuitous assertions of a religious innovator of the last century." Well, if it cannot, it cannot; if it can, it can—that is all there is to this argument. Those who see as the daring innovator sees, will follow him; others will not. "In the meanwhile it is well to bear in mind," says Max Muller, "that the universality of an error does not help in the least to make it a truth. It may prove useful to have learnt from history the elementary lesson that no opinion is true simply because it has been held by the greatest intellects, or by the largest number of human beings, at different periods in the history of the world."

God,—especially as a hundred other passages confirm it.

We shall next consider those passages which teach the invisibility of God. "No man," says John, "hath seen God at any time" (iv., 12). So also: "Whom no man hath seen or can see," says Paul, after telling us that God dwells in light which no man can approach (I Tim. vi., 15). The latter idea is confirmed in Exodus (xxxiii., 20), where the Lord says to Moses: "Thou canst not see my face, for there shall no man see me and live." His glory, expressed by Paul in terms of light, was so intense that it would have consumed Moses; so he was placed in the cleft of a rock and beheld the back of the Lord as he passed by.

Now if it could be proved that God is invisible to man—and this fact may be granted—would it thereby be proved that He is not a personal Being, an exalted Man? Not evidently to the mind of John, who, though he declares no *man* hath seen God, makes an exception of our Saviour (vi., 46), showing that the Father is in a form to be seen.

The fact is, that God and man are in different planes of being, the higher of which is invisible to the lower. If the idea be put in this form, viz., "Mortality cannot see immortality," all the apparent contradictions disappear, between the many instances recorded where God has been seen by man, and John's and Paul's emphatic denial that such a thing is possible; for then it will be seen that in all the instances where man has beheld God with his natural eyes, the latter did not appear in His glory, but functioned, for the time being, on the plane of mortality, and was therefore by so much not God; on the other hand, where man has seen God in His glory, it has been by dream, or vision, or other supernatural elevation of perception,—in which case man has, by so much, been more than mortal.

A notable instance of the latter is that of Moses, who, during the forty days and nights that he was with the Lord on Mt. Sinai, must have been raised to God's plane; for when he came down, his face shone with such effulgence that the people of Israel could not stand to look upon it. So also did Christ furnish examples of this law; for it seems that after His resurrection He became visible or invisible to whom He would; evidently according as He functioned on the mortal or the immortal plane.

Another argument against personality is sometimes drawn from the fact of God's immutability. The Scriptures represent Him as the same yesterday, to-day, and forever. "I am the Lord, and I change not," is the revelation of Him by Malachi (iii., 6); while James (i., 17) speaks of Him as the "Father of lights, with whom is no variableness or shadow of turning."

In so far as immutability is to be regarded as an absolute category, it inheres in Godhood, and is the very foundation of that infinite integrity on which is predicated the revelation that "God is a

God of truth and cannot lie." Before our Father attained to Godhood, He passed through mutations such as are inevitable in a course of psychic evolution; but when He attained to Godhood,—when His soul became perfectly attuned to the infinite harmony of the universe,—how could He be other than immutable? For change would then imply degeneracy.

But in a relative sense, God *is* changeable. Read the history of His dealings with the human race, and you will find it one long tapestry of mutation and change: of laws established and abrogated, ordinances ordained and set aside, commands and counter-commands. How, indeed, could He act the rôle of Providence, did He not change? How could He insure the eternal progress of His children, save by a course of progressive adaptation of the divine requirements?

In what way, then, is His mutability reconciled with His immutability? In this way: As respects the eternal principles underlying His purposes, He never changes; these form the very warp and woof of His divine perfection; but as respects the methods or devices for bringing about these purposes, He changes as the exigency requires; and the variations possible to His invention are practically infinite. How else could He bring them about?

It is by reason of this very principle of mutation in God that we perceive all things to be in a state of evolution here on earth. Nothing stands still; the law of life seems to be: Go forward, or the very forces of the universe will drag you back He who does not progress, immediately begins to retrograde.

And were it not for our faith, these very mutations would overwhelm us with doubt and fear; as it is, we know—all may know who will—that though the world seems to be going wrong, yet down upon the seething turbulence of life shines steadfastly forever the purposes of God, even as shines the sun above and beyond the storm and stress of the elements, which its very shining has indirectly served to set moving.

CHAPTER XXVI

HOW OUR FATHER BECAME GOD

HAVING examined, in the previous chapters, those aspects and concepts of the Universe, and also those texts of Scripture which seem to antagonize the personal or Christ-type of Deity, and found them not inconsistent with the Bible revelation of Him, I shall let that question rest, and assume that the only supreme being to whom earth-spirits owe allegiance is Jehovah, our Father in heaven, the immediate Creator and controller of this earth and all things in it.

But since by this conception He is made to belong to the same order of beings as Christ, His Son,—the same order, indeed, as man himself,—and must consequently have attained to Godhood or creative power, it becomes a pertinent question to consider how He reached such divine sovereignty. (1) Was He elected to the supreme place? Election may confer dominion,—it cannot add an iota to native ability; but is not dominion part of divine supremacy? (2) Was Godhood conferred upon Him? Ordination may give place and opportunity,—it cannot give creative power. But are not place and opportunity vital relations in creative power? (3) Did He attain to Godhood by the gradual development of powers inherent in His very being?

Whatever the answer shall be to these questions, one thing may be absolutely predicated on the start: He is God primarily by reason of supreme fitness; for Godhood, being omnipotence or the power to create in harmony with the infinite unity of the universe, is a thing, like brains, not conferrable by authority nor purchasable by money or influence. A being has either attained to this power, or he has not attained to it, by native self-effort. The universe itself could not give it to any man. A sufficient general answer, therefore, would be that God became God because He fulfilled the law of becoming perfect as His Father in heaven was perfect; or, in the terms of science, because He fulfilled the supreme requirements of psychic evolution.

But before considering specifically the meaning of these answers, let us see what we may learn from the analogy of human sovereignties; premising our investigation with this general consideration: that as man's institutions of law and government are deductions from his interpretations of nature and life—which be it remembered are expressions of God's ideals,—truth or the power analogous to Godhood is in these institutions to the extent that man has interpreted correctly, and afterward reasoned correctly on his interpretations; and it is needless to say on the other hand that error, and consequently instability, lurks in them to the extent that he has failed to grasp and generalize the full significance of the divine ideals. It follows, then, that any epoch of nature-study, any period during which multitudes of people depart from conventionalities, give attention to the innate significance of nature and human life,—must be characterized by rapidly changing human institutions, and their readjustment on lines more nearly in conformity with nature, as we say,—really more in conformity with the thoughts of God.

This is one way in which the text, "God rules among the nations of the earth" is made true; and, thank heaven, it is becoming more deeply and widely true every day throughout the world. The immediate conclusion, however, which I wish here to draw is: that in seeking an answer to the question how God became God, we are not to expect the light to break from some deep, occult cave of speculation, or even through some dark cloud of scriptural mystery, but rather from the very face of nature and of life; and if in scanning human forms of sovereignty, we shall discover the filagree shreds of truth, we may be sure that such forms, by so much at least, exhibit types of Godhood; which, after all, is merely a concreted, organized aspect of universal, absolute truth or harmony.

Consider, then, the first type which human sovereignty assumed—the patriarchal. Is there anything in this form which corresponds with a definite relation of God to man? Yes; it is the very relation which we revere when we pray: "Our Father who art in heaven." We may be certain then that this relationship is part of Godhood,—a part that could not have been neglected by our Father in the attainment of creative power.

But it is not all of Godhood, nor even enough to form by itself a safe basis for sovereignty. In human governments it failed because of the narrowness of its base: men were driven to sacrifice love, mercy, even truth itself to uphold mere blood or parenthood supremacy, and consequently civilization stood still.

In monarchical forms of sovereignty, which followed next, there must be an element of Godhood, since they have been so long and so widely tried by mankind. That element lies precisely in this circumstance: that abstract law, whether human or divine, will not execute itself. The king therefore resembles God as executor of law.

Unfortunately,—and here lies the weakness of monarchy as a basis for sovereignty—the king soon came to regard his own will as the sufficient source of authority. The people were in time debauched into the same conception; and, consequently, as truth, honor, life itself, were made subservient to the fear or favor of kings, civilization—which, be it remembered, represents the progress of God's social ideals — again stood still.

But the direst evil resulting from this form, was the universal reaction whereby God Himself came to be regarded as only a more absolute and less evadable King of kings, and the consequent power it gave to millions of priestly pretenders in every age and place, to extort obedience to anything which they could persuade or terrify mankind into believing was His will. And the world is yet in the shadow of this awful curse.

Nevertheless, after all is said, kinghood is part of Godhood; for like the king, God is supreme in power, and from His judgments there is no appeal. His autocracy, however, lies not in the fact that He is supreme-by-will, but in the fact that He is supreme-by-law—the very incarnation, as it were, of the truth and harmony of the universe; and consequently he who would escape falling "into the hand of the living God," need only conform to law as it touches him on all sides during every day of his life.

In pure democracy, the latest form of power, the basis of sovereignty is conceived to be the abstract quality of truth or right; in other words, the quality which became subservient by the degeneracy of the patriarchal and monarchical orders, is here, in theory at least, made supreme. But as truth or right means nothing save as apprehended by an intelligent being, and as experience proves that no one being can be trusted to its apprehension, democracy bases its sovereignty on truth as apprehended by all the people; in other words, upon what ought to be the highest conception of *relative* truth.

This is surely the noblest generalization of sovereignty yet attained by the race; and how near it comes to ideal Sovereignty is seen when we remember that the central fact of Godhood itself is *absolute* truth—truth as apprehended by a being in perfect accord with the universe.

Nor ought we to lose sight of this latter fact whenever we think of God: for though He is the Father of our spirits, and consequently deserves our love as the supreme Patriarch; and though He is King of kings, whose judgment, we ought to remember with fear and trembling, is absolute and final; yet, as when the people of a republic, in doing homage to their chief executive, reverence the authority rather than him who represents it, so in our worship of Deity, it is Godhood, the infinite power of the universe, rather than the exalted Man who wields that power, which should receive our devotions; if, indeed, the two concepts, eternally united as they are, can be divided in thought at all.

At first sight this may seem a supercritical distinction; but a little reflection will show that it is a point of view which has tremendous consequences in the shaping of our lives. For one thing in particular, it will tend to cure that neurotic disease in religion known as adoration, which is

How Our Father Became God 281

not truth-worship but person-worship; and in general it will teach us to reverence truth, the abstract relation, rather than the concrete forms with which it may be incidentally or temporarily related.

By this excursus into the analogies furnished by human sovereignties we have perhaps not directly advanced our answer to the question which is the thesis of this chapter, viz., How God became God; yet our time has not been wasted if we begin to see, even glimmeringly, that the answer is to be sought in life and nature, not in occult speculation; that in fact whatever is vital or thorough-going in the relations which men assume to each other, is nothing other than the reflex of that very power whose origin we are seeking.

Coming back then to our general answer, that Godhood is the supreme and final outcome of psychic evolution, or of eternal progress, to use the phrase common to Mormonism, it will be seen that the line of our enquiry is precisely this: that if we would know how God became God, we have only to study attentively the plan whereby man is enabled to become perfect as his Father in heaven is perfect. This plan has already been somewhat exhaustively laid before the reader in previous chapters. Here I need only make a summary.

It is self-evident, is it not, that power which culminates in the ability to create and control a solar system is attained only as a progressive acquirement; involving cycles of time of which, indeed, man can form no conception; but brought about, nevertheless, by processes of development of which the methods presented by his present life are fairly adequate samples.

As before pointed out, it is by means of our attrition with environment that we rise or fall,—counting by environment all those forces, spiritual or otherwise, not ourselves, with which the soul comes into relations. If we conquer, we rise toward Godhood by our added power; if environment conquers,—that is, if we flinch or fail in the trials of life,—we sink to a lower plane, because we have lost power.

Given, then, by our Father in heaven, an environment progressively differentiated so as to be matched with our growing powers; given on our parts a steadfastness of purpose which shall not fail, no matter what the temptation—a purpose represented by the mental attitude, "Father, thy will be done"; given as much of eternity as we shall need for this psychic evolution,—and what heights are there, within the compass of omnipotence, that man cannot scale?—Consequently, what heights that God did not scale in order to become God?

Note here that the very essence of victory over environment consists in these circumstances: (1) that we discover the law, or eternal significance, of that which opposes us. This part of our triumph we call knowledge. (2) That we put our own lives in harmony with the law so discovered. Knowledge is thereby transmuted into intelligence. It follows, therefore, that the measure of our intelligence at any time represents the degree to which we have attained Godhood: whence the truth of another aphorism in Mormonism becomes apparent: "The glory of God is intelligence."

There is no other real glory attainable by the human race. The glories of wealth, or beauty, or place, after which we mortals strive so madly, are mere shams—pitiful, temporary counterfeits—compared with the power of Godhood; for the glory of intelligence is the glory of manhood and womanhood, the glory of virility and power, and not of pretension; in short, the glory of character. The weakness of our civilization—though it is the strongest the world has ever seen—still lies in this—that ten thousand colleges and a million books enable us to see this glory but not to possess it; the education of the age teaches us to know, but does not give us the backbone necessary to do.

CHAPTER XXVII

THE FULLNESS OF PRIESTHOOD IS GODHOOD

LET us now consider more attentively the nature of those reciprocal relations, whereby God, on the one hand, prepares the environment for man's ascent, points out the way of using it, and even lends him the very power by which to rise; and whereby man, on the other hand, steadfastly subordinates his desires to his expanding sense of truth and right, making it the law of his life to say: "Father, thy will, not mine, be done."

It is very evident not only that co-operation between Instructor and instructed could not be closer, but also that without just such co-operation it would be impossible for man to become perfect as his Father is perfect. "Without me," said Christ, "ye can do nothing"—a truth which He enforced by this parable: "I am the vine, ye are the branches: as the branch cannot bear fruit of itself, except it abide in the vine; neither can ye, except ye abide in me" (John xv., 45).

No reasoning could be more cogent. As well cut off a branch and expect it to mature on its own account into a perfect tree, as to expect from any man, turned loose in the universe and refusing divine guidance, that he will in the end attain to Godhood.

Let us not, however, be of that narrow type of thinkers who believe that such reciprocal relations between God and man are not possible, to a limited extent at least, unless a man accepts the rites of religion. Darwin, Huxley, Tyndall, Spencer,—all the great naturalists,—are prophets in their way, as much as was Moses and Isaiah; for did they not bring truth into the world? Very important truth; truth that in one short century has transformed the civilization of the world.

What though they did not recognize the true God? It is rather creditable to their integrity—considering the impossible creature theologians made Him. Infidels, however, they were not; for, if they were agnostic as to the Law-giver, none surpassed them in reverence for the law; and so their Father in heaven, to whom they were blind in life, led them by the hand along rich paths of truth and will still lead.

Nevertheless, it is impossible that the laborers in the vineyard should go on forever without coming face to face with the Lord of the vineyard; and so the time is inevitable when these great lovers of truth must recognize with *Whom*, not merely with what, they have been in co-operation. Then they will have to make covenants directly with God, as one man with another, according to the rites and ordinances of the Gospel. Should they refuse, how could God assist them further in the acquirement of psychic power? For would He not, by doing so, be directly building up a power antagonistic to the unity and harmony of the universe? He not only would not—He could not do so; and, therefore, these men would from that day begin the process of undoing themselves. Being in opposition to God, they would have arrayed against them all the positive forces of the universe, and who could stand under such circumstances? For God, being the Creator of our environments, is essentially the universe to us.

It holds, therefore, as an absolute generalization, that without the Gospel or plan of salvation, no being can complete his psychic evolution. As to what the initiatory steps of this plan are,—the laws of adoption into the kingdom of God,—I must refer the reader to previous chapters. Here I desire to take up the theme implied by Paul when he said: "Wherefore let us cease to speak of the first principles of Christ, and press on to perfection; not laying again a foundation of repentance from dead works, and of faith toward God, of the teaching of baptisms, and of laying on of hands, and of the resurrection from the dead, and of eternal judgment: and this will we do, if God permit."

As already pointed out elsewhere, Mormonism, so far from contemplating a vacuous, inane future, characterized by idleness, and relieved only by the doubtful diversion of golden harps and the "beatific vision," looks forward to an after life filled with untrammelled opportunities for noble endeavor: the scientific investigation, or analysis and synthesis, of all that goes to make up world-building; the development of more and more perfect social relations for mankind; and the gradual integration of the psychic life of this planet, with the perfect life of other spheres. For, in the ultimate outcome of man, no perfection is to be attained by miraculous endowment. Causes must ever be adequate to effects.

During these ages of preparation he is to be a co-worker with angels in carrying out the plans of the Creator. It follows, therefore, that from the moment he makes covenants as a conscious co-operator with Deity, he becomes an agent of the Almighty; and in order that his acts shall have the same eternal significance that they would were they performed by divine Authority itself, they must be done by God's sanction. In other words, the Father must delegate to him part of His Godhood; which looked at from man's point of view becomes Priesthood.

From my thesis, "The fullness of Priesthood is Godhood," may be drawn the inference that the attainment of Godhood is through successive degrees of Priesthood. But hitherto the thought has been maintained that this supreme outcome of evolution is attained by man to the extent, and only to the extent, that he discovers and obeys law. What is the meaning, then, of its being attained through the medium of ordination? Simply this: Priesthood is God's official sanction for man's use of the degree of Godhood with which his obedience to law has invested him. Put it in this way: A man by assiduous devotion to legal training has fitted himself, say, for the position of judge on the Supreme Bench; in other words, the power of judgehood, to coin a word, is in him; but that does not make him judge,—the President's appointment only can do that. In like manner, the ordination of a man to the Priesthood is God's recognition of his right to win and use, by devotion to truth, so much of Godhood.

Painfully aware as I am of the trivial and artificial associations which the word priesthood must arouse through the reader's acquaintance with its use in history, literature, and contemporary religions, I hesitated long before using it to signify divine authority, or God's official sanction of man's attainments through self-effort. I shall be pardoned, therefore, if I take a little time to enlarge and dignify the connotation of the word in this new sense.

Hitherto he can have understood the word at best as standing for an order of men set apart to administer rites and ordinances, which, though unrelated or but superficially related to life itself, are supposed to be vital to man's welfare in the hereafter. In Mormonism, Priesthood is the badge or official sign of that conscious co-operation between God and man above referred to, without which his psychic evolution is, as we have seen, impossible; not a mere tacit feeling that he is so related to God, but a real, vital contract entered into by sacred covenant in holy places.

Accordingly, all male members of the Church in good standing hold some degree of the Priesthood; for every man is equally entitled to God's co-operation and guidance in the fruition of his psychic life. And since such fruition involves all aspects of law, officiation by authority of this sacred endowment is not confined to spiritual matters alone: whatever in life affects the temporal or eternal welfare of man may come under the guardianship and care of this divine investment. Indeed, as Priesthood is God's license for the ultimate attainment of Godhood, every man holding the sacred office must, if he realizes its solemn obligations, halt and ask, "Would God do the thing in contemplation?" ere he ventures to act upon it. Needless to confess, however, that in this, as in all other endeavors toward righteousness, practice at best only falters after precept.

By degrees of the Priesthood, mentioned above, are meant the various offices established by Christ, viz., Deacons, Priests, Teachers, Elders, Seventies, High Priests, Apostles, and so on. Each has its range of duties in relation to the temporal and spiritual welfare of the Church as a social organization; but the Priesthood, out of which these offices grow, has, as shown above, an eternal significance to the bearer himself,—or else no significance whatever, according to whether or not he magnifies its possibilities. The Priesthood of an Elder, for instance, is God's license for such a range of activities in the winning of Godhood, that a million years of psychic evolution will not exhaust them; yet the ordination itself adds nothing to the man's inherent power; it only gives him opportunity.

The assertion, sometimes made, that Mormonism believes salvation and exaltation can be won by the laying on of hands will thus be seen to be a slander. The position of the Church is this: while rites and ordinations add nothing in and of themselves, yet are salvation and exaltation impossible without them; for, as we have seen, psychic perfection depends absolutely upon God's co-operation; but God, being a perfected man and not a vague abstraction, enters into co-operation with lesser psychic beings by definite contract; rites and ordinations are His divinely appointed tokens of such contract. Being therefore essential to God's co-operation, they are essential to man's salvation and exaltation; and consequently the man who will not make definite covenants with God—he who vaguely trusts that if he lives a good, honest life, things will come out all right in the end—may not lose eternal life,—since there are a million lower altitudes while only one summit; but he will surely fail of becoming perfect as God is perfect.

I have just stated that the reception of Priesthood adds no power to a man. This needs qualification. While it does not increase the man's innate capacity or ability, it gives him dominion, and with dominion a key to the use of God's power through the medium of the Holy Ghost. Of two men possessed of equal dominance by natural acquirement, the one holding the Priesthood can do things which the other must not attempt. This general truth was illustrated by an incident in the life of Paul. The Apostle had been casting out devils in the name of Jesus, when certain sons of one Sceva, a Jewish high priest, attempted to imitate him. The result was disastrous. "Jesus I know," cried the evil spirit, "and Paul I know; but who are ye? And the man in whom the evil spirit was, leaped upon them, and overcame them, and prevailed against them, so that they fled out of that house naked and wounded."

Now as to the question of dominion resulting from the attainment of Priesthood, is not this precisely what John the Revelator meant when he said we should become "kings and priests unto God the Father" and reign forever and ever on the earth? (i., 6 and v., 10). Peter, in like manner (I Epistle ii., 5, 9), speaks of the saints as "an elect race, *a royal Priesthood.*" But Priesthood without dominion is meaningless; and Paul, as well as John in the above quoted passage, suggests the dominion, when he tells us that Christ's eternal place is above all "principality and power, and might, and dominion" (Eph. i., 4), whether in this world or in the world to come. What, then, are these principalities and powers in the world to come, if not subordinate delegations of divine authority? And if they are such delegations then they must be forms of dominion exercised by man in virtue of the attainment of Priesthood.

Again, what could be the purpose of such dominion, other than the dispensation to man of opportunities for the attainment of perfection? That Peter, Paul, and John saw these opportunities only in their aspect of social evolution was quite in keeping with the bias of their time. The natural world meant nothing, or little more than nothing, to the ancients. We, with clearer vision, feel now that to be a great scientist, a great inventor, is intrinsically more Godlike than to be a great king; and hence, by parity of reasoning, we include in God's dispensations of dominion to man, opportunities for doing and becoming, not only in the social world, but also in the natural world,—in short, in all other aspects which constitute supreme creative power.

My point, however, so far as this chapter is concerned, is this: Part of Priesthood is invariably dominion; and all of dominion, when it results from divine authority, is Priesthood. If I can show a similar correlation in respect of Godhood, then my thesis will be established. Such correlation must be seen by direct intuition, if seen at all. I ask then, Is not the universe related to God, as God is related to man? When He began the work of creating the solar system, was it not by a dispensation of dominion? Is it thinkable that He could create out of harmony, and without reference to the unity, of the universe? Plainly, it is not.

Dominion is part of Godhood, then, just as it is part of Priesthood; and these two ideas are therefore related as my thesis indicates. But do you realize the significance of this conclusion? It means this: that Priesthood, though it is a dispensation of God to man, is not something created by God; it is part of the infinite constitution of the universe itself. It is Godhood in small—Godhood to the extent that man's perfections fit him to wield it;[1] in other words, it is an eternal

---

[1] Incidentally, and by way of correcting a widely advertised misinterpretation of Mormonism, attention is called to the conception that any man holding the Priesthood and actually exercising the functions of divine authority, is virtually God within the limits of that authority; in the same sense that an officer of the government is virtually President of the United States, within the legitimate scope of his office. Mormonism holds no man infallible—God only is that; nevertheless the official acts of the Priesthood, if based on righteousness and within the scope of the authority delegated by God—are infallible,—as much so, as if God Himself had done them. This ought to make clear an exclamation by Brigham Young, to the effect that "Adam is our father and our God and the only God with whom we shall have [immediately] to do." That He is our father must be plain to believers in the Bible; that He is our God, in the sense that He will forever preside over the world that He

relation of intelligence; which fact I shall conclude by showing is also revealed in Scripture.

The reader cannot but have wondered at that curious passage in Hebrews (vii., 1, 2, 3), wherein Melchisedek, king of (Jeru) Salem, "priest of the Most High God . . . being first by interpretation king of righteousness, and after that . . . king of peace,"—is declared to be "without father, without mother, without descent, having neither beginning of days nor end of life: but made like unto the son of God; abideth a priest continually." He can hardly so far have stultified his intelligence as to have believed these categories true of Melchisedek, the man; they are easily reconcilable of Melchisedek, the Priest. What, indeed, can the words, "made like unto the Son of God,"—mean other than this: that as Christ received the fullness of Godhood, so Melchisedek received part; both of which (as this discussion has, I hope, made plain) are literally and truly, "without father, without mother, without descent; having neither beginning of days nor end of life,"—in other words eternal.

peopled, ought not to be a stumbling block; for such reverence to Adam in no way derogates from our Father in heaven, the Creator of many systems of worlds, nor from Jesus Christ, who by the appointment of the Father is supreme ruler over many worlds including our own.

CHAPTER XXVIII

IF NOT MORMONISM—WHAT?

TO Latter-day Saints who have been accustomed to looking at the human race as exhibiting while on earth the essential present, or time-link, in an endless chain of divine being, the conclusions reached in the preceding chapters will be regarded quite as matters of fact; but to the modern Christian world, long imbued with the notion that mankind is a subsidiary creation,—an order of being quite different from and inferior to that of God Himself, I can well imagine they will seem little short of blasphemous; and therefore, also that, though they cannot be refuted, they will not readily be believed and accepted.

It seems pertinent, therefore, to close the discussion with a chapter based on this point of view: Granted that these conclusions are false, what follows? What other teleological vistas, forward and backward, are left to the race?

As a preliminary, it may be remarked that whatever be the nature of those other vistas,—however unscientific they may seem by comparison—any holding of them up to view will not materially affect the multiplication of religions; for in respect of the tenet-creating tendency human beings may not unfitly be likened to a thrifty young orchard. The religious feeling is in them even as the sap is in the trees,—a sort of dumb, emotional potentiality ever seeking opportunity to express itself in forms of devotion.

Now, as there is evidently a natural evolution of the trees—into forms representing God's ideals, and crowned with luscious fruit; so there must evidently be a natural evolution of this religious feeling. And as a judicious orchardist can, by proper digging and pruning, materially assist the unfolding and fructivity of the trees, so there is manifestly a place for the pastor in the natural and spiritual evolution of mankind.

But note now the alternative: if the orchardist be actuated by artificial ideas, he may prune the growing tendency of his trees into all sorts of abortive forms—resembling nothing else in the natural world; with this penalty, however, that he will get no fruit. So also may the religious enthusiast,—guided by fantastic interpretations of Scripture, or the still more erratic conclusions of occult speculation,—prune and shape the emotional tendencies of his congregation. May—did I say? Has,—does; for how else can you account for the ten thousand varieties of psychic contortion that pass and have passed for religion among mankind?

That such abortive religions will never yield

fruits of eternal life—and by such fruits I mean increased present power in the individual: physically, intellectually, socially, morally, and spiritually—is best proved by the fact that they generally postpone such fruits to a hypothetical future; whereas, it is next thing to a truism that the religion which does not yield its rewards in the heaven of the Here and Now, will never—because it can never—yield them in eternity.

What, then, is the remedy for abortive religion-making? Precisely the same as that which we have already applied to abortive tree-culture. That remedy is to let God be true for every man; in other words, to let nature alone,—which involves finding out what is nature, and then removing all artificial obstructions, so that she may be alone. Are men less subject to natural law than trees? Do we prune and shape a growing tree by the speculations of seers and Mahatmas—or the vagaries of Christian Science? Then, in God's name, let us cease ignoring the laws of nature which constitute man's physical and spiritual environment; cease calling phenomena illusions—cease to go whoring after phantasmal "realities."

For if anything is fixed and certain, it is this: that he who rises above his present environment—his present sum total of impinging phenomena, if you please—is prepared for a higher, nobler sphere,—a sphere more difficult, and therefore more full of truth surprises. And the evidence is this, that his power of bliss is within him—not stored away in a hypothetical heaven; and he who lets present environments rise above him, must inevitably sink to a lower, cruder, more monotonous level. And again the evidence is this, that his weakness or damnation is within him—not locked up in some hypothetical hell.

Mormonism in taking such a stand merely voices what seem obviously the principles of common sense. They are, in fact, the principles which must underlie the application of scientific thinking to matters religious. If such thinking were made the criterion of religious truth, how, like punctured wind-bags, would the swelling spiritual "isms" of the day fall flat over the face of the earth!

To have weight or effect, however, such thinking would have to be applied by the religion-makers themselves, scientists being regarded as the natural enemies of religion. But if religious leaders were fitted by scientific training for such thinking, there would be no gas-blown theories of salvation to puncture. Men would have recognized long ago the natural connection between this world of ours with its varied phenomena and the education of the human soul for eternal life.

It will thus be found that religions of the unscientific kind have no teleological vistas either of the past or of the future; merely a precipitous starting-point, creation, with no indication of how or why, a more or less artificial earth-life, in

If Not Mormonism—What?

which the supreme good seems to be to get as little entangled with things earthly as possible, and lastly a final jump off—into heaven or hell. And as to the significance of these final states, we get little more of rational perspective than is contained in the child's "good-place" and "bad-place." It is true that, of heaven and hell word-painting, designed to dazzle or terrorize the sinner, we have lurid examples enough in the sermons of revivalism; but the moment they are subjected to three consecutive scientific questions, they shrivel and fade into what they are—mere reckless products of imagination gone mad.

And it is for this reason, no doubt, that the religions of the day deny the right of science to question them. The domain of religion is postulated as being a vague spiritual country beyond the territory of reason; whose methods of cultivation are so diverse from those of the intellectual that they present no analogies even, let alone examples, of common ground. Even so astute a thinker as W. T. Harris, United States Commissioner of Education, in an article opposing religious instruction in the public schools, recently published in a prominent journal, has fallen into this psychological error, saying:

> The principle of religious instruction is authority; that of secular instruction is demonstration and verification. It is obvious that these two principles should not be brought into the same school, but

separated as widely as possible. Religious truth is revealed in allegoric and symbolic form, and is to be apprehended not merely by the intellect, but by the imagination and the heart. The analytic-understanding is necessarily hostile and skeptical in its attitude toward religious truth. The pupil is taught in mathematics to love demonstration and logical proof, and he is taught in history to verify the sources and to submit all tradition to probabilities of common experience. The facts of common experience dealing with the ordinary operations of causality are not sufficient to serve as symbols of what is spiritual. They are opaque facts and do not serve for symbols; symbols are facts which serve as lenses with which to see divine things. On themes so elevated as those religious faith deals with, the habit of thinking cultivated in secular instruction is out of place. Even the attitude of mind cultivated in secular instruction is unfitted for the approach to religious truth. Religious instruction should be surrounded with solemnity. It should be approached with ceremonial preparations so as to lift up the mind to the dignity of the lesson received.

When we consider the nature of the ultimate facts which religionists seek to maintain, there is small wonder that they are driven to such dilemmas as the above respecting the nature of spiritual life. The God they postulate is so unlike any concept of experience that, by their own confession, He transcends all analogy. Indeed, "A God understood is a God dethroned," has long stood for a truism among them. Nevertheless, they are driven, perforce, to make this primal Mystery act, since the world is to be created and peopled, and religion must somehow come to bless mankind. Accordingly, they postulate subaltern mysteries, one after another; such as, that the earth was made out of nothing; that man's soul is the breath of Deity; that the transition between the natural and the spiritual world is abysmal; that man is saved solely by the merits of Jesus without reference to works; that heaven is so unlike earth that we can form no conception of it; and so on through all the vague categories of modern Christianity.

And as is their conception of God, so of a piece are all its corollaries; with the result that religion has become a ghostly creature, compelled to lurk only in those dark corners where the light of science cannot penetrate, and its priests a body of soothsayers afraid to speak with authority, save on matters beyond the province of verification; or else it has degenerated into a system of symbolism demanding constant soul-stultification on the part of its adherents: the holding of opposite views in science and faith,—justified on the thin assumption that the two planes of being are different!

Contrast with all this vacuity the positiveness of Mormonism,—the logical inevitableness of its doctrines; and instead of the mechanical cosmogony of sectarianism, opposed alike to science and reason, trace through the scheme of salvation, as taught by Latter-day Saints, that same golden thread which has unified the researches of science, the principle of evolution, or, as we call it, the principle of eternal progress; not evolution drifting along the line of least resistance, but evolution directed at every step by creative intelligence: Then ask yourself this question: "If Mormonism does not present the true scheme of salvation, where shall man turn to find it?"

CHAPTER XXIX

WHAT SECTARIANISM HAS TO OFFER

IN connection with the theme of the last chapter, call to mind the fact that the Church of Jesus Christ of Latter-day Saints was the one and only religion in all the world denied representation in the World's Congress of Religions during the late Chicago Fair. Was it not an unique, an enviable distinction to have thrust upon us? Christ spoke of a certain rock which had been rejected by all the builders, but which nevertheless became the chief corner-stone. Can you blame the Mormons for the unalterable conviction that in the restoration, through Joseph Smith, of the Gospel of Jesus Christ in its pristine purity, and with all its keys and powers, including authority to officiate in His name, God is fulfilling anew that very striking prediction?

And speaking of the modern builders' rejecting this stone of Mormonism, brings me to a consideration again of the occasion which led to the writing of this book: the concerted movements of various ministerial bodies with a view to "crushing" out our non-conformity. I trust that I have given these zealous imitators of Christ some rational idea of the real work before them. I hope that they will realize that the mud-slinging which they have indulged in during the past,—the Danite canards, the Mountain Meadow horror (deplored as much by Mormon as by Gentile), and the charges of Mormon ignorance and immorality, —will not suffice to aid them with any candid reader of these pages: They must meet the truths and arguments here set forth, or go back to their wooden creeds defeated.

Will they attempt it? No. Judged by their past record, they will appeal again to the refuge of lies; they will cull some fragments from this treatise which lend themselves to distortion and misrepresentation. These, taken from the context, they will overthrow and cover with ridicule, and then pose as champions. I do not speak thus bitterly against ministers in general; only against the tribe that conceive it to be evidence of holiness to attack and vilify the Mormons. May God still give me charity to remember that they are my brethren!

Mormonism presents to the world a new point of view for studying the meaning of life; a point of view so marvellous in its reach that it encompasses and ties together in one vast, rational unity all the truths known to the race.

But curiously enough, the ministers that come among us are the last people on earth who are willing or able to appreciate this point of view.

Such has been the nature of their education for the ministry that Mormonism offends them at every point. "Egregious materialism!" they exclaim. It is the only relief they can find for their offended sense of ministerial dignity.[1]

Poor stuffed and starched automatons of the

[1] "In the days of Joseph, to appear like a Prophet a man should, according to the popular idea, wear a long beard, long hair, and dress in an outlandish style. If he did not wash himself and clean and pare his nails, it would be all the better. He should not smile and be merry. When he spoke, his voice should be deep and solemn; when he walked, his tread should be slow and measured. If he lived in a cave it would suit many people better than if he lived in a house. He should be different from other men in every respect.

"Of course those who had these ideas of what a Prophet should be, were much disappointed in Joseph; for if a Prophet should talk, dress, and act in this manner, he was very unlike one. He wore no beard, did not have long hair, and was very cleanly in his person; he dressed with taste, had a pleasant face, a sweet smile, a cheerful and joyous manner, and was natural. He was the very opposite of what a religious bigot would think a Prophet ought to be; and he never took any pains to be otherwise.

"He was a great hater of shams. He disliked long-faced hypocrisy, and numerous stories are told of his peculiar manner of rebuking it. He knew that what many people call sin is not sin, and he did many things to break down superstition. He would wrestle, play ball, and enjoy himself in physical exercises, and he knew that he was not committing sin in so doing. The religion of heaven is not to make men sorrowful, not to curtail their enjoyment, and to make them groan, and sigh, and wear long faces, but to make them happy. This Joseph desired to teach the people; but in doing so, he, like our Savior, when he was on the earth, was a stumbling-block to bigots and hypocrites. They could not understand him; he shocked their prejudices and traditions."—GEORGE Q. CANNON.

theological seminary, with their upward-rolling eyes and teary voices, their ultra-specialized training and consequent narrow notions of religion as something connected with chapel services,—how could they be expected to estimate justly a religion which involves the sum total of man's ideas and activities; how appreciate the resultant social system, which is a more vital departure from the artificial holiness that, like the love-weed in our alfalfa, is blighting the healthy naturalism of our time,—than was the departure of science from the cosmogony of the Middle Ages?

How, with the bias of the seminary upon them, can they feel anything like Christian charity for a religion which figures neither as a divine gilding upon life, nor as a divine influx into life, but as a transplanting of divine life itself upon this planet; a religion which aims to sanctify and make holy every needful activity of man; a religion which counts law wherever found, whether in nature or in revelation, as equally the voice of the living God?

How, with their prim notions of ministerial broadcloth and immaculate shirt-bosoms, can they keep down a feeling of contempt for the Elder that plows and sows, the Seventy that shoes horses, the High Priest that plasters your house, the Apostle that superintends a factory or presides over a bank,—for a body of ministers, in short—comprising almost the total male membership of the church—that do, during week days, whatever the exigencies of life call upon them to do, and preach, if need be, on Sundays?

Even in the narrow field affected by these ministers, that of spiritual matters, Mormonism presents a depth and richness of soil which would bring a harvest to their starving congregations, could they but get away from their hackneyed texts and commentaries long enough to dig into it. As it is, what have they to offer in lieu of the systems they would crush? With what principles do they purpose to "reform, educate, and civilize" us?

It is conceivable that not all of these ministers have joined in the crushing crusade, but that some are in fact still intent upon our conversion by peaceable means. In order that these may be fore-armed, and so know how to approach us, I purpose confiding to them some prejudices of the thoughtful, intelligent Mormon, who is acquainted with the deeper principles of his own faith, and also with what may be gained of theirs from a study of their confessions of faith.[1]

[1] I am fully aware, however, that such creeds are not a just criterion of the best work being done by ministers of the Gospel. Indeed, where men are really helping to shape the social destiny of the race, the chances are ten to one, that they have overthrown their creeds and are drawing inspiration from the scientific thought of the age. For such men I have the greatest reverence, and feel sure they will not take to themselves what I have said against the narrow, bigoted preachers that make so much disturbance about reforming Latter-day Saints.

Well, then, to improvise an allegory, his own religion presents to him the aspect of a vigorous young tree; diversified in form and function, yet still bearing the stamp of a perfect unity; branch, and twig, and leaf, and flower, and fruit, each growing organically out of a greater something preceding; the whole filled and made alive by a mysterious power which is constantly sending its roots more deeply into the spiritual world, only to extend its beneficent sway more widely in the natural world.

Theirs—the religions of his would-be reformers—do not present to him the unity of even an artificial tree. They seem rather to be things wooden, built from timber cut for the most part during the dark ages, and nailed together—literally nailed—by the decrees of ecclesiastical councils. How some of these doctrines have hung to the rest of the illogical *ensemble*, during the enlightenment of the nineteenth century, is matter for wonder; as, for instance, the doctrine of the creation of the world from nothing, of the predestination of man to heaven or hell, and of the damnation of unbaptized infants.[1]

I have said that such are the relative aspects of his own, as compared with other religions, to the thoughtful, philosophical Mormon. But the

---

[1] It is gratifying to know that the same Sectarian Convention which resolved to open the crusade on the Mormons also pulled out from their creed the rusty nail represented by the last named doctrine.

effect is precisely the same with the Mormon who never reasons back to final causes; for in his dumb way he still feels, by a kind of blanket intuition, the living unity and essential rationality of the one, and the artificiality and ineffectiveness of the other.

Having pleaded guilty for myself and my co-religionists, to which definitely biased state of mind, I dare say, I have done the worst thing possible for our future peace and well-being; for what shall now restrain the rest of the body ministerial from giving up their angelic intentions toward us, and deserting to the contemplated crushing campaign previously referred to? Have we not numerous examples of the facility with which sectaries unite, when the object of attack is Mormonism?

Seriously, what is this crushing business to signify? Is the attack to be Scriptural? It dare not be—these ministers know that too well. Educational? Equally impossible. Political? Perhaps. But how shallow is the study of Mormonism which concludes that it can be swerved from its ideals by mere political circumvention! When a Mormon gentleman was refused his seat in the House of Representatives, the average minister no doubt rubbed his hands and chuckled at the crushing blow that had been dealt to Mormonism. What a piece of inane fatuity! It affected the health of the "octopus" no more than would the plucking of a leaf affect a tree. The real injury in such a case would be to the liberty and integrity of our beloved country.

But perhaps these holy men are dreaming of something more drastic; to which, indeed, political hindrances might be made a prelude. Perhaps disfranchisement, confiscation, expulsion, mob-violence, bayonets, wholesale massacres,—are among the responses they get to their pious prayers in our behalf.

Well, if crushing is in the womb of time for us, let it come. We are ready to a man to die, if need be, for our convictions. But let our persecutors not imagine that Mormonism would suffer. Individually we should merely transfer our efforts for mankind to the Church of the First Born in the spirit world—for this life is not the only sphere where the work of salvation is being carried on; and the very ranks of our enemies might be trusted for recruits to take our places here.

However, before they start this new crusade for the glory of God, let me commend to them the advice of one Gamaliel, a wise man in his day: "Refrain from these men and let them alone: for if this counsel, or this work, be of men, it will come to naught; but if it be of God, ye cannot overthrow it,—lest haply ye be found even to fight against God."

CHAPTER XXX

CONCLUSION: MORMONISM DESTINED TO HAVE THE
LAST WORD

BUT there is small need of anticipating so dire an outcome: Mormonism will always have the last word. For Mormonism is not an artificial system of religion—a formulary of tenets by men who assume a prerogative which even God himself does not exercise: that of pronouncing for all time what shall be right, what shall be wrong, in divine worship; cast-iron creeds which set out by muzzling Deity, that is, by denying the possibility of new revelation; creeds which cannot be modified with the exigencies of progress, and must consequently be abandoned in practice, though still held reverently (like a family skeleton) in theory. On the contrary, Mormonism is a living, growing organism, drawing its life and shaping its destiny from truth wherever and however found; a system which recognizes God as alike the author of nature and of religion, and holds law in equal reverence as the will of God, whether manifested in the natural or in the spiritual world.

Owing to this peculiar point of view, its position

becomes impregnable. Founded as it is in the very nature and constitution of the universe, it need fear no onslaught from mechanical systems of religion. Indeed, so far from being crushed by the vain sects that now cry for its destruction, it is destined to live and pronounce the *requiescat* on the last sham and conventionality of mankind which masquerades under the sacred forms of Christianity.

As a consequence, the attitude of Mormonism toward these same man-made sects, while full of charity, is nevertheless that of uncompromising non-affiliation.

My object in going to enquire of the Lord, [says Joseph Smith in the account of his first vision], was to know which of all the sects was right, that I might know which to join. No sooner, therefore, did I get possession of myself, so as to be able to speak, than I asked the Personages who stood above me in the light, which of all the sects was right,—and which I should join. I was answered that I must join none of them, for they were all wrong; and the Personage who addressed me said that all their creeds were an abomination in His sight: that those professors were all corrupt; that "they draw near to me with their lips, but their hearts are far from me; they teach for doctrines the commandments of men, having a form of godliness, but they deny the thereof." He again forbade me to join with any of them: and many other things did he say unto me, which I cannot write at this time.

This uncompromising point of view is generally held up by our opponents as evidence of the narrowness and bigotry of Mormonism. "Just as there are a hundred roads, all leading into Boston" —so runs a favorite analogy with sectarian ministers—"so there may be a thousand right ways into heaven. Once there, what matter by which route you came?" And under cover of this very thin analogy, they assume to settle God's infinite problem for Him, once for all; and because the Mormons stand aloof from such reasoning, they are hated for ignorance and want of Christian charity.

And when you come to look at it, how very exasperating is this attitude of non-affiliation! Had it not been for such aloofness here and there in the world, Christianity might long ago have been united in one universal love-feast!—the very condition enjoined by Christ upon his disciples as essential to salvation. And to think that now— now, right in the blaze of the twentieth century! —when such a unity in Christ is growing up in every land, we have a vinegar sect hid away in the fastnesses of the Rocky Mountains, sending out its emissaries to sow again the seeds of religious discord! Is it not damnable thus to interfere with the salvation of the human race? Why cannot these latter-day bigots join with us in a universal hallelujah chorus of heaven thrown open to all?

Why, indeed! And while we are in an emotional mood, let us stop to reflect how very sad it is that this novel method of scaling the battlements of eternal bliss has not been applied to all the social problems of the race from the beginning of time. For instance, think what treasures might have been saved, what precious lives spared, in the late Civil War, if the Union soldiers, instead of marching upon their brethren with sword and cannon, had united to free the slaves and save the Union, in the beautiful, holy, metaphorical way in which ministers of the Gospel propose to unite and save mankind! And no doubt they could have been persuaded to fight their battles in that glorious, ethereal way, had slavery seemed as vague, as impalpable, as far-off and impossible an evil as seems the sectarian hell, and the Union as chimerical and evanescent a good as seems the sectarian heaven.

But Mormons, with their very practical notions of salvation as a progressive coming into harmony with law, and of heaven as a progressive social regeneration of this world, cannot be persuaded to lay down the weapons of common sense, however narrow and bigoted they may seem in consequence. They are fated, therefore, to remain the iconoclast of modern religions, shams, and artificialities, intrenched though such shams may be behind solemn rite and sacred ceremony; the prophets of a new era for humanity—the era of life looked at as religion, of religion looked at as life.

Conclusion

Consequently, gentle reader, before you join the ranks of those who misinterpret the non-affiliation of Mormonism, ponder well this question: Can there be more than one true religion? If this question seems difficult, let me put another: Can there be more than one true science of chemistry? of botany? of zoölogy? of astronomy? of geology? Can there be more than one true history of natural phenomena?

Suppose the vague, chimerical systems of speculations, out of which the exact sciences have grown, were flourishing now, defended by the sophistry of long-haired mountebanks; and that each had its set of believers,—a thing by no means impossible,—what attitude would the real scientists of our day take toward them? Well, that is precisely the attitude Mormons are compelled to take toward the mediæval sects of religion that still linger among us.

But if scientists took so uncompromising an attitude toward the speculative charlatans, there would be social disturbance manifold. Now, suppose these mountebanks, feeling innately their impotence, should propose an armistice on the basis of some glittering generality, could scientists, in the interests of a false peace, conscientiously consent to give up what seemed to them the incontrovertible truths of nature? No more can the Mormons. There can be no unity (of life), either scientific or religious, save on the basis of truth. What passes for unity on any other basis is the unity of death.

If you concede, then, that there can be but one true religion, can you consistently remain a communicant in any sect that does not claim to be that one religion? To be true to yourself, what must be your attitude toward him who advocates a scheme of salvation merely as good as some other scheme? Does not this very admission prove his religion to be a mere man-made contrivance for attaining eternal life? A religion is divinely authorized or it is not,—there is no halfway ground. To assume that any religion is so authorized, leaves no alternative but to assume that all others are not. If the assumption is valid,—and each soul must determine that fact for himself,—such a religion is the greatest boon that can come to man; for what is it but an infinite plan for conquering the universe, with God Himself as guide? If it is not valid, it deserves no man's allegiance. Better the untrammelled contact of the soul alone and naked to the universe, —alert to truth because alone and because naked, —than the fatuous trust which blinds the senses through following one who assumes to see but sees not.

Do you want a minister of the Gospel to present a religion to you with less exacting demands on your faith than Mormonism makes? No, you answer; any iota less would prove it merely human. Why, then, condemn the Mormon Elder as narrow and bigoted for refusing to compromise? Does he not exhibit in his preaching the only virtue that can begin to inspire trust—that of speaking with authority? Suppose he should take the apologetic attitude. What then? He is either a coward or a hypocrite; the first, if he throws down the truth of God merely to placate men; the second, if he still assumes to be divine that which may be so thrown down.

While an uncompromising attitude in religion is not in itself a proof of divine authority, a compromising attitude—unless authorized by God Himself—is positive proof of man-made authority. When the time comes for me to apologize for Mormonism, then the time has come for me to drop Mormonism, if I would remain an honest man. For Mormonism is no mere do-the-best-you-can system of religion: it is either God's scheme of salvation or a colossal fraud.

But do not be too hasty in assuming that it is the latter. The true church must begin by making precisely the claims Mormonism makes. Anything short of that leaves it human by its own admission. Could we believe in the divinity of Christ, if He had compromised with the religions upon the earth in His day? Listen to His attitude in relation to the Sadducees and Pharisees: "O generation of vipers, who hath warned you to flee from the wrath which is to come!" "Woe unto you Scribes and Pharisees—hypocrites!" And so on. When did He ever abate one jot of His divine mission to curry favor with these "whited sepulchres" of sanctimoniousness?

And yet these were eminently holy and orthodox churches. It is doubtful whether those congregations of the present day, which out of the plentitude of their holiness have waged war upon Mormonism, can compare with their ancient brethren in punctilious sanctity. In contemplating the Mormons, however, they have the satisfaction of realizing just how the Pharisees felt toward Christ and His innovations; nor can there be any doubt that the Mormons on their side have had abundant opportunity of realizing just how the Pharisees acted!

The message of Mormonism to the world is equally unequivocal: "Come out of her, my people, that ye be not partakers of her sins, and that ye receive not of her plagues." And consistent with the declaration of the Lord to Joseph Smith in his first vision, this message is to all men, Christian, Jew, and Gentile, without reference to their affiliation or non-affiliation with other churches. To take a less comprehensive view of the mission of Mormonism is to doubt its divinity; and such a doubt immediately leads to the apostacy of the doubter.

In a former paragraph I stated that Mormonism looks with charity upon all churches; it does not hold that these churches are not good, or that they do not teach much truth; it holds only that they are not divine,—since there can be but one divine Church.

Nor do Mormons hold that the grace of God is

withheld from men not in the Mormon Church. Mohammedans may, by the grace of heaven, have a true testimony concerning the God of Abraham, Isaac, and Jacob; Christians, in addition to this, may, by the gift of grace, know that Jesus is the Christ; the Mormon, by a still fuller measure of grace, will know both of these things, and in addition thereto have a testimony of the tremendous fact that God has again spoken from the heavens, —has again set up His Church, "never more to be thrown down, or given to another people."

"It is written," says Christ, "that man must not live by bread alone, but by every word that proceedeth out of the mouth of God." Here precisely is where, in the estimation of Mormons, the Christian world are at fault; salvation is no longer by the dispensation of authority given to Peter and the Apostles. For God has spoken again and ushered in a new dispensation—the dispensation of the fullness of times.

The churches of the day are without divine authority: it was not in the purposes of the Almighty that the Apostles should transmit it. Whatever of good is in these man-made religions, fits men by so much for the new dispensation of God's will. The more of good men acquire,—either from churches or any other social factors,—the more nearly will they approach to living according to the requirements of this new dispensation; but when the time comes—be it in this life or the next—that they are ready to make those covenants with God which place them forever among the workers—and without which psychic evolution becomes ultimately impossible,—they will have to make them through the medium of the Church of Jesus Christ;—of which the Church of the Latter-day Saints is now the representative on this side of the veil.

Such, then, is the nature of the "last word" which Mormonism has over all other churches.

[*Advertisement*]

SOCIAL ASPECTS OF MORMONISM

AT first it was the intention of the author to combine in one volume an exposition of the fundamental principles of Mormonism and an account of the social system resulting from them. But ere long it became evident that to carry out this purpose would necessitate such a compression of both aspects as would be very detrimental to the subject.

It was therefore thought better to make two volumes, to be named, respectively, *Scientific Aspects of Mormonism* and *Social Aspects of Mormonism;* which, as will be seen, are related to each other as cause and effect. The latter, which I hope also to treat from the point of view of science and philosophy, ought to be of supreme interest to the student of sociology; for in Mormonism, as perhaps nowhere else in the world, is presented the aspect of a people shaping themselves along social lines through the momentum of a virile religious faith.

In the latter volume I hope to treat, somewhat at length, that social detail of past Mormonism which has received such tremendous emphasis in the speculations of mankind, and which the world will apparently not permit to subside into quiescence. I refer to plural marriage, which has really not had as yet a hearing on its own account. Such a reopening of the subject will not, however, be with any view to the recrudescence of the practice, but merely with a view to lifting the obloquy which now rests on the entire social system through a misunderstanding of this relatively insignificant feature.

APPENDIX A

SCRIPTURAL PROOFS OF PRE-EXISTENCE

THE doctrine of pre-existence, in the form invented by Buddha, has been held for thousands of years. Plato and Pythagoras taught it among the Greeks, it was a tenet of the esoteric religion of Egypt, and it is inculcated to-day by Theosophy. As presented by all these schools, the Hindoo notion remains essentially the same: man has a pre-existence by virtue of re-incarnation, again and again, in mortal or earth life.

The doctrine as held by the Latter-day Saints, while abundantly foreshadowed in holy writ, is new, so far as I have been able to discover, among the beliefs of mankind. The poet Wordsworth, in a moment of poetic inspiration, had this first estate of the soul revealed to him, as may be seen in the following noble stanza from his *Intimations of Immortality*.

> Our birth is but a sleep and a forgetting:
> The soul that rises with us—our life's star—
>   Hath had elsewhere its setting,
>   And cometh from afar,
>   Not in entire forgetfulness,
>   And not in utter nakedness,
> But trailing clouds of glory do we come
>   From God, who is our home.
> Heaven lies about us in our infancy;

> Shades of the prison-house begin to close
>   Upon the growing boy;
> But he beholds the light, and whence it flows,
>   He sees it in his joy;
> The youth who daily farther from the east
>   Must travel still is nature's priest.
>   And by the vision splendid
>   Is on his way attended;
> At length the man perceives it die away,
> And fade into the light of common day.

What a pity that the poet should not trust the truthness thus directly shining from God into his soul, rather than defer to the theological opinions of his time. See how he discredits his own inspiration:

> To that dream-like vividness and splendor which invest objects of sight in childhood, every one, I believe, if he would look back, could bear testimony, and I need not dwell upon it here; but having in the poem regarded it as a presumptive evidence of a prior state of existence, I think it right to protest against a conclusion which has given pain to some good and pious persons, that I meant to inculcate such a belief. It is far too shadowy a notion to be recommended to faith as more than an element in our instincts of immortality. But let us bear in mind that though the idea is not advanced in Revelation, there is nothing there to contradict it, and the fall of man presents an analogy in its favor.

Let us now proceed to examine whether the idea is or is not advanced in Revelation.

It will not be questioned that Jesus Christ had a pre-existence. The passages which prove this are so numerous, that every Bible reader must be familiar with them. He could not have been a "Lamb slain from the foundations of the earth," without having had a definite psychic existence, so as to accept such a divine mission. Indeed, He says Himself in so many words: "I came forth from the Father and am come into the world; again I leave the world, and go to the Father." Then, too, Christ's prayer: " Glorify thou me with the glory I had with thee *before the world was*," definitely fixes his pre-mortal status. (See John xvi., 28; also xvii., 5).

But Christ is called the "first-born among many brethren" (Rom. viii., 29) also the "first-born of all creatures." Manifestly a first-born implies a second-born; and if a second-born, then a millionth-born. Whence we draw the conclusion that Christ is our elder Brother; a conclusion further strengthened by Paul's remark: "For both he that sanctifieth [Christ], and they who are sanctified [mankind] are all of one: for which cause he is not ashamed to call them brethren."

This relationship between the Saviour and the saved is made clearer by other passages. For instance, Paul says: "Furthermore, we have had fathers in the flesh which corrected us and we gave them reverence; shall we not much rather be subject to the Father of spirits, and live?" (Heb. xii., 9) And Christ taught all men to pray, "Our Father which art in Heaven"; and lest there should be any doubt as to the significance of "our," He says on another occasion: "Say unto my brethren, I ascend to my Father and your Father; and to my God, and to your God." (John xx., 17) Other passages might be quoted to sustain the equal fatherhood of God, and the equal brotherhood of man with Jesus Christ. If, therefore, Christ had a pre-existence, it is fair to presume that His brethren and sisters also had one.

This latter fact becomes more than a presumption

when we consider passages like this: "Then the word of the Lord came unto me saying: 'Before I formed thee in the belly, I knew thee; and before thou camest out of the womb, I sanctified thee and ordained thee a prophet unto the nations'" (Jer. i., 4, 5.) Is it possible that such a commission could be made and the recipient not be in existence? John the Baptist was likewise chosen before his body was conceived upon the earth. So also was Ishmael; and so well was his character as a spirit known, and the character of the spirits allotted to his lineage, that the angel said: "His hand shall be against every man's hand and every man's hand against him" (Gen. xvi., 1)—a characteristic to which his race are true to this day.

Nor is Jesus Christ the only being called Son of God. Adam is equally so named. (Luke iii., 38). John says moreover: "Beloved, now we are sons of God, and it doth not yet appear what we shall be: but we know that when he shall appear, we shall be like him; for we shall see him as he is." (I John iii., 2); thus emphasizing the essential kinship of Christ and mankind.

Consider next this remarkable passage: "Then the Lord answered Job out of the whirlwind and said; 'Who is this that darkeneth counsel by words without knowledge? Gird up now thy loins like a man, for I will demand of thee and answer thou me: Where wast thou when I laid the foundations of the earth? Declare if thou hast understanding.'"

Job was evidently in existence at this time—a time when the earth was still in chaos,—just as we have seen was the case with Jeremiah, John the Baptist, Ishmael, and Jesus Christ. That the rest of mankind were also in that primeval state is made plain by one of the next questions put by the Lord: "Or who laid the corner-stone thereof, *when the morning stars sang together, and all the sons of God shouted for joy?*" (Job xxxviii., 1-7)[1]

Who could the sons of God have been other than the spirits begotten by our Father in heaven during pre-existence?—the very beings called sons of God afterward in their earthly estate. By no possibility of interpretation can the passage be made to apply to mortal beings; for the simple reason that the million (or billion) year epoch represented by the creation of the earth was just beginning. The figurative expression, "morning stars," would imply advanced spirits—spirits brighter or more intelligent by reason of longer existence in the organized spiritual estate. The fact that Lucifer was called a "son of the morning," gives additional color to this interpretation.

[1] By way of aiding the imagination to visualize this marvellous spirit-convention, with God the Father, and a host of angels and "just men made perfect" in their midst directing and controlling, it will be well to remember that a spirit is figured in Scripture to be the exact counterpart of the natural body, but impalpable. Nebuchadnezzar in looking into the fiery furnace, whither Shadrach, Meshech, and Abednego had been cast, exclaimed: "Lo I see four men loose, walking in the midst of the fire, and they have no hurt; and the form of the fourth [evidently a spirit] is like the Son of God." (Dan. iii., 25.) So also when Christ appeared after His resurrection, the apostles were "affrighted and thought they had seen a spirit"; but Jesus reassured them by saying, "Handle me and see; for a spirit hath not flesh and bones as ye see me have,"—proving therefore both points maintained above: the human form and the impalpability of a spirit.

Note the fact that these spiritual beings "shouted for joy." That implies not only a high degree of intelligence, but an immediate occasion for jubilation. The first fact we should naturally expect from long ages of psychic evolution previous to this event; the latter, or the occasion for jubilation, we assume to be the event itself; namely, the creation of a habitat for the second or mortal estate of these same spirits. What event, indeed, would be more likely to inspire shouts of joy than a new world in which psychic evolution might go on? For these spirits understood, perhaps more clearly there than they do here the absolute need of a second or mortal estate in order to attain the perfection of their Father in heaven.

But out of this glorious inauguration of a new world grew discord as well as joy—if I may be permitted to bridge by modern revelation two important events mentioned in Scripture. In fact, it was precisely here that the war in heaven had its origin. For when the question of how mankind should be saved from the abyss into which it was necessary to plunge them, "Lucifer, a son of the morning," proposed to do it by taking away man's free agency and making him do right, as the birds fly southward in winter; this plan not being accepted, he declared war against God and Jesus Christ, leading one-third of the spirits of heaven with him. How they were cast out of heaven and became the Devil and his angels of darkness is told in the twelfth chapter of Revelations. Jude also alludes to this same event in these words: "And the angels which kept not their first estate, but left their own habitation, he hath reserved in everlasting chains, under darkness, unto the judgment of the great day."

That the beings called angels in these two passages are in fact spirits, is manifest from many passages in which they are called evil spirits, unclean spirits, devils, and so on; as also from the fact that they could possess mortal bodies. The word angel in its generic sense, stands for any supernatural being, whether spirit or resurrected personality, who fulfils a commission of the Almighty. That angels may be spirits is expressly pointed out by Paul in the question: "Are they not all ministering spirits, sent forth to minister for them who shall be heirs of salvation?" (Heb. i., 14). By parity of reasoning, apostate spirits, —spirits who have ceased to minister in the service of God and have become enemies of that service, would naturally be called fallen angels, as we have seen they are.

The doctrine of pre-existence has now, I trust, been fully established by Scripture. Space will not permit me to enter more deeply into the social life of that first estate. But the mere fact of a pre-mortal life itself throws a wonderful light upon the present life of the spirit, and also upon the life which is to come.

APPENDIX B

CONTRADICTIONS RESULTING FROM THE ATTEMPT TO CHRISTIANIZE THE GOD OF BUDDHA

IF from the origin of the Universe [says Herbert Spencer [1]] we turn to its nature, the like insurmountable difficulties rise up before us on all sides—or rather, the same difficulties under new aspects. We find ourselves on the one hand obliged to make certain assumptions; and yet on the other hand we find these assumptions cannot be represented in thought.

When we inquire what is the meaning of the various effects produced upon our senses—when we ask how there come to be in our consciousness impressions of sounds, of colors, of tastes, and of those various attributes which we ascribe to bodies, we are compelled to regard them as the effects of some cause. We may stop short in the belief that this cause is what we call matter. Or we may conclude, as some do, that matter is only a certain mode of manifestation of spirit, which is therefore the true cause. Or, regarding matter and spirit as proximate agencies, we may attribute all the changes wrought in our consciousness to immediate divine power. But be the cause we assign what it may, we are obliged to suppose some cause. And we are not only obliged to suppose some cause,

[1] *First Principles*, pp. 36–43.

but also a first cause. The matter, or spirit, or whatever we assume to be the agent producing on us these various impressions, must either be the first cause of them or not. If it is the first cause, the conclusion is reached. If it is not the first cause, then by implication there must be a cause behind it; which thus becomes the real cause of the effect. Manifestly, however complicated the assumptions, the same conclusion must inevitably be reached. We cannot think at all about the impressions which the external world produces on us, without thinking of them as caused; and we cannot carry out an inquiry concerning their causation, without inevitably committing ourselves to the hypothesis of a First Cause.

But now if we go a step further, and ask what is the nature of this First Cause, we are driven by an inexorable logic to certain conclusions. Is the First Cause finite or infinite? If we say finite we involve ourselves in a dilemma. To think of the First Cause as finite, is to think of it as limited. To think of it as limited, as necessarily implies a conception of something beyond its limits: it is absolutely impossible to conceive a thing as bounded without conceiving a region surrounding its boundaries. What now must we say of this region? If the First Cause is limited, and there consequently lies something outside of it, this something must have no First Cause—must be uncaused. But if we admit that there can be something uncaused, there is no reason to assume a cause for anything.[1] If beyond that finite region over

[1] This ground does not seem to me well-taken. The moment we apply it to the analogues of Causation, viz., to Time and Space, it reduces itself to an absurdity. Thus, "If we

which the First Cause extends, there lies a region, which we are compelled to regard as finite, over which it does not extend—if we admit that there is an infinite uncaused surrounding the finite caused; we tacitly abandon the hypothesis of causation altogether. Thus it is impossible to consider the First Cause as finite. And if it cannot be finite it must be infinite.

Another inference concerning the First Cause is equally unavoidable. IT must be independent. If it is dependent it cannot be the First Cause; for that must be the First Cause on which it depends. It is not enough to say that it is partially independent; since this implies some necessity which determines its partial dependence, and this necessity, be it what it may, must be a higher cause, or the true First Cause, which is a contradiction. But to think of the First Cause as totally independent, is to think of it as that which exists in the absence of all other existence; seeing that if the presence of any other existence is necessary, it must be partially dependent on that other existence, and so cannot be the First Cause. Not only however must the First Cause be a form of being which has no necessary relation to any other

---

admit that there can be space beyond a hypothetical beginning of space, there is no reason to assume space for anything"; and so of time. The fact is, all finite ideas of creation involve both time and space, and we are compelled to use them, even though we know that in an absolute sense these concepts are infinite, and as such incomprehensible to man. When philosophers shall rest causation on precisely similar grounds, we shall have an end of those barren problems which one moment assume the character "It is," and the next, "It is not." Man's mind no more demands a first cause than a beginning to space and time.

form of being, but it can have no necessary relation within itself. There can be nothing in it which determines change, and yet nothing which prevents change. For if it contains something which imposes such necessities or restraints, this something must be a cause higher than the First Cause, which is absurd. Thus the First Cause must be in every sense perfect, complete, total: including within itself all power, and transcending all law. Or to use the established word, it must be absolute.

Here then respecting the nature of the Universe, we seem committed to certain unavoidable conclusions. The objects and actions surrounding us, not less than the phenomena of our consciousness, compel us to ask a cause; in our search for a cause, we discover no resting place until we arrive at the hypothesis of a First Cause; and we have no alternative but to regard this First Cause as Infinite and Absolute. These are inferences forced upon us by arguments from which there appears no escape. It is hardly needful however to show those who have followed thus far, how illusive are these reasonings and their results. But that it would tax the reader's patience to no purpose, it might easily be proved that the materials of which the argument is built, equally with the conclusions based on them, are merely symbolic conceptions of the illegitimate order. Instead, however, of repeating the disproof used above, it will be desirable to pursue another method; showing the fallacy of these conclusions by disclosing their mutual contradictions.

Here I cannot do better than to avail myself of the demonstration which Mr. Mansel, carrying out in detail the doctrine of Sir William Hamilton, has given in his *Limits of Religious Thought*. And I gladly do this, not only because his mode of presentation cannot be improved, but also because, writing as he does in defence of the current Theology, his reasonings will be the more acceptable to the majority of readers.

Having given preliminary definitions of the First Cause, of the Infinite, and of the Absolute, Mr. Mansel says:—

But these three conceptions, the Cause, the Absolute, the Infinite, all equally indispensable, do they not imply contradiction to each other, when viewed in conjunction, as attributes of one and the same Being? A Cause cannot, as such, be absolute: the Absolute cannot, as such, be a cause. The cause, as such, exists only in relation to its effect: the cause is a cause of the effect; the effect is an effect of the cause. On the other hand, the conception of the Absolute implies a possible existence out of all relation. We attempt to escape from this apparent contradiction, by introducing the idea of succession in time. The Absolute exists first by itself, and afterwards becomes a Cause. But here we are checked by the third conception, that of the Infinite. How can the Infinite become that which it was not at first? If Causation is a possible mode of existence, that which exists without causing is not infinite; that which becomes a cause has passed beyond its former limits.

Supposing the Absolute to become a cause, it will follow that it operates by means of freewill and consciousness. For a necessary cause cannot be conceived as absolute and infinite. If necessitated by something beyond itself, it is therefore limited by a superior power; and if necessitated by itself, it has in its own nature a necessary relation to its effect. The act of causation must therefore be voluntary; and volition is only possible in a conscious being. But consciousness again is only conceivable as a relation. There must be a conscious subject, and an object of which he is conscious. The subject is a subject to the object; the object is an object to the subject; and neither can exist by itself as the absolute. This difficulty, again, may be for the moment evaded, by distinguishing between the absolute as related to another and the absolute as related to itself. The Absolute it may be said, may possibly be conscious, provided it is only conscious of itself. But this alternative is, in ultimate analysis, no less self-destructive than the other. For the object of consciousness, whether a mode of the subject's existence or not, is either created in and by the act of consciousness, or has an existence independent of it. In the former case, the object depends upon the subject, and the subject alone is the true absolute. In the latter case, the subject depends upon the object, and the object alone is the true absolute. Or if we attempt a third hypothesis, and maintain that each exists independently of the other, we have no absolute at all, but only a pair of relatives; for coexistence, whether in consciousness or not, is itself a relation.

The corollary from this reasoning is obvious. Not only is the Absolute, as conceived, incapable of a necessary relation to anything else; but it is also incapable of containing, by the constitution of its own nature, an essential relation within itself; as a whole, for instance, composed of parts, or as a substance consisting of attributes, or as a conscious subject in antithesis to an object. For if there is in the absolute any principle of unity, distinct from the mere accumulation of parts or attributes, this principle alone is the true absolute. If, on the other hand, there is no such principle, then there is no absolute at all, but only a plurality of relatives. The almost unanimous voice of philosophy, in pronouncing that the absolute is both one and simple, must be accepted as the voice of reason also, so far as reason has any voice in the matter. But this absolute unity, as indifferent and containing no attributes, can neither be distinguished from the multiplicity of finite beings by any characteristic feature, nor be identified with them in their multiplicity. Thus we are landed in an inextricable dilemma. The Absolute cannot be conceived as conscious, neither can it be conceived as unconscious: it cannot be conceived as complex, neither can it be conceived as simple; it cannot be conceived by difference, neither can it be conceived by the absence of difference: it cannot be identified with the universe, neither can it be distinguished from it. The One and the Many, regarded as the beginning of existence, are thus alike incomprehensible.

The fundamental conception of Rational Theology being thus self-destructive, we may naturally expect to find the same antagonism manifested in their special applications. . . . How, for example, can Infinite Power be able to do all things, and yet Infinite Goodness be unable to do evil? How can Infinite Justice exact the utmost penalty for every sin, and yet Infinite Mercy pardon the sinner? How can Infinite Wisdom know all that is to come, and yet Infinite Freedom be at liberty to do or to forbear? How is the existence of Evil compatible with that of an infinitely perfect Being; for if he wills it, he is not infinitely good; and if he wills it not, his will is thwarted and his sphere of action limited.

Let us, however, suppose for an instant that these difficulties are surmounted, and the existence of the Absolute securely established on the testimony of reason. Still we have not succeeded in reconciling this idea with that of a Cause: we have done nothing towards explaining how the absolute can give rise to the relative, the infinite to the finite. If the condition of casual activity is a higher state than that of quiescence, the Absolute whether acting voluntarily or involuntarily, has passed from a condition of comparative imperfection to one of comparative perfection; and therefore was not originally perfect. If the state of activity is an inferior state to that of quiescence, the Absolute, in becoming a cause, has lost its original perfection. There remains only the supposition that the two states are equal, and the act of creation one of complete indifference. But this supposition annihilates the unity of the absolute, or it annihilates itself. If the act of creation is real, and yet indifferent, we must admit the possibility of two conceptions of the absolute, the one as productive, the other as non-productive. If the act is not real, the supposition itself vanishes.

Again, how can the relative be conceived as coming into

being? If it is a distinct reality from the absolute, it must be conceived as passing from non-existence into existence. But to conceive an object as non-existent, is again a self-contradiction; for that which is conceived exists, as an object of thought, in and by that conception. We may abstain from thinking of an object at all; but, if we think of it, we cannot but think of it as existing. It is possible at one time not to think of an object at all, and at another to think of it as already in being; but to think of it in the act of becoming, in the progress from not being into being, is to think that which, in the very thought, annihilates itself.

To sum up briefly this portion of my argument. The conception of the Absolute and Infinite, from whatever side we view it, appears encompassed with contradictions. There is a contradiction in supposing such an object to exist, whether alone or in conjunction with others; and there is a contradiction in supposing it not to exist. There is a contradiction in conceiving it as one; and there is a contradiction in conceiving it as many. There is a contradiction in conceiving it as personal; and there is a contradiction in conceiving it as impersonal. It cannot, without contradiction be represented as active: nor, without equal contradiction, be represented as inactive. It cannot be conceived as the sum of all existence; nor can it be conceived as a part only of that sum.

. . . .

Some do indeed allege [says Mr. Spencer] that though the Ultimate Cause of things cannot really be thought of by us as having specified attributes, it is yet incumbent upon us to assert these attributes. Though the forms of our consciousness are such that the Absolute cannot in any manner or degree be brought within them, we are nevertheless told that we must represent the Absolute to ourselves under these forms. As writes Mr. Mansel, in the work from which I have already quoted largely—"It is our duty, then, to think of God as personal; and it is our duty to believe that He is infinite."

That this is not the conclusion here adopted, needs hardly be said. If there be any meaning in the foregoing arguments, duty requires us neither to affirm nor deny personality. Our duty is to submit ourselves with all humility to the established limits of our intelligence; and not perversely to rebel against them. Let those who can, believe that there is eternal war set between our intellectual faculties and our moral obligations. I for one, admit no such radical vice in the constitution of things.

Mr. Spencer's conclusion could not have more force for Latter-day Saints if it had been stated by the Prophet Joseph Smith himself! Nor need Dean Mansel have confused his soul by holding, at one and the same time, a truth borne in upon his heart, and its contradiction borne in upon his intellect, if he had not given up the God of the Bible. The conceptions of Deity held by the Latter-day Saints involve no such contradictions.

INDEX

Absolution, and confessionals, etc., 175; and indulgences, 174; and progress, 171, 177
Adam and Eve, 86, 87
Adam, God, 293
All born innocent, 172
All things created for man, 68
Altruism, 229
America, discovery of, not accidental, 111
Angels, guardian, 44, 127, 205
Anglo-Saxons descendants of Ten Tribes, 99
Anthropomorphism, 32, 248
Anti-Mormon hostility ends in disappointment, 7
"As man is God once was," etc., 88
Atonement of Christ, 166, 167
Authority, ascribed to personality, 106; preaching with, 316; rather than individual reverenced, 280

Baptism, a covenant, 175; and divine authority, 179; and sectarianism, 179; and sprinkling, 182; evidence of divine wisdom, 178; exhibits man's psychic life, 182; logical necessity of, 173; symbolical, 180, 181; token of forgiveness, 178; universal application, 179
Beatific Vision, a Presbyterian's view, 217; Catholic view, 216

Being born is being judged, 117
Beings, intelligent, three classes, 131
Blavatsky, Madame, 31
Book of Mormon, 209
Bookworm, 152
Buddha and soul evolution, 25; god of, contradictions of, 330
Buddha's abstractions, 16
Buddhist and Mormon idea of creation compared, 263
Buddhistic Karma, 170

Cain, descendants of, 94, 101
Carlyle's ridicule of St. Augustine's idea of God, 23
Carlyle, Thomas, 31, 62
Causation and mind, 264
Cause and effect inherent, 263
Changes in passing from first to second estate, 120
Character and inclinations, divergence of, 125
Characters, great, fore-ordained, 126
Christ, and divine authority, 169; and Godhood, 169; and law of liberty, 99; and mercy, 166; and the Father, 248; and truth absolute, 213; concepts relating to, 243; express image of Father, 33; our brother, 165, 325; uncompromising, 317

Christian delusion, 59, 60
Christian God Mormon Holy Ghost, 48
Christian Science, error of, 140
Churches not social or racial workshops, 17
Church, organization, 197; survival, criterion of, 8; the, its rites and ordinations, 290
Civilization and psychic alternations, 156
Compromise must be authorized by God, 317
Covenant, children of, 131
Created and uncreated, 26
Creation, and Buddhist god, 37; and Mormon conception of God, 38; and spiritual essence, 36; first, spiritual, 70; mediæval notion of, 65; motive of, 64; order and time of, 66; problem of, 67; science and theology on, 64; second, mortal, 71; seven-day period, 65
Creative action, how sprung forth, 28
Creator, vague, 241; Dean Mansel's exposition of, 334
Creeds and scientific thought of age, 307
Creeds' failure to perceive repentance, 158

Damnation, meaning of, 58
Darwin, Chas. R., 61, 69, 285
Death and resurrection, time between, 224
Declaration of Independence, criterion of judgment, 91
Deluge, necessity of, 94, 95
Depravity, total, 54
Development, man's co-operation necessary to, 190
Divine, allegiance, restrictions of, 268; attributes, reception of, 260; authority, absence of, 319

Doctrine and covenants, 209
Earth, this, a school, 55
Eddy, Mary Baker G., 31
Education, and intelligence, 149; and repentance merge, 163; conception of, 148; psychological classification, 153; secular, and environment, 163; true and false, 152
Ego, importance of, 82, 83; subject to God, 84; the, 55; the (Joseph Smith), 80
Ego's capacity for faith and repentance, 84
Egypt and Babylon, civilization of, 95
Emerson, Ralph Waldo, 31
Energy, conservation of, 47; conservation of, and Joseph Smith, 205; persistence and transmutation of, 244
Enoch and social harmony, 97
Enthusiasm masquerades as supreme religious virtue, 7
Environment, evolution of, 76, 85; first spiritual, 84; its influence on Greeks and Chinese, 110; new continuation of old, 120; shapes destiny, 75; suited to degrees of intelligences, 85
Eternal City, 221
Eternal progress, 39
Evils, all, causes of, 145
Evolution, dual, of natural world, 69; defined, 61; eternal progress, 62, 302
Existence, purpose of, 69
Experience, law of, 24, 236
Experiences, natural, and soul evolution, 202

Fairness, Mormon policy, 5
Faith, alone dead, 190; an abstracted quality, 146; and repentance, heralds of eternal life, 160; conditions necessary to operation of,

Index 341

Faith (*Continued*)
133; effects of, 152; essential characteristic of, 83; fundamental principle of religion, 133; how developed or destroyed, 143; in God, scientific aspect of, 129; in law unifies, 145; meaning of, 136; necessary to psychic evolution, 135; quality necessary to conviction, 138; truthness, and conviction, relation of, 139; types of, 136, 141; without works, 141

Father, and Son, presence of, 223; Son, Holy Ghost, unity of, 266

First cause, 253, 331; incomprehensible, 262

Fiske's, John, idea of God, 45, 46

Forces, negative, reactionary, 256, 257; spiritual and physical, 198

Fore-ordination, 125

Forgiveness, and its token, 174; and remorse, 172; different tokens of, 175

Forms, dwarfed (animal and vegetable), 226

Free agency, 81

Future life, activities and possibilities of, 286; and the arts, 221; natural epochs of, 224; work of, 220, 221

Genius, etc., 47

Geocentric theory, 241

Gifts, possession and manifestations of, 124

God, absurd conception of (St. Augustine), 20; Adam, 293; and Godhood, 63; and His supremacy, 50; and inspiration, 209; and modification of will, 43; and organic processes, 229; and power to create, 254; and psychic evolution, 177; and the affairs of men, 213; and the animating principle, 36; and the Bible, the Koran, 209; and the Holy Scriptures, 208; a personal being, Bible doctrine, 32; "as spirit" misinterpreted, 16; Athanasian conception of, 29; Bible type of, Mormon type, 22; Buddha's idea Christianized, 235; Buddhist conception of, 28, 31; Christ, 253; Christ-type of, and science, 234; Christ-type of, inspiration to righteousness, 16; "coming to," 184; compared to earthly father, 43; definite, tokens definite, 177; demanded by reason, 243; eternal, 236; fatherhood of, 325; father of spirits, 171; Greek conception of, 16; how God became, 281; how He rules among nations, 105; how our Father became, 275; how seen by Moses, 272; idea of, mediæval times, 21; infinite, 236; in His glory, how seen, 272; in the sense of Godhood, 255; invisibility of, 271; "is a Spirit," 270; justice of, in teaching effects of sin, 119; known as man becomes like Him, 18; known to man through Christ, 167; manifestations of, 242; man's conception of, bounded by experience, 18; man's dual relationship to, 170; man-type of, the only reasonable type, 22; medium of manifestation of, 47; modern Christian conception of, 28, 30; modern Christian idea, difficulties of, 235; modern Christians and science, 244;

God (*Continued*)
  Mormon conception of, 14; Mormon conception of, sources other than Scripture, 32; mutability of, 273; omnipotence and omnipresence of, 15; one and many, 238; our Father, 55; pantheistic conception of, difficulties of, 34; Paul's restriction, 267; personal idea of, how relinquished, 31; personality of, 19, 24, 34; personal, philosophical difficulties to concept of, 232; planned destiny of nations, 112; postulated incomprehensible, 300; prescribes tokens, 176; real revelation to man, 19; scientific concept of, 31; scriptural conception of, how operative in nature, 34; shapes destiny of individual, 117; shaping destiny of mankind, 89; subjectively, objectively, 219; supreme-by-law, 171; the source of power, 169; to be like Him implies progression, 19; true conception of, vital to unity, 18; two surviving conceptions of, 28; unreasonable type of, overthrown, 22; vague, tokens vague, 176; what is He? 234
God's, ideals, expressions of, 276; immutability, 272; personality, noblest ideal of, 19; will and phenomena, 48
Godhead, 252; and psychic evolution, 281
Godhood, alone not God, 259; and kinghood, 279; and organized psychic being 258; and patriarchial government, 278; and priesthood, 284; as incarnated, 245; dominion part of, 292; inoperative unless incarnated, 258; real meaning of, 251
Gods, plurality of, 261
Goethe's Mephistopheles, 57
Golden Rule, 100
Gospel, and psychic evolution, 286; new dispensation of, 319
Government, democratic, 279; monarchical, 278
Governments, divine, and fitness to rule, 265
Grace, 219; and damnation, 192; and infinite energy, 204; and the spirit of God, 198; and truth, 260; means of psychic evolution, 212; of God not restricted to members of Church, 319
Grecian civilization and worship, 102
Greek nemesis, 171

Hades and Paradise, 228
Hamilton, Sir William, 333
Hamitic, civilization, 96; energy expended in early days of world, 107; race, future of, 104
Harmony with law yields power, 130
Harris, W. T., U. S. Commissioner of Education, 299
Hate an element of bigotry, 6
Hatred of Mormons unites opposing sects, 4
Healing, phenomena of, 139
Heart-power needed in schools and world, 151
Heat waves, 200
Heaven, and hell within you, 298; a state of harmony, 57; endurance of, 39; order of, and church government, 223; perfect social harmony, 222; the *here* and *now*, 56; we create, 222
Heliocentric theory, 241

Index

Hell, experiences of, 59; state of discord, 57
Heredity, physical and spiritual, 125; possibilities of, 121; spiritual, supreme, 127
History, principle of interpretation of, 108
Holy Ghost, and energy, 203; and existence, 49; and instinct, 223; and symbolism, 215; as medium, 205; differentiations of, 204; involves a token, 214
Hubbard, Elbert, millennium, 7
Huxley, Thos., 285

Ideal, Gospel, 92; individual-liberty, 98; modern, 97
Idealization and expression, 193
Ideals, false, of Old-World civilization, 92; man goes to nature for, 21
Idolatry and attendant evils, 118
Ignorance, and knowledge, 149; conception of, 148; the negative of law, 155
Imitators, 194
Impulses, unexpressed, smother, 208
Inalienable rights, 91
Infidels, 285
Inspiration, 47, 210
"In the beginning was the Word," 259, 260
Intelligence, and radiancy, 228; eternal, 79; how measured, 283; in materials unthinkable, 50
Intelligences working in spirit world, 74

Japheth and descendants, 101
Japhetic race, future of, 104
Jehovah, 238, 242, 267
Jews and their influence on nations, 111

Job, 327
Jordan, Dr. David Starr, 56

Kingdom, of God and threatening dangers, 197; of God, Christ's definition of, 185; of God, Jewish conception of, 186; of God, potentially within man, 196
Knowledge transformed to power, 152

Law, and government, human institution of, 277; and phenomena, 155; criterion of, 163; the harmony of the universe, 157; voice of God, 306
Liberty, outcome of different race, 93
Life, dependent on human law, 21; eternal, dependent on divine law, 21; eternal, how possible, 155; demands power, 149; man's power to analyze, 75; place of religion in, 51; opportunities of earth and future, 72; pre-existent, present, and future, transitions of, 76; result of dual creation, 69; two aspects of, 225
Light waves, 200
Loeb, Dr., 74
Lucifer, 256; and his angels, 328

Makers' appreciation and joy, 221
Man, a child of God, 15; become God, 261; brotherhood of, 162, 325; co-eternal with God, 78; distinguished from brute creation, 151; must co-operate with God, 130; same order of being as God, 55
Man's appearance on earth, 86, 87; spiritual life a process of evolution, 78

Mansel, Dean, 263, 333
Mansions, many, 221
Matter and spirit same entity, 63
Melchisedek, the high-priest, 294
Millennium and social-equality, 100
Mind and body deformities, 226
Ministers, and crushing of Mormonism, 307; Utah, have declared war, 7
Missionary system produces cosmopolitanism, 5
Mormon, and Christian philosophies, common ground of, 45; and social growth, 233; anticipations a socialized future, 223; principles of virtue, 115
Mormonism, a shaping factor of world, 116; and common sense, 298; and education, 150; and natural and spiritual law, 199; and science coincide, 12; and sociological evolution, 130; and World's Congress of Religions, 303; an organic religion, 232; a scientific religion, 9; a transcendent system of evolution, 61; charitable though uncompromising, 312; crushing of, 7, 303, 309; destined to last word, 311; difficulty to substitute, 308; if not, what? 295; faith and reason, 242; finds in life commentary on Scripture, 23; for all, 318; hatred of, unites opposing sects, 4; highest standard of righteousness, 112; holds other churches as not divine, 318; not an artificial religion, 311; offends ministers, 305; requires no apology, 317; social aspect of, 321

Mormons among great of Shemitic race, 114; desire Christian unity, 183
"Morning stars sang together," 327
Moroni, angel, 227
Mortality cannot see immortality, 271
Motive, impelling, in man, 83
Mutation and earth evolution, 273
Mysteries, 301

Nebuchadnezzar, 89
Necessity of mortal world, 107
Newton, Sir Isaac, 64
"No man can be saved in ignorance," 147

Occasion for writing book, 1
Omnipotence, omniscience, and omnipresence, 219, 258, 259
Oppression, revolt against, 99

Pantheism, 32
Paradise and Hades, 228
Parents draw spirits they deserve, 120
Pastor moulds opinion of his congregation, 3
Perdition, sons of, 58
Perfection, God's help necessary to, 192; implication of, 262; man's possibilities of, 187
Phenomena, are illusory, 10; explained by heredity and fore-ordination, 125; man fitted to apprehend, 11; natural, and Buddhistic philosophy, 33
Physical, and mental defects, causes of, 124; science and man's pre-eminence, 67
Plato, 21
Polytheism, 238

Powers, positive, negatively used, 162
Prayer, and modern Christian God, 40; meaning and conditions of, 40, 41; philosophy of, 207
Prayers, 175; by whom considered, 43
Preaching, dogmatic, futility of, 147
Pre-existence, advanced by revelation, 324; memory of, 172; scientific doctrine of, 105; spiritual proofs of, 323
Pre-existent state, oblivion of, 123
Priesthood, grants dominion, 291; infallibility of, 293; license for Godhood, 290; offices of, 289; ordination to, 288
Prodigal man, 164
Progress and environment, 282
Prophets, false notion of, 305
Psychic, evolution and analogies in nature, 187; life of earth and other spheres, 287; sensation and electricity, 200

Reason for crushing Mormons not new, 6; why sectarian ministers do not unite, 5
"Reform" demands "Conform," 7
Religion, abortive, 296; and domain of reason, 299; and living faith, 52; artificially cultivated, 296; a social factor, 54; birth of, 26; in the public schools, 299; life itself, 55; Mormon conception of, 55; natural, 297; of would-be-reformers, 308; only one true, 315; reason for existence of, 12; unscientific, unworthy of credence, 9; varied forms of, how developed, 191; warp and woof of life, 53
Religions, false, 202; Godliness of, lost, 195; withered, 196
Religious, bigotry a past vice, 6; feeling seeks expression, 296; societies and will of man, 195
Remorse, awakened, 164; why felt, 170–171
Repentance, and absolution, 170; and cults of to-day, 158; and education identical, 147; and emotion, 169; and forgiveness, 160; and revelation, 169; brings man to God, 163; conformity to ideal, 160; essential characteristic of, 83; implies righteousness, 156; sequence of, 157; what involved, 161
Resurrected bodies, 229; of infants, 231
Resurrection, life after, 224; now in process, 231; potentiality of spirit, 231
Retrogression and advancement, 76
Revelation, 210; and law, 157
Righteousness, alone upholds organic systems, 4; artificial, 53; defined, 157; the secret of Mormon thrift, 4
Right, requisites of, 202
Roman civilization and worship, 102

Salvation (Joseph Smith), 156; and divine worship, 208; and eternal bliss, 156; and grace, 189; comes through intelligence (Joseph Smith), 149; education a means of, 158; imaginary, 52; impossible through ignorance, 155; latent elements of,

Salvation (*Continued*)
154; meaning of, 154; Mormonism's practical notion of, 314; tendency of age toward, 182; through sacrifice, 150; unity essential to, 313
Scattering from Babel, results of, 108, 109
School, God's, ideally fitted, 154
Schools, artificial contrivances, 149; fated by fads, 154
Science, and eternal energy, 199; and faith, beginning of, 199; skeptical, 12; woof and warp of, 11
Scripture, and the mystical 209; growing and expansive, 211; mediæval doctrine of, 210; misinterpreted, 189–190
Sectarianism, what, has to offer, 303
Sectarian ministers the originators of strife, 304
Secular organizations originators of social movements, 17
Selfishness and power, 161
Self-reliance not offensive to God, 192
Seth, descendants of, and priesthood, 95
Shemitic, civilization, 97; influences on Latin races, 102, 103; race, future of, 104; race preservers of the great religious ideals, 101
Sin, and ignorance, 158; and relative righteousness, 55; and the devil, 255; penalty of, 118; unpardonable, 58, 257; unstability of, 4
Smith, Joseph, 9, 78, 149, 156; and cosmic forces, 47; as a prophet, 305; first vision, 246
Social evolution in spirit world, 188

Social world, problems of, 221
Solar system, a product of cause, 28; necessity of, 66
Souls, Nathaniel-like, 165; selfish, 165
Sound waves, 199
Sovereignty, misconception of, 278
Species, derivation of, 66
Spencer, Herbert, 31, 230, 337
Spirit, and parentage deserved, 119; form of, 81; presence of, 224
Spirits, classified in premortal state, 116; self-classification of, 105, 107
Spiritual, and mortal, union of, 71; counterpart, 227; evolution, nature of, 185
Superstition, false faith, 144; Middle Ages cast seed, 6

Telepathy, divine, 205
The hereafter and intelligent beings, 216
Theories, philosophic, supplant living faith, 17
Theosophists and Christ, 168; and prayer, 40
Things, duration of, conditional, 154
Thoughts and emotions organically conveyed, 206
Time, and space, 25; and space, without beginning or end, 264
Token, characteristics of, 178; essential to salvation, 178
Truth, and truthness distinguished, 138; defined (Joseph Smith), 9; interpreted by God, absolute, 12; interpreted by man, relative, 12; known by experience, 24; Mormon apprehension of, 12
Truthness, man's range of, 201
Tyndall, John, 285

Unity, of natural phenomena, 134; of sectaries in attacking Mormonism, 309; spiritual and social, 134, 135
Universe full, 26

Vanity, 214
Virtue as reward, 162

Wordsworth and pre-existence, 324

Wordsworth's *Intimations of Immortality*, 323
Works, lifeless, Christ's denunciation of, 195; without grace dead, 193
World, natural and spiritual, 225
Worlds, formation of, 26

X-rays, 201

Printed in the United States
65023LVS00007B/55